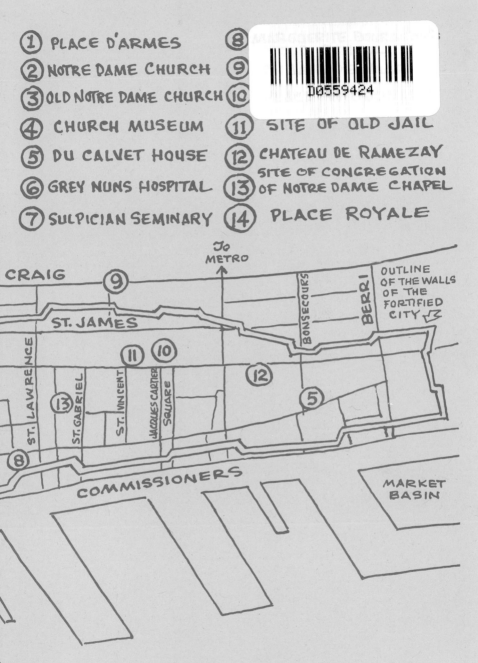

1. PLACE D'ARMES
2. NOTRE DAME CHURCH
3. OLD NOTRE DAME CHURCH
4. CHURCH MUSEUM
5. DU CALVET HOUSE
6. GREY NUNS HOSPITAL
7. SULPICIAN SEMINARY
8. MARGUERITE BOU...
9.
10.
11. SITE OF OLD JAIL
12. CHATEAU DE RAMEZAY
13. SITE OF CONGREGATION OF NOTRE DAME CHAPEL
14. PLACE ROYALE

To METRO

CRAIG

ST. JAMES

ST. LAWRENCE

ST. GABRIEL

ST. VINCENT

JACQUES CARTIER SQUARE

BONSECOURS

BERRI

OUTLINE OF THE WALLS OF THE FORTIFIED CITY ☞

COMMISSIONERS

MARKET BASIN

ST. LAWRENCE RIVER

Montreal:

The Days
That Are No More

Other Books by

EDGAR ANDREW COLLARD

The Art of Contentment (Editor)
The McGill You Knew
Call Back Yesterdays
Montreal Yesterdays
Canadian Yesterdays
Oldest McGill

Montreal:

The Days
That Are No More

EDGAR ANDREW COLLARD

Illustrations by John Collins

Doubleday Canada Limited
Toronto

Doubleday & Company, Inc.
New York

1976

ISBN: 0-385-11002-2
Library of Congress Catalog Card Number: 75-42858

Design by Maher & Garbutt Ltd.
Printed and bound in Canada by The Bryant
Press Limited.

Second Printing

To Elizabeth, my wife,
for the gathered happiness
of the years

FOREWORD

This is a book of "little things"—the story of a few square miles. It is a local history; and in French local history is called "petite histoire."

There are many kinds of history. Certainly the more analytical kind, drawing from many facts conclusions about broad movements and trends, is of great importance and necessity. In generalizations, however, something inevitably is lost. What is lost most of all is the sense of history as experience. For experience lies in the here and now. No one experiences as abstraction, a theory, a generalization. Experience lies in the moment that is lived, the place that is known. And experience itself is not little. It is life.

I can never forget an address by Stephen Leacock before the Canadian Historical Association. "A thing to which this association ought specially to devote its attention," said Leacock, "is the encouragement of what may be called local history."

He went on to speak from his own experience. As a boy on an Ontario farm he had been taught to think of history as the story of Greece and Rome, or of the Napoleonic Wars. He did not realize that the old grave among the brambles at the foot of the farm was history. It never occurred to him that this old grave recalled a time in the days of early settlement when there was no consecrated burial ground and everyone must bury his own dead.

"Fifty years have passed since the time of which I speak," he said, "and my point of view has changed. I value none the less the great historical epics of a Macaulay or a Gibbon. But I find myself drawn more and more to the charm and meaning of the history of little places. Who lived here first? Who first set the stones that lay beneath the simple frame of that log-house? How did life feel for these first-comers? Such queries and such reflections . . . may well fill the reflecting mind with wonder and interest. For after all, the life of the individual has in its silent passage to the end the same infinite mystery and the same unfathomed meaning as the life of a nation."

I have often thought of these words of Stephen Leacock as I have gone about Montreal. Quite ordinary-looking streets and street corners, and the dark stones of old buildings half hidden from view, have taken on new meaning by knowing what happened there in the long ago.

I can never pass the corner of Notre Dame Street and McGill without recalling that here stood the Récollet Gate and through that gate the forces of the American Revolution marched into Montreal to take possession of the city on a November day in 1775, when "the streets were stiffened with cold."

Nor can I ever walk along Sherbrooke Street near the head of Fort Street without glancing at one of the stone towers among the trees beyond the wall of the Séminaire, knowing that two Indians lie buried in that tower—converts in the

Indian mission maintained on the slope of the mountain by the Sulpicians in the seventeenth century.

Down by the waterfront on Windmill Point I know I am at the spot where duels were fought near the windmill; and on the waterfront of Lachine I am standing on the shore where the fur traders put out in their canoes every spring on the long journey into the Northwest.

The real drawing power of this history of places, this sense of locality, lies in the way it evokes the mystery of existence and what has well been called "the poetry of time." The English historian, George Macaulay Trevelyan, expressed it when he said: "The appeal of history to us all is in the last analysis poetic. But the poetry of history does not consist of imagination roaming at large, but of imagination pursuing the fact and fastening upon it."

And the fact that is most evocative relates to experience—to what happened at some point of time and in some particular place. It is what happened in the yesterday that was once today and in the locality where we now live. In few cities is the history of localities more rewarding than in Montreal, where life has been lived for centuries in these few square miles on an island—an island at the crossroads of a continent's history.

For thirty-two years I have written an article on the history of Montreal every week for the editorial page of *The Gazette*. Material drawn from these 1,700 articles form the basis of this book, though revised, expanded and adapted in the light of subsequent research. For kind permission to use this material, and the sketches of John Collins, I am very grateful indeed to *The Gazette* and to Southam Press Limited.

Edgar A. Collard
Montreal, Quebec
7 January, 1976

CONTENTS

Part Two. Americans' Montreal

Part Three. Adventures and Ordeals

Part Four. Persons and Places

Part One

The
French Régime

John Collins SKETCHBOOK

ST. PAUL
and
ST. DIZIER

ONE

The Brides Who Came by Shiploads:
The King's Girls

THEY WERE CALLED "the King's Girls"—"*les filles du roi.*" And it was King Louis XIV who had sent them out to New France. The colonists were in need of wives. The king was supplying them. Between 1665 and 1673 about 1,000 arrived.

In Montreal, as in Quebec, these girls from France had to be housed and cared for until the young colonists had a chance to make their selection. Marguerite Bourgeoys, founder of the Congrégation de Notre Dame, brought many to her house on St. Paul Street—the house where she had her school and was forming her group of nuns. This stone stable, converted into a schoolhouse, stood at what today is number 50 St. Paul, at the point where St. Dizier Street ends. One detachment of King's Girls was so large that this building could not hold them. Some had to be taken to a neighboring house she had bought from Charly-St. Ange.

Louis XIV wished to see New France grow, but he did not

wish to depopulate France itself. The answer lay in sending enough young girls to the colony to marry the male settlers. Then New France could provide for its own increase.

The plan met with the approval of the Roman Catholic Church. A community with an excess of bachelors was hard to keep in order, and respectable. Marriage with its responsibilities, and the influence of the wives, would give sound, sensible, hard-working standards of living. Most of the arrangements for selecting the King's Girls were made by correspondence between Jean Talon, the first Intendant of New France, and Jean-Baptiste Colbert, the minister in France charged (among many other things) with the development of the colony. Talon had clear ideas about the type of girls needed. They should be strong enough for work in the fields or, at the very least, have some aptitude for manual labor. They should also be reasonably good-looking, for, after all, they were coming to be brides. "The girls destined for this country," wrote Talon, "besides being strong and healthy, ought to be entirely free from any natural blemish or anything personally repulsive."

Nor would good health and good looks be enough. These girls must have good moral character. The colony did not want girls of easy virtue. On this point Colbert agreed with Talon. He saw that it was "important in the establishment of a country to sow good seed."

The King's first plan was to dispatch to New France girls who were already being supported by the state—those (mostly orphans) being maintained in institutions in Paris. At first this plan seemed ideal. At one and the same time the state at home would be relieving itself of the expense of maintaining these girls, and they would be given new lives in the colony. Experience, however, proved the plan mistaken. Orphanage girls, brought up in the sickly air of Paris, could not stand the rough conditions, the incessant hard work of pioneer households.

A new plan was adopted. Country girls would be sent instead. In 1670 Colbert wrote to the Archbishop of Rouen: "As in the parishes about Rouen fifty or sixty girls might be found who would be very glad to go to Canada to be married, I beg you to employ your credit and authority with the curés of thirty or forty of these parishes, to try to find in each of them one or two girls disposed to go voluntarily for the sake of a settlement in life."

This plan worked far better. Good, healthy, honest girls were recruited. But precautions and procedures were necessary to keep this mass shipment of girls from coming to be regarded as something loose and ribald. The migration was severely regulated; the candidates carefully screened; an atmosphere of grave responsibility was encouraged. A few girls of doubtful background were able to get themselves into the shipments. In Quebec, after some of them had been married to the colonists, they were found to have husbands at home. This loophole was closed. Colbert ordered that any girl joining the *filles du roi* had to produce a certificate. In this certificate the curé or magistrate of her parish in France had to certify that she was free to marry.

On their long journey over the Atlantic the girls were accompanied and supervised by matrons or guardians, chosen for their piety and probity. Such a pious duenna was Madame Jean Bourdon, widow of the attorney-general of New France. At times Madame Bourdon had her problems. Though most were decent girls, they were vigorously young and, together in large numbers, mischievously lively. On one of the crossings the 150 girls "gave her no little trouble," and some of them were "very rude and hard to manage."

Marguerite Bourgeoys knew far better how to manage them. Apart from her experience and success as a teacher, she had already crossed the ocean, in returning from one of her visits to France, with a group of the King's Girls. She was a woman of deep understanding of human nature, less interested in repression than in setting an example by her own character and manner, and influencing by sympathy and affection. So far from feeling that a shipload of *filles du roi* would be an harassing problem, she welcomed the chance to show kindness to them. She heard another detachment was about to arrive at Montreal. "As they were to be the mothers of future families," she wrote, "I thought it only right that they should be brought together in a safe place, and that of all others, the Blessed Virgin's house ought to be open to her children. Full of this idea, and scarcely waiting to consult the sisters, I hastened to the shore to meet these girls and to take them to our house. It was too small to accommodate them all. It was therefore necessary to take them to the little house bought from St. Ange where I was obliged to stay to give them the necessary instruction."

While the girls were with Marguerite Bourgeoys she not only watched over them and taught them the catechism, but probably gave what brief instruction she could on household skills, and interviewed the young men who came looking for wives. On many of the marriage contracts her neat, small handwriting appears. The contracts are often dated from the "parloir de la Congrégation."

The procedure in Montreal was much the same as in Quebec. The King's Girls were kept under supervision in one place. The young men came for wives. They had to deal first of all with the "directress." They had to make known their possessions and means of livelihood. A girl had the right to decline any suitor. The first question the girls asked was generally whether the young man had a farm. A notary and a priest were at hand. After the marriage contract had been drawn up and duly signed and witnessed, the marriage took place. Under the old French custom each bride was supposed to have a dowry. The King had not neglected his duty. Each of the King's Girls had "the King's Gift." It might be as much as a farmhouse, with provisions for eight months. More often it was fifty livres in household supplies, together with a barrel or two of salted meat.

The bachelors did not always marry the King's Girls by desire or free will. The law drove them to it. In New France the bachelor was a marked man—a public enemy, an antisocial character, a citizen shirking his duty. Colbert was firm in his instructions to Talon in 1668: "Those who may seem to have absolutely renounced marriage should be made to bear additional burdens, and be excluded from all honors; it would be well even to add some marks of infamy." Talon provided severe penalties for unmarried men. They were forbidden to hunt, fish or trade with the Indians. Nor were they allowed to go into the woods on any pretense whatever (probably to prevent them from finding temporary satisfaction with Indian women).

An instance of what might happen to an obstinate bachelor was seen in the case of François Le Noir of Lachine. He was haled before a judge. The charge: though a single man he had been trading with the Indians at his house. François Le Noir admitted his guilt. But he promised to marry within three weeks after the arrival of the next shipment of *filles du roi*. If he failed then, he would donate 150 livres to the church at Montreal and an equal sum to the hospital. Under this agreement Le Noir was permitted to trade, but still forbidden to go into the woods. When the *filles du roi* arrived the following year, he married Marie Magdeleine Charbonnier from Paris.

King Louis XIV not only promoted marriages in New France by providing the colonists with wives; he also provided strong inducements for large families. His scale of baby bonuses was generous, even if the qualifications were exacting. Any of the colonists having ten living children born in lawful wedlock (none a priest or in a religious order) were eligible for a pen-

5

sion of 300 livres a year. If they had twelve children, the pension rose to 400 livres. Parents in New France were required by law to see that their sons were married by eighteen or nineteen, their daughters by fourteen or fifteen. Any father failing to comply, and failing to give a satisfactory explanation, was fined. He had then to report to the authorities every six months to explain any further delays.

This public emphasis on prompt marriages had some extraordinary results. In Montreal, about 1672, a widow had the banns of her next marriage proclaimed immediately after her first husband's death. Normally, the banns of marriage had to be proclaimed three times; but in her case the two later readings were dispensed with. She had "her second marriage arranged and carried out before her first husband was buried."

The premium set by the state on prompt marriage and frequent childbirth proved effective. Largely because of such policies, the population of New France more than doubled between 1666 and 1676.

In the story of the King's Girls Marguerite Bourgeoys stands out as the figure of compassion. The girls never seem to have regarded her as a guardian, matron or duenna—someone there to curb and intimidate them. She was their friend, doing all she could to understand and help. When the girls left her house on St. Paul Street and went out to make homes for themselves, they left with affection for her. They often came back to visit her, and for advice and encouragement.

Among the King's Girls were many very young, not much over sixteen. They had left their homes in France and their mothers for a long and dangerous sea journey, were put on display and suddenly married on slight acquaintance, and had to make abrupt adjustments to a new way of life. Marguerite Bourgeoys became a mother to them in the rough, strange land.

SKETCHBOOK

John Collins

GATE
OF THE
SULPICIANS

TWO

The Strong Man of St. Sulpice:
Dollier de
Casson

ABBÉ DOLLIER DE CASSON, the Superior of the Sulpicians in Montreal, was so strong that he could lift two men at one time—a man with each of his hands. He was a towering, commanding figure. "This is a man!" the Indians conceded in tribute.

The Indians had good reason to show him respect as a priest. He was not a missionary to be mocked. One winter night, while on a mission by the shore of the Bay of Quinté, he was kneeling at his prayers. A young Indian tormented him; his jests were obscene. Dollier de Casson did not even rise from his knees. His right arm shot out. The Indian was knocked sprawling over the ground. The missionary resumed his prayers. No one interrupted him.

It was this giant of a man who built the Sulpician Seminary in Montreal—the ancient stone manor house on Notre Dame Street at Place d'Armes, to the west of Notre Dame Church. He launched the construction of it about 1680. The Sulpicians first occupied it some five years later. The building was later extended, mostly in the eighteenth century. But the core that Dollier de Casson built is still there. It is the oldest building in Montreal, and one of the oldest in all North America. After nearly three centuries it is still used for its original purposes.

The construction of this Seminary was, in its way, characteristic of Dollier de Casson. He was a resolute man; he made up his own mind; he acted without hesitation. The Sulpicians in Montreal, he believed, were miserably housed. They deserved a new building suitable to their needs—a building appropriate to their position as the priestly seigneurs of the whole Island of Montreal. It was true that the headquarters of the Sulpicians was in Paris. Any important decisions should be made only after approval had come from there. But in the seventeenth century an entire year was often needed for an inquiry from Montreal to be sent and an answer from Paris received.

Dollier de Casson, as the Sulpician Superior in Montreal, was scarcely patient enough to proceed so slowly. He preferred to go ahead on his own initiative—he had a way of acting first and seeking approval afterward. In this independent spirit he had gone ahead with constructing the Seminary in Place d'Armes. The letters from Paris were severe with protests. They complained that Dollier de Casson was involving the Sulpicians in embarrassing debts. He must practice greater economy.

Though the Sulpicians at the headquarters in Paris frequently had reason to be unhappy with Dollier de Casson's willful decisions in Montreal, they were well aware that he was incomparably the best man for the post. He had been assigned to a hard role. The population of Montreal was growing, but much of it was mixed and floating. It was a community not only of settlers but of the come and go of fur traders and voyageurs, of Indians and soldiers, or adventurers of all sorts.

And it was a place of controversies—controversies among the different religious orders and among the imperious officials appointed by the King. The Superior of St. Sulpice in Montreal had to be a strong man, dedicated and devout, but with a knowledge of the world. The management of the Sulpicians' business and the defense of their rights, as well as of their missionary work, demanded a well-tempered zeal, a practical attitude, a capacity to be both dignified and good humored.

Dollier de Casson met all these complex requirements. He had the rare advantage of having been a soldier before he became a priest. In France he had served as a captain under the great commander, Marshal Turenne. He had been praised by the marshal for daring and resolution in danger.

As Superior of St. Sulpice in Montreal he gave an example of soldierly daring and resolution. It was on the evening of the day of Pentecost in 1671. Vespers had been said; the bells of "Le Salut" had not yet been rung. Word came that a horrible fight was going on in the street. Dollier de Casson at once ran out; M. de Frémont, curé of the parish, went with him. They came upon two men in a clinch, swaying and struggling; one man's head streamed with blood. A little group stood about, looking on, doing nothing.

The fight had been going on for some time. It began when Sieur de Lormeau, on a stroll with his wife, encountered Sieur de Carion. Both men were military officers: Lormeau was an ensign, Carion a lieutenant. Each hated and had quarreled with the other. That Pentecost evening de Carion insulted de Lormeau as they passed, spitting out the word "Coward!" "Coward yourself!" shouted de Lormeau. "Get away from here!"

The fight was on. Sieur de Carion drew his sword; Sieur de Lormeau drew his. Their swords clashed three or four times. Then the two men moved in for the clinch. Hatred convulsed them; both were fit to murder. De Carion seized his sword blade like a dagger. He tried to plunge the point into de Lormeau's stomach. De Lormeau's peruque slipped off. The sight of the bare head gave de Carion a new idea. He grabbed his sword by the hilt and smashed the pommel, blow after blow, on de Lormeau's unprotected head. Blood spurted.

Madame de Lormeau, appalled and scared, looked about for help. She ran to Charles Le Moyne's house nearby. On that evening Charles Le Moyne had two gentlemen to dinner: Picoté de Belestre and a merchant of Rochelle, named Baston. The dinner party was startled when Madame de Lormeau burst in. "Murder! Murder!" she screamed. "Come out, M. de Belestre, come out!" All three gentlemen leapt up from the table. In the street they saw the grappling pair. All three tried to pull them apart. The fighters, locked in their hatred, could not be budged. Picoté de Belestre stood back, panting and disgusted. "Since you won't break it up," he said, "then go right ahead and kill yourselves, if you want to." A servant of de Carion's arrived with a sword. He brandished it but did not strike. A friend of de Carion's (an ensign in the same company in his regiment) came up. He lunged at de Lormeau with his sword. Charles Le Moyne protested.

At this moment Dollier de Casson ran up. Everything changed the moment he arrived. He risked the swords; he asked no one's aid. He laid his big hands upon the fighters. With a heave he wrenched them apart. Then he faced them, as a priestly peacemaker.

Dollier de Casson could be a hero, but he was never a fool. He knew there are times when courage makes no sense. One day, when serving in the French army, his regiment was under heavy fire from the enemy's batteries. Suddenly he became aware that one of the enemy's gunners was in the act of applying his match to a cannon trained directly at him. As an officer, Dollier de Casson had to set an example to the men under his command. Military etiquette of the day was strict. An officer under fire must not run away; he must not throw himself ignominiously on the ground. But Dollier de Casson did not relish the idea of standing still to have his head blown off. Instantly he drew out his handkerchief. He dropped it at his feet. He bent low to pick it up. The cannon ball whizzed harmlessly over his head. His dignity and his life had both been preserved.

After he had completed his training for the priesthood at St. Sulpice in Paris, Dollier de Casson naturally was selected for service with the Sulpicians in Canada; for not many young priests had as much useful experience with the rough life of the world. He had hardly arrived in Canada than he was appointed a military chaplain in the war with the Iroquois. He later accompanied La Salle on an exploring expedition to Lake Erie—an area he claimed in the name of the King. He had gone with La Salle to seek out Indian tribes for missionary work. For a man who had mingled in the commotions of the world, the solitude of the forest brought release into spiritual peace. "I would rather die in the midst of the forest," he said, "in accord with the will of God, as I believe I am, than among all my brethren in the seminary of St. Sulpice." But he was not to be left to missionary work in the wilderness. He was summoned back. In 1671 he was appointed Superior of St. Sulpice in Montreal.

No superior could have been more active. In addition to all the day-to-day business of the Sulpicians he launched a series of projects. He founded Notre Dame Church in Place d'Armes—the church that served (with extensions) until after the present Notre Dame Church was opened in 1829. After the church, he built the Seminary nearby. As the Sulpicians were the seigneurs and administrators of the island, he sponsored secular projects as well as ecclesiastical. He begun to dig the first Lachine Canal to bypass the Lachine Rapids. He seems to have completed more than half of it. But stern complaints about the cost came from the headquarters in Paris and he had to abandon the work. Dollier de Casson was also Montreal's first town planner. He laid out the first ten streets, with the aid of the notary and surveyor, Bénigne Basset. He marked and named Notre Dame Street, St. Paul and St. James, and such cross-streets as St. Joseph (now St. Sulpice), St. Peter, St. François (later St. François-Xavier) and St. Gabriel. In some cases (as with St. Paul Street) he incorporated old trails, but he more clearly defined them and gave them names. He compelled the observation of his plan. Some of the settlers wanted to sow crops where his streets had been formally laid out. He prevented them.

Dollier de Casson's talent and energy found still another expression: he wrote the first history of Montreal. It was probably written in the winter of 1672-73. At that time Montreal was only about thirty years old. He could learn about its earliest days from people still living. Had he not set down the living tradition much of the story of Maisonneuve, Jeanne Mance, Marguerite Bourgeoys and the soldier Closse would have been lost forever.

His own personality comes through his history. As an old soldier, he writes with zest and understanding of the skirmishes with the Iroquois. And as a very human, good-natured man, he notes with amusement the oddities of human nature. He was delighted with the story of Madame Primot. The Iroquois had attacked her. Hands and feet were her only weapons. An Iroquois flung himself on her to take her scalp. Dollier de Casson records that she "caught hold of this monster so forcibly by a place which modesty forbids us to mention that he could not free himself." He beat her over the head; she sank into unconsciousness.

By this time the French settlers had time to run to her rescue. The Iroquois made off. One of her rescuers raised her in his arms. As soon as Madame Primot became aware of what was going on she gave him a smashing blow. "What are you doing?" asked the others. "This man but wished to show his friendly feeling for you without thought of evil. Why do you hit him?" She answered: "I thought he wanted to kiss me."

Dollier de Casson enjoys his amusement. But he hastens to add a pious comment: "The depth of the roots which Virtue implants in the hearts of her chosen is indeed marvellous . . ."

Dollier de Casson died in 1701 in the Seminary he had built at Place d'Armes. The funeral oration referred to his "easy and kindly conversation," and how he had "without trick or affectation softened all hearts." His had been "an imposing authority which no one could withstand."

John Collins SKETCHBOOK

NOTRE DAME
CHURCH

THREE

The Chief They Called "the Rat": Kondiaronk

THEY CALLED HIM "the Rat." He was Kondiaronk, a chief of the Hurons. But he was far more: he was among the greatest of Indian chiefs. He manipulated the course of history according to his own schemes. The other Indian tribes, the French governors, even the English colonies to the south—all were affected by his moves and motives. He died in Montreal in somber grandeur. In the old Notre Dame Church in Place d'Armes he was buried with unequaled picturesqueness, in a singular unity of sorrow.

Kondiaronk could be as cunning, as furtive, as vicious as any rat. If provoked, he could tear gruesome wounds. But if allied to large, diplomatic plans, he could become the enlightened statesman. His mind seemed to think more quickly than others, to see farther.

Frontenac, as Governor of New France, often invited the Rat to his table. He wanted to give his officers the pleasure of hearing the chief's swift replies. In conversation he would be deliberately challenged. His repartees were "always animated, full of wit, and generally unanswerable."

The French historian, Le Roy de La Potherie, had known him. He wrote: "Few could have a greater acuteness of mind than he, and had he been born a Frenchman he was the type of man to manage the most ticklish affairs of a flourishing state." Along lines very similar was the appraisal of the Jesuit historian, Father Pierre-François de Charlevoix. He wrote that "it was the general opinion that no Indian had ever possessed greater merit, a finer mind, more valor, prudence or discernment in understanding those with whom he had to deal."

The Rat was the chief of the Hurons in the Michilimackinac area, near Lake Huron and Lake Michigan. The main enemies of his people were the far stronger Iroquois. His hope of security lay in war between the Iroquois and the French. So long as the Iroquois were fighting the French, the Hurons would be safe from annihilation. If the Iroquois and the French declared peace, the Iroquois would be free to turn on the Hurons. They could wipe the Hurons out.

The French needed allies, and the Rat pledged his support on one primary condition: the war should not be ended until the Iroquois were destroyed. The Governor at that time, Marquis de Denonville, agreed. To fulfill his role in this alliance, the Rat organized a war party against the Iroquois. With a picked band of Hurons he was bent on "distinguishing himself by some brilliant achievement." He visited Fort Frontenac (now Kingston), where he heard news that astounded him. The French commandant told him that Denonville was actively negotiating a peace treaty with the Iroquois. The Governor was even then in Montreal, awaiting the arrival of ambassadors representing the Iroquois nations.

The Rat realized that Governor Denonville had double-crossed him. But he had perfect Indian composure—he betrayed neither surprise nor anger. "It is well," he said to the commandant at Fort Frontenac. He immediately laid his own plans to kill these negotiations between the French and the Iroquois. He prepared to ambush the Iroquois peace delegates on their way to meet the Governor in Montreal. He took them by surprise, slaying some, capturing the rest. He then told his Iroquois prisoners that the French had sent him to waylay them. The Iroquois protested. They declared they were delegates on their way to a peace conference with the French. The Rat at once pretended to be astonished, horrified, angry. Governor Denonville, he said, must have made use of him to lay a trap for the Iroquois delegates; he had been made the instrument of the Governor's perfidy.

Without a moment's delay he released his captives. He loaded them with gifts. "Go, my brothers," he exclaimed, "go home to your people. The Governor has made me do so black a deed that I shall never be happy till your five tribes take a just revenge upon him." He kept only one of the Iroquois party. It was an Indian custom. One of his Hurons had been killed in the skirmish. The Iroquois gave him one of their warriors in exchange.

He then carried out the second stage of his plot. He hurried on to the French fort at Michilimackinac. The commandant at that remote post had not been informed that the Governor was negotiating a peace treaty with the Iroquois. He believed that the old war was still going on. The Rat took advantage of his ignorance. He declared that his Iroquois prisoner (the one exchanged for the Huron killed in the skirmish) was a spy. The Indian tried to explain that he was not a spy but a member of the peace party. The Rat said he must be crazy. The commandant called out a firing squad and had the Iroquois shot. The Rat then took another Iroquois, an old man long held prisoner at Michilimackinac, and set him free, urging him to go back to his people, to tell them what he had seen at Fort Michilimackinac: that the French were shooting Iroquois even while they were pretending to make peace with them.

Governor Denonville found himself struggling in the net of embarrassments the Rat had woven for him. He did his best to explain to the Iroquois that he had no part in the attack on the peace delegates, and no part in the shooting of the Iroquois in the fort at Michilimackinac. But the Governor, in the midst of delicate peace negotiations, found himself at a sudden disadvantage, trying to make his explanations sound convincing. He had other troubles. Many of the Iroquois had never favored a peace with the French. They were now delighted to have a pretext for renewing the war. Further still, the Governor of the English colony of New York, Sir Edmund Andros, was exerting all possible pressure on the Iroquois not to come to terms with the French but to remain allies of the English.

The Rat had accomplished exactly what he had set out to do: he had killed the peace. The Iroquois remained uncommitted for a while. Then came the night of August 4, 1689. A storm of rain, turning at times to hail, beat down over the Island of Montreal. The settlers at Lachine, nine miles west of the town of Montreal itself, huddled indoors. None of them was about in such weather. Lachine, as one of the outlying settlements, was protected by three forts. But on that wet night the garrisons had been driven to take shelter also. Some rumors had come to Montreal that the Iroquois might be turning to war again, but they were discounted. Governor Denonville was in Montreal on a visit. A number of officers from the forts on the island were in town to see him. No one was on the alert.

On that August night the same storm that had driven settlers and soldiers indoors acted as a cover for 1,500 Iroquois as they landed on the waterfront at Lachine. They beached their canoes. Undetected, they moved into the village. Groups of them surrounded most of the houses. At a given signal they screamed the war whoop. The settlers could not help one another. As each house was surrounded, each man had his own battle to fight. Some houses were broken into at once; the settlers were killed in their beds. Others barricaded their doors; they put up a fight. Their houses were set afire; they were forced out and seized the moment they appeared.

The Iroquois made no effort to hurry away. The soldiers still drowsed in Lachine's three forts. The noise of the storm drowned all shouts and screams; the direction of the wind carried all sounds of the fight away from them. The Indians lighted fires. The slow torture of chosen victims began. The attack had been made at dawn on August 5; the morning became a festival of cruelty.

When Lachine was reoccupied, the French saw what the Iroquois had done. The Sulpician, Abbé de Belmont, was an eyewitness. He described the charred remains of women impaled on stakes, children roasted in red-hot embers. He saw burned houses, slaughtered cattle. Frontenac (who returned to New France as Governor before the end of the year) wrote in his report that the settlers were "brained, burned or roasted, some being devoured, while the wombs of pregnant females were laid bare to snatch their infants, and other atrocities committed of a shocking and unheard of nature."

When word of the attack on Lachine reached Montreal a sortie was made against the Iroquois. But the troops were pulled back by the Marquis de Vaudreuil, commander of the forces in the colony. Governor Denonville had ordered him to take no chances. Vaudreuil interpreted the orders strictly. Any serious attempt to drive off the Iroquois was given up. Most of the settlers and soldiers withdrew into the forts. Week after week the Iroquois were almost free to roam about the island, pillaging houses and carrying off anyone they could find. They left at their leisure in October, two months after the massacre. As they set out in their canoes across Lake St. Louis they gave ninety yells to announce they were carrying away ninety prisoners. As they passed the forts they shouted: "You deceived us! Now we have deceived you!"

The Rat had proved his superb cunning. He had saved his Hurons by preventing their enemies, the Iroquois, from coming to terms with the French. By his plotting he had led Iroquois and French to believe each had been deceived by the other. The Rat, however, was more than a Machiavelli. By scheming, he had done what he considered necessary for the preservation of his people. But he then rose to grander solutions. He came to favor a vast peace settlement—one not merely between the French and the Iroquois (which would menace other tribes by leaving the Iroquois free to attack them), but a treaty that would make peace between the French and all tribes, and between each tribe and all the others. He took part in the preliminary negotiations. Then he made ready to attend the final gathering.

This great peace conference, one without precedent, was opened in Montreal on July 25, 1701. Some 1,300 Indian peace envoys arrived. They came from points as far away as Wisconsin in the far west, from Acadia in the east. They were greeted with salutes from the guns. Evergreen boughs had been stacked for them. They used the boughs to make wigwams for themselves. By this time Denonville had gone; the colony had a new Governor, Louis-Hector de Callières. He was busy for weeks welcoming the Indian delegations, and going through the elaborate preliminary rituals of treaty-making.

In all these proceedings the dominant figure was the Rat. He was there not only as the leader of his Hurons; he was the spokesman for a number of other tribes. The peace gathering could not have been held without him; without him, it could not hope to succeed. Father Charlevoix wrote in his history that on the Rat Governor de Callières had "built his main hope of successfully terminating his great work. He was almost exclusively indebted to him for . . . this assemblage, till then unexampled, of so many nations for a general peace."

Then came a crisis. The understanding had been that, as a gesture of good will and good faith, all the tribes would bring with them the prisoners they held from other tribes. The Rat had persuaded the tribes under his influence to bring their Iroquois prisoners. The Iroquois, by contrast, arrived without the prisoners they had taken. The Rat was disappointed, humiliated. The whole conference could have broken down then and there, had he wished.

The time came for him to address the gathering. He was gravely ill with fever, too weak to stand. They brought him a folding stool. It did not give him enough support. They brought a large, comfortable armchair. They offered him wine; he preferred syrup of maidenhair fern. He recovered a little and began to speak. His voice was weak. But all were eager to hear him. They drew close, listening attentively, in a respectful hush.

Once again the fate of New France was in the hands of the Rat. He rose to the moment. He described "with modesty, and yet with dignity" the steps he had taken to bring a lasting peace among all the nations. He made them see the necessity of such a peace, the advantages it would bring to each of them. Then, turning toward the Governor, he called upon him so to act that no one could ever accuse him of betraying the trust placed in him. His voice failed. He ceased speaking. The vast and varied audience applauded. They carried him, still in his armchair, to the hospital, the Hôtel Dieu. Early the next morning he died. And he died a Christian, offering his prayers, receiving the sacraments. He had been converted to Christianity by the Jesuit missionary, Father Etienne de Carheil. He himself often preached at Michilimackinac, never, it was said, "without fruit."

The death of the Rat profoundly moved the whole peace gathering. Minor disputes were softened, the main purposes strengthened. All joined to honor the Rat in his death. The French carried his body from the Hôtel Dieu to his wigwam. It was laid on a beaver skin. Though he was a Christian, he was lying in state in a unique gathering of scores of Indian tribes. By his side, with a gun and a sword, was laid a kettle. It was for his use in the world of spirits. The Iroquois, his worst enemies, came to pay tribute. They arrived in solemn procession. Sixty of them sat on the ground around him. One of them spoke, declaring it a day of grief. They performed the sorrowful ceremony of covering the body.

The funeral the next day had all the strange grandeur of mingled rites—the rites of the town and the wilderness. The senior French captain in Montreal, Pierre de Saint-Ours, led the funeral train with a military escort of sixty soldiers. Sixteen Huron warriors followed, marching four-and-four. They wore robes of beaver skin; their faces were painted black for mourning; their guns were held reversed. Next came the clergy. After them came six war chiefs, bearing the body. The pall was strewn with flowers. On it lay a plumed hat, a gorget, a sword. His brothers and children walked behind his body, then the chiefs of the tribes. The wife of the Intendant of New France, Madame de Champigny, was there, accompanied by Vaudreuil, who had been appointed Governor of Montreal. Staff officers brought the procession to a close. The funeral service took place in Notre Dame Church in Place d'Armes. When his body was buried in the crypt, volleys of musketry were fired in his honor.

In the solemn aftermath of his death the negotiations for the peace treaty were concluded. The Iroquois were never again a menace to the French, or a threat to the very existence of other tribes. As they had agreed to remain neutral in any war between France and England, the English in North America had lost their allies and one of their principal means of attack and defense. The French were able to extend their effective control into the west and down the Mississippi, enjoying a new security.

It has been said that no man knows today exactly where lie the bones of the Rat. The old Notre Dame Church, where he was buried in 1701, stood just north of today's Notre Dame Church. It covered Notre Dame Street and extended into Place d'Armes. The old church was demolished in 1830. But this is not to say that the bones were scattered and lost. They were gathered up and buried again in the new church. Today the bones of the Rat lie somewhere under the concrete floor that now covers Notre Dame's huge crypt.

John Collins SKETCHBOOK

ST. LAWRENCE
and NOTRE DAME

FOUR

The Prisoner of God:
Jeanne Le Ber

ON AUGUST 5, 1695, a strange procession moved through the streets of Montreal. It was the strangest procession Montreal had ever seen. None stranger has been seen since.

Jeanne Le Ber, a young woman of thirty-three, was going from her home (and her family was one of the richest in all New France) to the chapel of the nunnery, the Congrégation de Notre Dame. She was to enter a cell behind the altar. There she was to vow to shut herself up for the rest of her days, by a self-imposed sentence of solitary confinement.

On that August evening, vespers had been chanted in the parish church in Place d'Armes. Then a procession was formed, at the head of it the clergy walked. It made its way to the Le Ber house in St. Paul Street, where Jeanne was at prayer. She came out, wearing a long woolen gown bound at the waist by a black belt. Her father came with her. He was then sixty-one years old—an advanced age at that time when life expectancy was brief. He was compared to Abraham or Jephthah of the biblical stories. He, as they had done, was leading his child as a victim to the sacrifice. Yet she was going by her own choice and insistence. He walked with her through the streets to give public witness that he honored his only daughter for her decision to spend the rest of her life as a dedicated recluse. But before the end of the ceremony in the chapel he was overwhelmed by anguish. He hurried back to his house, unable to see his daughter disappear into the cell that would be her living tomb.

What happened at the chapel of the Congrégation de Notre Dame was described in a signed document by Dollier de Casson, Superior of the Sulpicians in Montreal and Vicar General of the diocese. He stated in this document that he wished to set down the facts, that generations to come might know of this young woman's extraordinary self-sacrifice:

"I declare that on the fifth day of the month of August last, which was a Friday, the feast of Notre Dame des Neiges, I blessed a little room with its little door and grille for Mademoiselle Jeanne Le Ber. . . . I declare that after the benediction which I pronounced in my quality as grand vicar, before the clergy as well as all the sisters of the congrégation, and other people from outside, I made a brief exhortation to which she listened on her knees, after which I led her to the above-mentioned little apartment in which she locked herself up at once . . ." At that ceremony one of her spiritual directors did not soften his words. Jeanne Le Ber was to regard herself as already dead—dead to the world. "You are dead," he said, "and enshrouded in your solitude as in a tomb. The dead do not speak, nor are they spoken to."

This decision by a young woman to shut herself up for life, to live as though she were dead, was all the more remarkable because she gave up so much. She was not only the daughter of Jacques Le Ber, a very rich man; she was rich in her own legal right, for her father had given her a lavish dowry. Jeanne was regarded as one of the most eligible young women in New France. She was an aristocrat, as her father had used his wealth to acquire a patent of nobility from King Louis XIV.

Though Jacques Le Ber and his wife were both pious, they had not at first recognized the depth of their daughter's religious feelings. They had begun to prepare her for a life in society and the prospect of marriage. Her mother one day gave her an elaborate headdress in the latest fashion. Jeanne said she would wear it if told, as an act of obedience, but she begged to be allowed to dispense with it. God would be her witness that she wore it against her will. She began to go to parties. But she would retire to carry out her resolution to pray at fixed times every day and to recover her awareness of the sovereignty of God.

Such tendencies were not new. Even as a child of five or six she had gone again and again to visit her godmother, Jeanne Mance, at the Hôtel Dieu. She also had long religious talks with the Superior, Mother Catherine Macé. She surprised the nuns by her interest in the mysteries of religion and the originality of her comments. For three years she was sent by her parents to be a boarder at the Ursuline Convent at Quebec, where her aunt was one of the teachers. The nuns noticed her extreme seriousness at all religious services. Already the withdrawal from the world was becoming evident. When made a gift of a cushion adorned with ribbons, she tore the decorations from it and flung them on the floor. She explained that she hated such worldliness. When chosen as one of the performers in a biblical play at the convent, she was horrified by the gaudy robe she would have to wear, and burst out crying.

After she returned to Montreal, and grew older, the withdrawn, introverted tendencies became more and more pronounced. When proposals of marriage came, she reacted with revulsion. Under the protection of the Holy Virgin she would present to God her own most precious treasure—her own person. Her sense of the vanity of the world reached a crisis. She had become the close friend of a nun at the Congrégation de Notre Dame—a young girl, Sister Marie Charly. Her friend died suddenly. The sight of the corpse chilled any remaining attraction Jeanne might have had to the world, and made God the one reality. She now decided to give up the world, to become a recluse.

She sought advice from her spiritual adviser, Abbé François Seguenot. He suggested an experiment in seclusion, a limited vow for a term of five years. She withdrew into a room in her father's house. She would leave only to go to mass. She decided to express her humility publicly: she would wear a plain gray robe and bow down to kiss the floor of the church at the elevation of the Host. Her spiritual adviser may have suspected something too self-conscious in these public demonstrations. He recommended that she go to High Mass no more, but attend the first mass only, when few were present.

Her style of seclusion mingled austerity with a rich girl's privileges. On the side of austerity, she practiced the customary afflictions of the zealous: the hair shirt and the scourge. On the side of privilege, she lived under her father's roof; she continued to eat meat (which strict zealots generally gave up); she retained her own money and attended to her own business affairs; and she had an attendant in her cousin, Anna Barroy, who waited upon her in her room and accompanied her to and from the church. At times she modified her seclusion and saw visitors, though usually only for some religious purpose.

Despite such compromises it became evident that these five years of seclusion were more than the indulgence of a passing emotional disturbance. Her severance of family ties became awesome. In the autumn of 1682 her mother lay dying. Jeanne refused to leave her room to visit her, though they were both under the same roof. She appeared only after her mother's death, kissed her dead hand and turned away. When the five years were ended and she was freed from her vows, she declined to take charge of the household for her widowed father. On the contrary, she decided to make her temporary vows perpetual: she chose to remain a recluse for the rest of her life. She continued to live in seclusion in her father's house under the same conditions as before. The detachment shown at her mother's illness was seen again when her brother, Jean Vincent, was wounded in a skirmish with an English and Iroquois war party near Fort Chambly in 1691. He was brought home to die, but Jeanne would not leave her room until he was dead. She then came out to aid the preparations for laying out the body, and withdrew as quickly as she could.

Obviously Jeanne Le Ber was not acting on impulse when she decided to go to a cell behind the altar in the chapel of the Congrégation de Notre Dame. Her vocation as a religious recluse had been thoroughly tested in her father's house over a long period. As Dollier de Casson (who led her to her cell in the ceremony at the chapel) was to emphasize, she was not beginning a new way of life but was carrying on the vocation of solitude "she had followed at home the greater part of her life, but especially the last twelve or fifteen years." The lack of impulse was also seen in the detailed legal agreement drawn up between her and the Congrégation de Notre Dame. The document was prepared by the notary, Bénigne Basset; Dollier de Casson signed as a witness. It provided for an exchange of benefits. Jeanne Le Ber would make a large capital donation, enough to meet the cost of building and decorating a chapel for the Congrégation. In addition, she would pay the Congrégation, as a sort of rent, an annual sum of seventy-five livres.

In return for these benefits the Congrégation would have to fulfill a list of stipulations. Nothing was left vague; everything was spelled out. First of all, the chapel would have to be constructed in a style she preferred. It would be a replica, as far as possible, of the chapel at Loretto in Italy—the chapel said by tradition to have been the house of the Virgin Mary, miraculously transported to Italy by angels. Then Jeanne Le Ber described the accommodation she needed. Directly behind the altar she was to have three rooms. They were to be constructed one above the other; all were to be ten by twelve feet. The lowest room would have two doors. One would lead to the sisters' garden, the other into the chapel. The second door would have a grille built into it. Through this grille she could see the altar; through it she could make her confession and receive communion. The room above would be her bedchamber. She would place the head of her bed on the side nearest the tabernacle; only a thin partition would separate her from the Blessed Sacrament on the altar. The top room would be where she would do her needlework for the churches.

She made further stipulations. The Congrégation was to provide her with food, clothing and fuel. It would arrange to have someone wait upon her, whenever her lady-in-waiting, Anna Barroy, was absent. And it would offer daily intercessions on her behalf. She was to be accepted as a member of the Congrégation and be known as Sister Le Ber. But she would not be required to follow the communal rules of the order; she would live her own life in seclusion. Marguerite Bourgeoys, who had founded the Congrégation, had been, since Jeanne's childhood, one of the chief influences on her life. She now welcomed her into her order. "I was delighted," she wrote, "when Mlle. Le Ber entered our house . . ."

Jeanne Le Ber seems always to have been aware of her rank as a rich and aristocratic young woman. Not everyone with a vocation for solitude could command it in so grand a manner. Since she retained possession of her private wealth, she preserved her privileged position by making gifts from time to time to the Congrégation and to other religious institutions. Only at the approach of death did she see fit to dispossess herself of the remainder of her money. No doubt she was also aware that the respect in which she was held by all, from the Bishop down, was due to her social position as well as to her exemplary piety. Yet she may also have recognized that the very prominence of her social rank made her example all the more influential and conferred upon her sacrifices a power for good they would not otherwise have had.

At times strictness of solitude was relaxed, generally that her influence might be felt. She would sometimes address the nuns at their recreation period after supper. She would speak to them through the grille in her cell. But as soon as the bell rang, announcing that the recreation period was over, she would become silent, not even waiting to finish a word she had begun to speak. The Bishop of Quebec, Monseigneur Saint-Vallier, came to visit her. He brought with him two Englishmen, one of them a Protestant minister. The minister asked what had prompted her to follow a way of life so restrictive. She pointed to the Blessed Sacrament, glimpsed through the grille in her cell door. That, she said, was the magnet that drew her.

Jeanne Le Ber did not cut herself off completely from what was going on in the outer world. She was appealed to in the crisis of 1711. The English were advancing against New France: a fleet was mounting the St. Lawrence to Quebec, an army was moving overland toward Montreal. Jeanne embroidered a banner to be carried in battle. On one side was an image of the Virgin Mary, on the other an exhortation to faith in the Virgin's intercession. Abbé de Belmont publicly blessed her banner as a symbol of hope. The invasion ended in disaster. The fleet sailing against Quebec was scattered and wrecked in a storm. When the land force moving against Montreal heard the news, it retreated. Jeanne Le Ber's banner was said to have saved the colony—the banner with her declaration of faith in the Holy Virgin: "She is as terrible as an army in battle array. She will help us to vanquish our enemies."

In the anxieties of 1711 Jeanne Le Ber also wrote a prayer. It has been recited every day ever since in every chapel of the Congrégation: "Queen of Angels, our Sovereign Lady and our very dear Mother, we, thy daughters, confide to thy care all our houses and all our possessions. We trust that thou wilt not suffer thy enemies to molest us, for we are under thy protection, and we place unbounded confidence in thee. Amen."

Even if Jeanne Le Ber never lost her sense of aristocratic rank, and even if a touch of the theatrical marked her way of life, the rigor of her austerity for twenty years at the Congrégation could never have been borne without intense religious zeal. When she died her clothes were such rags that they would not dress her in them even in her coffin. Her stockings she made for herself; she used remnants of prickly wool left over from the clothes she made for the poor. She made her shoes from the straw of Indian corn; it was cheap; it also kept her footsteps silent as she walked near the altar at night, when the chapel was empty and she could pray alone in front of the Sacrament. She slept on a mattress of straw. She would never allow it to be moved; it became harder and harder. She did not wish to use sheets. Her pillow, stuffed with straw, was covered with the coarsest cloth. She had an aversion for medicines. Yet whenever she had to take any with a foul taste, she refused to rinse her mouth, but let the taste linger.

Though she had stipulated that she must have a door from her lowest cell into the sisters' garden, she never seems to have gone into the open air or stood under the sky. It is said that she would not even look out of a window. One of the Sulpician priests, in writing of her, said she lived even more severely than the hermits of olden days; for they not only had gardens, but permitted themselves to take walks in the woods. The unhealthiness of her environment was recognized. As this

Sulpician writer said, "the close air of so small a room contributed to many of her infirmities."

Jeanne Le Ber's days in her cell behind the altar at the Congrégation's chapel were not spent in idleness; every hour had to be accounted for. From Easter to All Saints' Day she rose at four o'clock in the morning; from All Saints' Day to Easter at four-thirty. After dressing, she prayed for an hour. She then listened to the Mass through the grille in her lowest cell, her arms spread out like a cross. From nine to nine-thirty she read some religious book. From ten to eleven she prayed. At eleven she read a chapter of the New Testament, then searched her conscience. At eleven-thirty she dined.

So passed every morning. The afternoon hours were also allotted. At one o'clock she said vespers and compline. A half-hour was spent in religious reading. At four she spent an hour in prayer. At six o'clock she supped, taking this meal, like all others, on the floor. At seven she said her rosary and several other prayers aloud. At eight-thirty she went to bed. At midnight she always arose, left her cell and went into the chapel. At that hour all the nuns had retired for the night. The door of the chapel was locked. She was entirely by herself. In the dark silence she would prostrate herself for an hour or more before the altar. Even on the bitterest winter nights, when silence and cold seemed to deepen together, she would never spend less than a hour in worship in the unheated chapel.

Every interval of the day not spent in prayer or reading she gave to needlework. She made altar frontals, bouquets of artificial flowers and sacerdotal vestments for the churches in and about Montreal. The gorgeousness of her silk embroidery was in contrast with the horrid drabness of her surroundings. Specimens of her handicrafts have survived. Some are preserved in the Motherhouse of the Congrégation on Sherbrooke Street; others are on display in the museum at the back of Notre Dame Church in Place d'Armes.

In the autumn of 1714 Jeanne Le Ber was seriously ill. She was feverish and breathed with pain. She received the last rites of the church, but was determined that the long solitude of her life should not be broken at the end by the attentive flutterings of the ordinary deathbed. She asked the nun sent to nurse her to go into the chapel and take her place before the altar, that she might be more alone. She asked, too, that the curtains be drawn that not even the light should come to distract her. In the silence and darkness of the little room Jeanne Le Ber died on October 3, at nine o'clock in the morning, in her fifty-third year.

Many years before, her father had asked the sisters of the Congrégation that he might be buried in the chapel his daughter had built. Though his daughter had left him to go into seclusion, he had been permitted to visit her twice every year, and he had once expressed a wish that she would come back to him in her death. On October 5 Jeanne was buried in the chapel, at her father's side.

After her death the greatest evidence of the sincerity of Jeanne Le Ber was disclosed in the life of her written by Abbé de Belmont. He said he had learned from her spiritual director that she had derived little satisfaction from her life of seclusion, or from her prayers. In her earlier days, while a recluse in her father's house, her prayers had brought her sweetness and tranquility. But all the last twenty years of her life—the years spent in her cell behind the altar—had been passed in arid gloom. Little warmth or light had come to her to relieve or reward the austerity of her devotion. By sheer force of perseverance, by steadiness in her vows, she had gone through her religious exercises, and her needlework for the churches, forsaking or neglecting none of her duties. And when she felt the end drawing near, she had redoubled her devotions, knowing that the time was at hand when she might be delivered not only from the rigors she had imposed upon herself, but from that long night of the soul through which only her unyielding will had carried her for twenty solitary years.

Nothing remains of the chapel built for the Congrégation de Notre Dame by Jeanne Le Ber. It was destroyed by fire in 1768. The City of Montreal, in 1912, extended St. Lawrence Boulevard through the old grounds of the Congrégation south of Notre Dame Street. Anyone going along that section of the boulevard is passing near, if not over, the site of the chapel where Jeanne Le Ber spent her last twenty years as "the prisoner of God."

John Collins SKETCHBOOK

LA SALLE
MARKER
LA SALLE BOULEVARD

FIVE

The Man with the Iron Hand:
Henri de Tonty

THEY CALLED HIM "the Man with the Iron Hand." And he
did have a metal hand. Some said it was copper; some, brass;
some, silver. Others insisted it was really iron. Whatever it
was, he concealed his metal hand inside a glove. It was a
handicap undoubtedly. But it was an asset too. When he
brought his hand down upon an opponent's skull, it fell with
stunning force. The Indians came to respect him. They had
no knowledge of artificial hands; they only knew that inside
that glove he had terrible striking power. They called him
"strong medicine."

Henri de Tonty was "the Man with the Iron Hand." He
lost his right hand serving in one of the campaigns of King
Louis XIV of France against the King of Spain. It was shattered
when a grenade exploded during the battle of Libisso. Tonty,
it is said, did not wait for a surgeon. He cut off the remains
of his right hand with his left.

The unshakable nerve of Tonty was seen in this self-performed surgery. Of all the fur traders, explorers and empire builders who set out from Montreal into the wilderness in the seventeenth century, none surpassed the dependable resolution of "the Man with the Iron Hand." Yet he seems to have been no giant of a man. He was described as small and slight—only his will power gave him towering stature. Said one of his contemporaries: "He is beloved of all the *voyageurs* . . . he is the man who best knows the country . . . he is loved and feared everywhere."

Henri de Tonty was not a Frenchman but an Italian. His name was actually "Tonti." In 1647, his father, a Neapolitan banker, took part in a popular revolt against the tyranny of the Spanish viceroy. He seized the fortress of Gaeta. During this revolt, and in this fortress, Henri was probably born. After the uprising failed, the Tontis escaped to France. When old enough, Henri had gone into the French navy. When the war against Spain ended, he found himself discharged, poor, maimed.

It was just at this time that influential friends recommended him to René Robert Cavalier, Sieur de La Salle. About to embark upon a stupendous project in New France, La Salle was looking for a dependable lieutenant, someone to support him in all risks and troubles. At first he was hesitant about a man with only one hand, and a left hand at that. But in later years he wrote (apparently to Abbé Renaudot, one of those who had recommended Tonty):

"M. de Tonty has always been so dependable in his dealings with me, that I cannot overstate my joy in having him with me. ... He has surpassed my highest hopes. ... His honesty and strength of character are well enough known to you, but perhaps you would not have believed him capable of doing things for which a strong constitution, a knowledge of the country, and the free use of two arms seem absolutely necessary. Nevertheless, his energy and ability make him capable of anything."

La Salle needed a lieutenant with the qualities he had found in Tonty. His own mind and temperament had serious defects. He could not remedy them. He needed someone with the practical executive capacity he lacked, and someone who would not be driven away from him by his moody arrogance. Tonty met his requirements. He was capable; he was loyal. Between the two men grew a bond so strong that each was ready to risk his life for the other—and did.

In Montreal today La Salle has many memorials. A monument to him stands on the waterfront at Lachine—the settlement given the outlandish name of "China," ridiculing La Salle's early belief he could find somewhere in the interior of North America a new route to the riches of the Far East. A cairn and a metal standard mark the site of his old seigneurial homestead on the Lower Lachine Road, just east of the high embankment of the railway bridge. On the Island of Montreal a municipality is named after him, several streets and a boulevard. His name has been taken by all kinds of businesses, even a taxi association.

Henry de Tonty had many connections with Montreal. Here he acquired his trade goods and equipment; here he engaged his *voyageurs*; here he carried out negotiations and signed legal documents; here he shipped his furs; here the governor consulted him about strategy in the Indian wars; here his brother Alphonse had settled; here Tonty himself lived for the winter of 1684-5 and wrote his narrative. Among Montrealers this man with the gloved right hand must have been a familiar figure.

It was not, however, until 1950 that Tonty was honored in Montreal. On July 19 the executive committee named de Tonty Street after him. It is appropriately placed—near the park called Louisiane.

La Salle was a man of gigantic plans. Though he had courage and imagination, he yet wanted the patience and realism, the sense of organization, to carry them out. His critics encouraged the belief that he was mad—a man never to be relied upon. They spread rumors that he was "fit and ready for the madhouse." Even when La Salle was planning his first expedition, a shrewd Sulpician priest warned that he was "known to be somewhat changeable," and might abandon the whole project "at the first whim." And near the very end of his career another of his critics remarked: "There are very few who do not believe that he is crazy. I have spoken of it to people who have known him for twenty years. Everyone says that he has always been something of a visionary."

Such comments were only partly just. La Salle thought in such expansive terms that he seemed, at times, to be claiming the whole interior of North America for himself. While such plans could be ridiculed as visionary, they were also a threat to those with interests of their own in the same vast region. If La Salle's aims had not had such imperial scope, he might have aroused less uneasiness and had fewer rivals. Yet it remained true that his reach was always exceeding his grasp. He was seeking to do things beyond any man's scope. In Tonty he found the only one who would try systematically to put foundations under his castles in the air. As has been said, "while La Salle conceived, Tonty achieved."

Of even greater importance than Henri de Tonty's loyalty to La Salle's plans was his loyalty to La Salle himself. Tonty was the only true and lasting friend La Salle ever had; he knew he "was the only officer who did not abandon him."

The Jesuits had observed La Salle's difficult disposition during the nine years he had spent preparing himself to enter their order. They had found him bad-tempered, autocratic, rigid, taciturn, generally unsociable. Undoubtedly he had unusual talents (notably in mathematics) and a potential for zeal. For nine years they tried to discipline his restlessness, to bring his impulses under control, to regulate his irritability. La Salle left the Jesuits on March 28, 1667. As the Jesuits said, he was characterized by "inquietus."

A man with such a temperament was unsuited to take command. He provoked resentment among his followers. The expeditions he led into the wilderness were marked by mutterings and mutinies. In the end he was murdered by one of his own men. Henri de Joutel, a member of his party, wrote that all his fine qualities were "counterbalanced by a haughtiness of manner which often made him insupportable, and by a harshness towards those under his command which drew upon him an implacable hatred, and was at last the cause of his death." Gloomy, withdrawn, bitter and tactless, La Salle found only one person who would stand by him through the years, even under desperate conditions. It is easy to understand why he said of Tonty: "I cannot overstate my joy in having him with me."

La Salle was a young man in his twenty-fourth year when he left the Jesuits. He had spent nine years of his life training for a vocation he had abandoned. He had no training for any other. As a native of Rouen, he turned naturally to New France. Normandy had supplied the colony with many of its settlers. The church of New France was a dependency of the archdiocese of Rouen. La Salle also had family connections. As uncle was in the Company of One Hundred Associates, the group of rich men formed by Cardinal Richelieu to promote trade and settlement in New France. And his brother was a Sulpician priest in Montreal.

La Salle came to Montreal in 1667. The Sulpicians granted him a seigneury. It was a large property facing the waterfront, where the Lower Lachine Road now runs. He received the land for nothing, on the condition that he would encourage settlers and carry out the customary seigneur's obligations. But living the life of a seigneur, fixed in one spot and supervising the details of a community, soon proved as incompatible with his temperament as his novitiate with the Jesuits in France. His restlessness was provoked and tormented by living always in sight of the river—a river whose mysterious connections might lead on to immense discoveries. If he was ever to begin his explorations, he would need money. And if he was to raise money, it would have to be by selling his seigneury. He sold it back to the Sulpicians, for though they had given it to him for nothing, he had brought about many improvements.

La Salle was now to devote himself to exploration and the fur trade. His vast schemes for the American interior obviously needed official approval and support at a very high level. He found the backing he needed in the old Comte de Frontenac, Governor of New France. Frontenac was himself difficult, overbearing, quarrelsome. But he was also a big man, capable of large views—a man who welcomed daring and enterprise. He believed that the valley of the St. Lawrence was only a small part of the realm that ought to be claimed in the name of Louis XIV. He also had his own share of avarice; by private arrangements with La Salle, he could have a share in the profits of the fur trade.

After exploring and trading on the Great Lakes, La Salle grew restless again. He had far grander plans. He would develop the whole interior of the continent and explore the Mississippi to its mouth. These plans he had taken to the court at Versailles in 1677. There he presented dazzling possibilities. The tremendous interior of the continent would be opened to trade and communications. The English would be prevented from coming over the Allegheny Mountains. If French power could be extended to the mouth of the Mississippi, the power of Spain might be curbed in that region. La Salle gave his proposals a final attraction: they would cost the king nothing. The project could be supported if La Salle was granted trading rights in the area.

The king granted his requests "since we have nothing more at heart than the exploration of this country, through which, to all appearances, a way may be found to Mexico . . ."

La Salle returned to Montreal, bringing with him Henri de Tonty, who was to be his lieutenant in achieving the impossible. And his project *was* impossible. He had to finance it on borrowed funds. Only rapid returns could satisfy his creditors. When difficulties and misfortunes delayed revenues, his creditors began to close in upon him.

Tonty's first assignment in the New World put him to the test. La Salle began to construct a ship to transport furs on the Great Lakes. The work was begun on the Cayuga Creek on the Niagara River. Though La Salle saw the work started, he soon had to leave for Fort Frontenac to attend to his business problems. Tonty was placed in charge at the creek, in the midst of a wilderness.

Tonty was menaced, anxious, harassed. The shipbuilders had been tampered with by La Salle's enemies. They were truculent, hard to manage, tending to mutiny. The Seneca Indians disapproved of the project; they feared it might somehow be used to their disadvantage. They loitered about—a sinister, unnerving shadow. One of them, pretending to be drunk, broke into the camp. He attacked the blacksmith; the blacksmith held him off with a red-hot iron bar. As the ribs of the ship arose, the Indian menace increased. Rumors reached Tonty: the Senecas would set fire to the ship before it could be launched. All his men were put on the alert.

Everything had conspired against Tonty: the isolation of the wilderness; the meager food; the piercing wintry cold; the disaffected grumblers; the haunting Indians. Yet when La Salle returned to Cayuga Creek early in August he found his ship, the *Griffon*, of about forty-five tons, had been launched in the spring, taken up the Niagara River and anchored below the current at Black Rock. The loss of the *Griffon*, laden with furs, later in the year was to be another of La Salle's misfortunes. But in building her, Tonty had done his job under great difficulties, and he had done it well.

Tonty was now assigned a very different role. A number of La Salle's traders had deserted, carrying away furs with them. Tonty rounded them up. La Salle then set out with Tonty to build a fort in the interior. They moved into the Illinois country and built Fort Crèvecoeur on Lake Peoria. There the construction of another ship was begun—a ship for the exploration of the Mississippi. But La Salle's failure in leadership was soon seen. He provoked resentment among his men. Rumors began to go about: he was a ruined man; they would never be paid; there would be no sense in serving him any longer. La Salle left to bring back supplies and trade goods. He placed Tonty in charge. Tonty was doing his best to maintain order, but a letter was brought to him from La Salle, instructing him to examine a huge rock on the Illinois River—Starved Rock. Perhaps, La Salle suggested, a far stronger fort could be built there. Tonty followed instructions. But he had to leave Fort Crèvecoeur at a bad time. The men soon mutinied, demolished the fort and disappeared.

Tonty was stranded in the wilderness, with only a few followers. He decided to serve La Salle's interests in another way: he would try to conciliate the Indians. If La Salle's plans for the interior of America were ever to succeed, the Indians of the region, the Illinois, would have to be allied with him, not only in trade but to resist the menacing Iroquois, traditional allies of the English. But the Illinois were suspicious of La Salle and his intentions in their territory. To give them reassurance, Tonty settled down among them in their village on the shore of the river.

The air was tense. At any time the Iroquois might begin pressing into the Illinois country. English and Dutch traders had been supplying them with guns and ammunition. In the Iroquois hunting grounds game was growing scarce; they would be moving westward.

On a September day in 1680 Tonty saw an Indian running into the village. He screamed a warning. The Iroquois were closing in to attack them. The Illinois gathered around Tonty, accusing him of treachery. So recently from Europe, he knew little about Indians, but, as a Récollet friar said, he showed "courage and intelligence." He assured the Illinois he was on their side; to prove it, he would go with them to fight the Iroquois.

When the Illinois moved out to fight, the Iroquois had already emerged from the woods and were advancing across the prairie. Well armed, they opened fire with their guns. Tonty saw at once he must prevent a battle. His Indians, with nothing but bows and arrows, would be massacred. He tossed aside his gun and went forward in the wild hope that he might be able to parley with the Iroquois and somehow persuade them to draw back. Two Frenchmen and an Illinois Indian were willing to go forward with him. But he commanded them to fall back. He went on alone, unarmed, holding a wampum belt.

The Iroquois closed around him. His swarthy Italian complexion, and his wilderness dress, made him seem at first like an Indian. A young Iroquois stabbed at his heart. The blade, striking a rib, glanced aside. Blood spurted from the gash. A chief noticed his ears. He could not be an Indian, the chief called out; the ears had not been pierced.

Tonty was led behind the fighting line. The battle never ceased. He could hear the crackle of the fire, the shouts. He did his best to parley. Speaking was hard; the blow had made him bleed from the mouth. His one chance was to point out that the Iroquois, though long the enemies of the French, were at that time bound by a truce. The Illinois Indians were under King Louis' protection. If they killed the Illinois, they would be making war on the king's allies.

No orderly parley was possible. Interruptions bewildered him. An Iroquois plucked his hat from his head. He put it at the end of a gun, ran to the front line and displayed it to the Illinois. The Illinois thought he had been killed; they fought more furiously than before. Then reports came that Frenchmen were among the Illinois. They were firing on the Iroquois.

Tonty thought he was done for. "I was never," he said, "in such perplexity; for at that moment there was an Iroquois behind me, with a knife in his hand, lifting my hair as if to scalp me. I thought it was all over with me, and that my best hope was that they would knock me on the head instead of burning me, as I believed they would do."

It seemed a time to stretch the truth. Tonty told the Iroquois that the Illinois were 1200 strong. Sixty Frenchmen were in reserve at their village, ready to join the battle. This story had a surprising effect. Tonty was released with a wampum belt of peace. He came out from among the Iroquois, back toward the Illinois, holding the belt up in the air. The sounds of battle died away. Bleeding and shaken, he staggered among his allies.

The Iroquois had made truce with Tonty only to plan attack later. But Tonty had not failed. He gave most of his Indian allies the chance to escape. He himself set out with his men to make his way northward, to get back to La Salle. Winter had set in. They tried to feed themselves by digging roots out of the frozen ground. They grew weak and hopeless. Nothing remained but to have the courage to face death. Tonty would lead them back to a deserted Indian village they had passed. There they would shelter themselves in an abandoned wigwam and die by a warm fire. Friendly Indians, the Ottawas, rescued them in time.

Meanwhile La Salle had set out on a desperate search for Tonty. When he came into the Illinois River he was coming into a deathland. The devastation of the Iroquois invasion was everywhere. The Illinois village, where Tonty had lived, was covered by wolves and vultures. And nothing but ugly ruins remained of Fort Crèvecoeur. The ship he had been building was abandoned. Across its side the mutineers had written: "Nous sommes tous sauvages . . ." No trace of Tonty could be found. He could hardly be alive in that forsaken and ravaged land.

There was nothing for La Salle to do but to head northward again, hoping somehow he might appease his demanding creditors and gather his resources for another effort. But he had, in Tonty, lost his greatest asset. Tonty, in his narrative, speaks of their inexpressible joy, when they at last found each other at Michilimackinac.

La Salle now laid new, audacious plans. His project had hitherto been wrecked by disasters. It could be saved only by some sensational achievement. He would be the first to explore the Mississippi to its mouth and claim immense new regions for the king. He would prove that this river would offer a new means of communication to the heart of the continent, far better than the St. Lawrence route, closed half the year by ice. In the autumn of 1681 La Salle went to Montreal to make his will. He left everything to a cousin, to whom he was deeply in debt. He was counting on Tonty's help in the dangers of the voyage. Shortly before he left he wrote to a correspondent in France: "I hope to write more at leisure next year, and tell you the end of the business, which I hope will turn out well: for I have M. de Tonty, who is full of zeal . . ."

On February 6, 1682, La Salle led his expedition to the shore of the Mississippi. About a week later the ice broke up.

He and his men put out in their canoes. The climate grew steadily warmer. They had started in biting cold. Soon they found themselves in a sort of premature springtime. The sun became sultry, the air balmy, the foliage rich, the flowers brilliant. They came into crocodile country. La Salle and his men lived largely off crocodile meat.

On the journey Tonty was the one who visited the Indians and negotiated with them. At one point Indians lined the bank, their bows grasped at the ready. Tonty offered to go to them with a pipe of peace. He landed with a few men and the Indians responded with friendship. They wished to demonstrate their good will by joining hands. Tonty, with his one hand, was embarrassed. He told his men to join hands for him. La Salle, seeing the peaceful reception, came ashore also. They went to the Indian village and spent the night there.

Near the end of their journey they knew they were drawing near the sea; they could smell brine in the air. The river divided itself into three branches. La Salle chose the one to the west; Tonty took the middle one; another member of the expedition, Dautray, took the one to the east. All three of them came out into the Gulf of Mexico.

The moment had come to claim and name the new land for the king. And La Salle did it in style. He dressed himself grandly for the occasion; he brought out a special costume—scarlet trimmed with gold. He mustered his men under arms. They sang the joyful, thankful hymns of the church, the *Te Deum*, the *Exaudiat*. La Salle set up a column and a cross. In a loud voice he proclaimed in that wilderness: "In the name of the most high, mighty and invincible Prince, Louis the Great, by the grace of God King of France and of Navarre, Fourteenth of that name. I . . . do now take, in the name of his Majesty and his successors to the crown, possession of Louisiana . . ." The moment his proclamation ended, the air quivered with volleys of musketry, shouts of *"Vive le Roi!"* La

Salle drew up a *procès verbal*—the official description of the proceedings. Henri de Tonty signed it.

The Louisiana claimed by La Salle on that April day in 1682 was vastly more than the state as it is today. It comprised the center of the North American continent, from the Gulf of Mexico northward to the Great Lakes, and from the Allegheny Mountains in the east to the Rockies in the west.

On the return journey up the Mississippi illness forced La Salle to go ashore to recover. He sent Tonty on to Quebec to announce the news of the discovery. The reception was not what had been expected. Frontenac was gone. A newly appointed governor, Le Febvre de La Barre, had allied himself with La Salle's worst enemies. In his letters to France he poured scorn on La Salle's discoveries, doubting they were real. He said La Salle owed money to everybody and had set himself up in the wilderness like a king among a pack of vagabonds.

Having done his best in Quebec to report La Salle's explorations, Tonty returned to the Illinois River. He now largely took over the organization of the fur trade for La Salle, who admitted that he had "neither the habit nor the inclination to keep books." Tonty, as businessman, was enterprising, systematic, thorough. As headquarters for their trade, Tonty built a fort on impregnable Starved Rock, at the height of all-season navigation in the Illinois. The post was named Fort Saint Louis. The location was strategic. It would stand as a barrier to the intrusion of English and Dutch traders, who were finding their way into the Illinois country through the Cumberland and Ohio valleys.

Tonty demonstrated the breadth and vigor of his policies. He engaged in intricate diplomacy. He traveled extensively among the Illinois and other Indians, making firm contracts with them, to counteract English and Dutch influences. To develop his trade and to assure defense he united the different western tribes in an alliance. He then induced them to abandon their scattered villages and to settle in the shadow of Fort Saint Louis. Through his efforts a great federation was created. In the rock's shadow were 300 cabins, sheltering about 20,000 Indians.

Meanwhile, however, Governor La Barre had been effectively undermining La Salle's authority. He interfered with the supplies of trading goods for La Salle's headquarters. Finally he sent Chevalier de Baugy to take over command of Fort Saint Louis. Faced with this new challenge, La Salle decided to go directly to Versailles and lay his case before the king.

Louis XIV's faith in La Salle had been clouded by La Barre's persistent misrepresentations. Yet La Salle found he had arrived at Versailles at a good time. The King was being annoyed by the Spaniards. They had been interrupting French ships at sea, even seizing and imprisoning his subjects. La Salle, having described his journey of discovery to the mouth of the Mississippi, now proposed an expedition by sea, to establish French power on the shores of the Gulf of Mexico. He also pretended, with whatever motives, that the gold mines of Spanish Mexico lay nearby; they could be attacked by an expedition from the mouth of the Mississippi.

La Salle's proposals found a ready reception. This time La Salle was not thrown upon his own finances. The king provided a large naval vessel of thirty-six guns, another vessel of four guns, a store-ship and a ketch. The expedition, under La Salle's command, was to sail with a hundred soldiers, as well as mechanics, laborers, settlers, missionaries.

In all his plans La Salle had made one fatal mistake: he did not bring Henri de Tonty with him. He had a reason. The king had restored La Salle to his trading powers at Fort St. Louis, and La Salle felt Tonty was needed to carry on the business. The absence of Tonty's loyalty, his resolution, his practical competence and counsel was seen at once, even before the expedition put out to sea. A position of command brought out all La Salle's worst impulses. He became suspicious, secretive, changeable, offensive. The commander of the principal ship was an experienced and rather good-natured naval officer, Taneguy Le Gallois de Beaujeu. La Salle even refused to tell him the expedition's destination. Sieur de Beaujeu had never encountered such a man before. He wrote privately to the king's minister to complain. But he promised to do his best: "I shall go straight forward, without regarding a thousand whims and 'bagatelles.' . . . I shall humor him, as I have always done, even to sailing my ship on dry land, if he likes."

The ships reached the Gulf of Mexico. But they could not find the Mississippi. La Salle, guiding the course, had gone four hundred miles beyond the Mississippi's mouth. He reached the entrance to Metagorda Bay. Here, he was convinced, was the way to the Mississippi. Sieur de Beaujeu offered to help in any way he could, though he had long endured every provocation. He suggested he might go to Martinique for provisions and reinforcements. But La Salle, arrogantly confident he had reached his destination, dismissed him, and he sailed.

Soon afterward, La Salle realized his mistake. He was not at the mouth of the Mississippi. He did not know where he was or where he should go. The ships had gone. No help would be coming. The whole party was in appalling isolation, in the midst of the unknown. There was only one hope: he would have to make his way northward to find help. But he would have to go by the Mississippi. First he would have to find in which direction the Mississippi lay.

La Salle did not know that Tonty had set out to rescue him. As soon as he had heard at Fort Saint Louis that La Salle had reached the Gulf of Mexico, Tonty was determined to find out if he was safe and the render him any aid he could.

He came down the Mississippi, expecting to find La Salle established somewhere near its mouth. But he reached the gulf without finding any trace at all. He sent exploring parties along the shoreline, east and west. There was nothing but emptiness and silence.

Tonty had no clue as to where La Salle might be. He gave a letter to an Indian chief on the Mississippi—a letter he was to give La Salle if he should appear. He showed his respect in a gesture of tenderness and loyalty. On the shore he found the pillar La Salle had set up in 1682. It had toppled and rolled down into the water by the shore. He recovered it and set it up again, on higher ground.

As Tonty, frustrated, made his way back to Fort Saint Louis, La Salle had never needed him so desperately in his life. La Salle had set out with a few of his men. Despair and hate gripped the little group as it struggled farther into the unknown. Grievances festered. La Salle's leadership, though resolute, was as harsh as ever. And his nephew, Moranget, was given to bullying and browbeating the men. La Salle did nothing to deter him. A man named Duhaut was plotting a mutiny.

La Salle had sent a party on ahead to uncover food he had left in a cache. Moranget was one of them; so was Duhaut. The day they were to return came and passed. La Salle had a presentiment of evil. He went out with an Indian guide and a friar named Douay. The friar later said that La Salle talked all the way about faith and the providence of God. "Suddenly," he went on, "I saw him overwhelmed with a profound sadness for which he himself could not account. He was so much moved that I scarcely knew him."

They reached the encampment of the men sent on ahead. La Salle saw two eagles circling in the air. He knew what it meant. He fired his gun and pistol to summon anyone around.

One of the men appeared. La Salle demanded to know what had happened to his nephew. The man was insolent. Le Salle went at him, to teach him respect. A shot rang out from the tall grass. La Salle staggered and fell, shot through the brain by Duhaut, who had been crouching hidden, like an Indian. The mutineers insulted his body. They stripped it of clothes and dragged it among bushes. There they left it to wolves and vultures.

Tonty's loyalty did not end with La Salle's death. When he learned that La Salle was dead, but some of his party might still be alive, he went to succor them. Reverses overwhelmed him. Most of his men deserted; he lost his ammunition in crossing a river; the Indians refused to provide guides. He came back through flooded country, sometimes wading up to his neck in water. Food ran out; he was forced to eat his dogs. He came down with fever. "I never in my life suffered so much," he said. Though he failed, he had done his best. No one else made the slightest effort to come to the help of any survivors of La Salle's expedition.

Tonty, having done all he could for La Salle while he lived and for La Salle's followers after his death, gave his own life in the end in serving La Salle's grand plan for a French post at the mouth of the Mississippi. Louis XIV had revived the scheme. Under the Montreal-born brothers, Iberville and Bienville, French colonies were established. Tonty joined efforts to establish French power on the gulf. His skill with the Indians proved valuable in negotiations to win the Chickasaws from English influence from the Carolinas. But a supply ship from Havana brought the yellow fever. Tonty contracted it. He died near Mobile in 1704.

Tonty was more than La Salle's lieutenant. He has a place of his own in the development of North America. But his most attractive quality remains his loyalty. He never ceased to perceive La Salle's greatness; he never failed to compensate for La Salle weaknesses. Tonty won tributes of his own. "He is a lad of great enterprise and boldness who undertakes a good deal," said Governor Denonville. Tonty had a far higher tribute for La Salle. To him La Salle was "one of the greatest men of this age."

John Collins SKETCHBOOK

PLACE ROYALE

SIX

The Traders on The Waterfront:
The Fur Fairs

FOR ABOUT 150 years—from the middle of the 17th century till the last years of the 18th—a grand Indian fair took place every summer in Montreal. The fairground was the "common"—the long strip of land between the waterfront and the southern wall of the town (where Commissioners Street now runs). Montreal has had many fairs since then, even a world exposition. But none has equaled the primitive picturesqueness, the motley vividness, the ceremony, noise or lively bargaining, even the rowdiness and alarm, of these Indian fairs on the waterfront.

Every spring Indians by hundreds gathered from the west for a rendezvous at Michilimackinac or Green Bay, in the region of the Great Lakes. They often descended on Montreal in one massive flotilla. The flotilla of 1693 was made up of more than 400 canoes. These Indians journeyed to Montreal over a water route of 1,000 miles or more. Their coming was hailed. The economic prosperity of Montreal, even its economic survival, depended on the fur trade. If these Indian flotillas failed to arrive, the town (at least during the 17th century) would be faced with ruin.

Above the Lachine Rapids some of the French settlers would come out to welcome the Indians as they paddled into view. Enterprising traders tried to set up booths at Lachine to do some deals with the Indians before they went on the next nine miles to the Montreal waterfront. This sort of advance trading, or preview, was against the law. The trade was regulated by the government. Montreal was its recognized center. Other recognized fur fairs were held at Sorel, Trois Rivières, Quebec and Tadoussac. But Montreal, as an outpost thrust out toward the west, was in the best position. Its fur fairs transcended all others.

When the Indians reached Montreal they set up their tepees, made fires for their kettles and unpacked their bundles of peltries. But the fair did not open without ceremonies. The Governor of New France would be present. He would make a special journey upstream from Quebec. Wearing his plumed hat, his scarlet cloak, he sat in state on the fairground in an armchair. The Indians formed a ring around him, in the order of their tribes. The calumet—the pipe of peace—was passed round. The song of the calumet was sung.

The governors lent their prestige to the annual fairs at Montreal not only because of the economic importance they had for the colony. These gatherings at Montreal of Indians from many tribes gave the governors an opportunity to parley with them, to confirm them in their alliance with the French. The fairs were also an opportunity to deal with complaints and grievances.

The value of the fairs for such diplomatic negotiations was seen in 1670. A precarious peace had been worked out between the French and the Iroquois. But three French soldiers had murdered three Iroquois. They first made the Indians drunk to steal their furs from them; then they killed them. Three other French soldiers had murdered an Iroquois chief. The motive was the same: to steal the furs. It was a crisis. The Iroquois threatened to end the peace treaty with the French, to unbury the hatchet. Sieur de Courcelle, the Governor of New France, placed his hope in the next annual fur fair at Montreal. When the Indians had assembled on the Montreal waterfront he spoke to them. He made a speech with cleverness and vigor, pausing from time to time to make appropriate gifts. Then he proceeded to prove to the Indians at the fair that justice would be done. The French soldiers who had murdered the Iroquois chief were led out. They were lined up and shot as the hundreds of Indians at the fair looked on. The Indians were placated. The fair had proved its usefulness. In no other way could so many Indians be assembled to see an execution carried out.

Once the governor's preliminary ceremonies and parleys were over, trading began in earnest. For much of the bargaining, the Indians came into town. Negotiations were brisk on the marketplace, La Place Royale. This ancient marketplace is still there, now a city square, close to the waterfront, between St. Paul and Commissioners streets.

The fair was an advantage to the Indians and French traders alike. The merchants of Montreal set up their little shops and offered trade goods in a variety the Indians could hardly expect from the French traders who traveled into the wilderness in their canoes. For the people of Montreal, and for those who came in from round about, the fair was a superb chance to obtain furs without the trouble, cost or risk of trading expeditions into the distant Indian country.

Beaver was the favorite; it fetched the best prices. Otter, marten, mink were also in demand. Moose hides had a market, as did bearskins. A certain number of buffalo skins were brought to the Montreal fur fairs, but they took up far too much space in the canoes for the price they would bring. The great period of the buffalo skins lay still far in the future, after transportation overland had been developed.

Dealers on the waterfront needed interpreters to deal easily with the Indians. Interpreters with fluent knowledge of the Indians languages were in competitive demand. They usually asked for payment in a proportion of the furs bought.

As for the Indians, they could satisfy their needs in the little shops on the fairground. They could equip themselves for a year. Their purchases were of two kinds: the necessary and the ornamental.

Among necessities, the Indians bought muskets, powder, shot or musket balls. By the middle of the 18th century they had become so dependent on their guns, and so little skilled in the use of bow and arrow, that one observer believed "they would starve to death" if the Europeans refused to supply them with muskets and ammunition. They gradually became dependent on European cloth for their clothing. They bought woolen blankets, linen shirts, and blue, red or white cloth. They gave up making hatchets or knives of stone or bone in favor of those manufactured in Europe. In the same way, they cast aside their own clay pots in favor of brass or copper kettles.

Such utilitarian articles were only part of the trade goods bartered for furs at the Montreal fairs. Much of the trading was in jewelry or coloring for self-decoration. Indians, men and women, loved earrings: brass, tin, silver. They were eager for cosmetic paints. Cinnebar (a heavy crystallized red mercuric sulfide) did well in the Indian trade. They would paint themselves with it, sometimes their shirts as well. When vermillion was introduced into the trade, the Indians thought no other color could compare with it. Verdigris was often used in painting their faces. To aid them in their make-up, and as a means of judging the effect produced, the Indians liked to have looking-glasses. Peter Kalm, visiting Montreal in the 1750's, wrote: "The Indians like these very much and use them chiefly when they wish to paint themselves. The men constantly carry their looking glasses with them on all their journeys, but the women do not. The men, upon the whole, are more fond of dressing than the women."

The best bargaining lure of all in the fur fairs in Montreal, as elsewhere, was brandy or rum. The Church authorities condemned it; they struggled to bring it to an end. The traders insisted that it was essential. If any trader would not offer brandy to the Indians, the Indians would go off to trade with somebody else, probably with the Dutch colonists or the English. Without the trade in liquor, there would be no certainty of trade in anything else. After nightfall at the Montreal fairs the Indians, growing wild with rum or brandy, might have menaced the whole town. But the gates of the town would be closed; otherwise, as one writer observed, they "might have been tempted to commit great outrages, and would have kept the inhabitants in a continual state of alarm."

The fur fairs on the Montreal waterfront continued to be held in the early years of the British Régime. They were described by an English traveler, G. Taylor of Sheffield, who came to the fair in September, 1768. Though he had been in North America only a few months, he purchased some trade goods in New York and came north to take part. "We found the town ... very full of people," he wrote, "even from the remotest parts of the Northern provinces; traders that reside almost above a thousand miles distant, and Indians that came sixteen to eighteen hundred miles."

The commanding officer of the garrison in Montreal presided. He took the precaution of placing guards here and there to preserve order. It was a necessary arrangement, for liquor was being traded on all hands. The Indians immediately consumed their rum. "They have their rum in a keg," Taylor observed, "the bung of which they set to their mouth, drinking round and never quitting it till the vessel be quite emptied. This brings on a temporary madness; and, so long as it continues, they are guilty of the most enormous excesses."

Though liquor dominated the trade, it did not monopolize it. Descriptions of the Indians picture how many other trade goods they bought with their furs. They were dressed mostly in European clothes, decorated with European paint and ornaments. The English traveler, John Palmer, gives such a picture of the Indians he saw on the Montreal waterfront: "The morning after I came here, six or eight large canoes, manned by at least eight Indians each, and loaded with peltry, arrived. The Indians were dressed in all their finery: blue leggings, trimmed with scarlet list, a gay printed shirt, or black or common blanket thrown over their shoulders, and a gaudy yarn sash round their waists; some had their faces painted red and black, etc.; some had plates of silver on . . . and almost all had pendulous earrings."

The fur fairs on the Montreal waterfront were primarily a feature of the French Régime. Toward the end of the 18th century they dwindled away. A few Indians might come from time to time with furs and trade them as best they could. But the annual fairs had gone. The Montreal traders dealt with the Indians at their posts in the Northwest and brought the furs back to Montreal in their own canoes.

The great trading on the waterfront was over. How great it had been is seen in the official records. At least 100,000 fur-bearing animals would be slaughtered in a single year to supply the flotilla of Indian canoes that came to Montreal for the fair.

John Collins SKETCHBOOK

OLD BUILDINGS
NORMANT STREET

SEVEN

The Mother of the Homeless:
Mme d'Youville

EARLY IN THE morning of the 24th of December, 1771, a young man was working on the farm of the Grey Nuns at Châteauguay. He was feeding the animals and distributing the hay more carelessly than usual. He heard the voice of Mother d'Youville, the Superior of the Grey Nuns. "My son," she said, "don't waste the hay!" He looked about him. Nobody was to be seen.

Yet he could not mistake that voice. He used to accompany Mother d'Youville when she made her frequent tours of inspection over the farm. He had often heard her instructions, for she observed everything and superintended the whole management. The young man was perplexed that morning of December 24 when he heard Mother d'Youville speak but could not see her. Later he spoke to others of his weird experience. He was told that Mother d'Youville had died a few hours before at the Hôpital Général in Montreal.

If Mother d'Youville had spoken after her death, she could have spoken in no way more characteristic. Prudent, efficient management had been her aim and practice; attention to detail had been imperative. When the Grey Nuns in Montreal learned of this experience of the young worker on the community's farm in Châteauguay, they were convinced she had truly spoken, and spoken with a purpose. These words were adopted by the Grey Nuns as a sort of motto: "Don't waste the hay!"

Only by strict and orderly economy had the immense charitable work of Mother d'Youville been possible down through the difficult years. She had set about caring for all the wretched and miserable, the poor, the old, the forsaken. In Montreal the saying among the people for anyone in trouble was: "Go to the Grey Nuns, they will do something for you." For all her work she had little money. If she was not to turn away those who came to her for shelter, she had to make the most of what was available. Nothing was to be wasted. Waste was a sin against the needy. Mother d'Youville had little use for the show or parade of good works—the sort that gave generous help today and was bored or indifferent tomorrow. True charity meant organization, a firm will, routine and no nonsense. It would never do to waste the hay.

Mother d'Youville gave her life to the care of the miserable because she herself had known misery. Though well born in the colony of New France, her life had been a succession of humiliations. Her father, Christophe Dufrost, Sieur de La Jemmerais, the son of a noble family in Brittany, came to Canada as an officer in the army and served in the border wars. Her mother was a daughter of the seigneur of Varennes. But Mother d'Youville's father died young, leaving a large family and little money; for his pay as an officer, while enough to support a family, had not been enough to create an estate.

After the father's death the family seems to have lived by

the grace and favor of friends and relations. By the use of influence and the generosity of others Marie-Marguerite was able to spend two years at the Ursuline Convent in Quebec. When she came back to her home in Montreal she made a little money by selling her needlework. These embarrassments did not prevent her from entering into an active social life. At that time rank counted for more than money in the colony; she still enjoyed the higher rank by right of birth. After a few years of vivaciously fashionable life she entered into a marriage that seemed to offer distinction and ease.

Her husband, François d'Youville, was the son of Sieur de La Découverte, the inheritor of a fortune. François d'Youville's portrait hangs today in the museum at the Château de Ramezay. It depicts a young man self-assured to the point of conceit, capable of much charm, but likely to be ruthless and self-centered. And so he was. It proved a harsh marriage. She never had a home she could call her own. Her husband took her to live with his mother in a house facing the marketplace. He was much away from home in his trade with the Indians. She was left with a mother-in-law who was grasping and unfeeling and interested in nothing but hard cash.

Even François d'Youville's trade distressed his wife. He established a post at Ile-aux-Tourtes, where he sold "firewater" to the Indians. This liquor trade was against the law. But his father had been a friend of Governor Vaudreuil, and Vaudreuil protected him. When Vaudreuil died, he lost his immunity and his post. About this same time, however, his mother died. At once he squandered the money her penuriousness had saved; it disappeared at the gambling tables. Dissipation wrecked his health. He died when scarcely thirty.

For Marguerite d'Youville it had been a wretched married life. She had only exchanged the insufficiency of her mother's home to suffer from parsimony in her mother-in-law's. From her husband she had known only hardhearted treatment. He had not troubled to turn up for the baptism of their first child; he had even been away when the child was born. When several of their children died in infancy, he gave no consolation. He left her with a debt of 10,812 livres and expecting a sixth child, who died soon after birth. To support herself and her two surviving children, she kept a little shop.

Unhappiness turned her mind to religion, and her religion turned her to helping other unhappy people. Her first charities were all voluntary, even to taking a poor blind girl into her house. She raised money for her charities largely by her needlework and by operating her little shop.

Her efficient charity attracted the attention of Monsieur Louis Normant du Faradon, Superior of the Sulpicians and Vicar General. He believed she had the potential to take over the direction of a charity that had failed—the Hôpital Général of the Charon Brothers.

This hospital had its origin toward the end of the 17th century. A young merchant, François Charon de la Barre, having made a sizable fortune, decided to devote his life and his money to the care of the disabled, the old, the infirm. He joined with others to found and endow a hospital. It was on land granted by the Sulpicians at Pointe à Callières, near today's Place d'Youville. François Charon meant well and did some good compassionate work; but the management of the hospital was confused, erratic and frustrated, partly because of incessant disputes with government authorities. After his death the management sank into total incompetence. Large debts were accumulated, both in France and in New France.

Monsieur Normant considered Madame d'Youville as the one chosen by Providence to reorganize the Hôpital Général. But he felt that Madame d'Youville first needed greater experience. He advised her to gather other devout women about her as associates, to establish a little hospital in a house, and to carry out the work in a sort of informal religious community.

Montreal in the 18th century was full of local cliques and rivalries. If Madame d'Youville was becoming the protégé of the Sulpicians, this was reason enough why the factions opposed to the Sulpicians would turn upon her as their target. A struggle had begun over which group would take over the direction of the declining Hôpital Général.

When Madame d'Youville and her associates went into the street a crowd surrounded them, jeering, insulting, tossing stones. The memory of her dissipated and unscrupulous husband was revived. The implication was that he and she had been two of a kind. As he had illegally sold liquor to the Indians, she, it was said, had kept up the trade. More than this, she and the women working with her were drinking freely themselves. They were called "the Grey Sisters" though she and her associates wore no nuns' costumes but only plain, ordinary dress. The Sisters of Charity in some of the towns of France had been called "Les Sœurs Grises," because of their gray costumes. The French word "gris" has two meanings—"gray" or "tipsy." By calling Madame d'Youville and her charitable workers "the Grey Sisters," though they were not dressed in gray, the slander was clear: they were "the Tipsy Sisters."

This and other slanders inflamed the factional spirit so bitterly that one day a Récollet (Franciscan) monk publicly refused to give communion to Madame d'Youville and her hospital workers. A priest has the right to deny communion to flagrantly open and scandalous sinners. She and her workers were being treated, even before the altar, as notorious reprobates. Nor were her feelings spared even when the house where she was caring for the homeless burned down. "Don't you see that violet flame?" people in the crowd were saying. "It's the firewater intended for the Indians that's on fire!"

How deeply these slanders had entered into Madame d'Youville's soul was seen many years later, when she was at last permitted to organize her workers into a recognized religious order. The King had believed that New France had too many religious orders already. In 1750 an attempt had been made to force a merger of her work in Montreal with the Hôpital Général of Quebec. In 1755, however, permission was granted to found her own order, the Sisters of Charity (la Congrégation des Sœurs de la Charité de l'Hôpital Général de Montréal). She had to decide the color of the robes the sisters would wear. She chose gray. The gray robes would be an everlasting reminder of the humiliations they had suffered at the hands of their enemies. And these gray robes would fulfill the words of the Gospel: "Blessed are ye when men shall revile you, and persecute you, and say all manner of evil against you falsely. . . ."

The Hôpital Général of the Charon Brothers had been falling into ruin. By 1748 only two of the brothers were left. Both were in their sixties. The dilapidated building held only four inmates: the oldest eighty-eight, the youngest seventy-three. These old men vegetated wretchedly in a corner of the ground floor. Rain was blown through the gaping windows; it seeped through the ceilings and dampened the accumulated dirt.

Action could be delayed no longer. The Sulpicians had prevailed over their opponents. They had persuaded the government to give Madame d'Youville and her workers a chance to show what they could do to get the hospital into order.

Madame d'Youville, and her few associates, took over the debt-burdened ruin. She had to direct the work from a distance, for she was confined to her bed or a chair by a knee injury. For eighteen days her associates worked from five o'clock in the morning until the sound of the Angelus in the evening. They cleaned the building; they took an inventory of its meagre assets. For repairs Madame d'Youville had to borrow money; new debts were added to old. When the hospital was ready on

October 7 she was brought to it on a stretcher in a cart.

Madame d'Youville gave the widest, most compassionate definition to her Hôpital Général. Hers was a hospital in the sense of being an "hospice," or shelter. Her welcome was to all the homeless. Her first care was mostly for the old and the chronically disabled, whatever their age might be. Other needs appeared; she broadened her work to include them. She cared for the insane; separate accommodation was set up for them. She was asked by the Intendant to take charge of the "fallen women" sentenced by the courts. This she did; their quarters came to be known about town as the "Jericho." She grew increasingly concerned about abandoned infants. She had seen one lying half buried. And on a winter's day she saw another frozen in the ice of the little Rivière St. Pierre near the hospital; a dagger was still sticking in its throat. She took upon herself the care of all unwanted infants. They were often left in a basket at the hospital's door.

In the Seven Years' War, as France and England struggled for possession of North America, wounded soldiers and prisoners had to be cared for. This work, too, she carried out. She began it at the request of the Government. The Intendant Bigot promised she would be paid for it. But Bigot found ways of keeping much of the money for himself. She then had to decide whether to give up the work or to carry it on as another of her charities, and somehow to find the money herself. For her there was really only one answer: she would carry it on, whether paid for it or not.

Her charity was impartial. She cared for wounded English soldiers just as she cared for the French. When these English prisoners recovered from their wounds or illnesses, she provided work for them. Some she employed as orderlies in the English ward in her hospital; others she put to work on the farms of the Grey Nuns at Pointe St. Charles and Chambly. The word "l'Anglais" ("the Englishman") was added to their

Christian names. A number of these prisoners settled among the French Canadians. This is believed to account for some of the families today named "l'Anglais," or "Langlois."

Mother d'Youville was also active in rescuing English-speaking captives from the Indian allies of the French. In 1757 she paid a ransom of 200 livres for the release of an English soldier named John. In the following year she took charge of a little Irish girl named O'Flaherty. One of the Sulpician priests had rescued her from the Indians; they had already bound her to the post and were about to light the fire. This Irish girl was educated by the Grey Nuns. She joined the order and lived till 1824.

Mother d'Youville even went so far as to hide English soldiers being pursued by Indians. In the border warfare, skirmishes might take place near the hospital, which was outside the walls of Montreal. Some of the English, hotly pursued, sought sanctuary in the Hôpital Général, and Mother d'Youville never turned them over. She would hide them in the cellars, feed them in secret and let them go when the moment came when they could make good their escape. One day she and her nuns were sewing a tent in the hall of the hospital. A terrified English soldier burst in upon them. Without saying a word she lifted a corner of the tent. She motioned for him to crawl under it. An Indian with a tomahawk rushed in. She calmly pointed to the door. The Indian dashed outside; he went off searching for his victim in the fields.

The question naturally arises: How was Mother d'Youville able to meet the costs of caring for so many helpless people? Her work was always expanding. She never turned anyone away. She did not hesitate for a moment even when a fire destroyed all but the walls of the Hôpital Général in 1765. Standing outdoors, with the helpless gathered about her, she called upon them to sing the great song of thanksgiving to God: "We will recite the Te Deum on our knees, to thank

74

God for the cross he has sent us." The hospital was rebuilt; the work went on.

The explanation lies in Mother d'Youville's ability to combine boundless charity with rigorous business management. From the start, money was raised with needlework. This work was expanded when she began to undertake contracts for the Government. She and her nuns made military uniforms, officers' lace and braid, decorative fringe, army tents. She also made sails for fishing boats. Among her best customers were the fur traders; they needed goods for bargaining with the Indians. Every year, in the spring days when the voyageurs were about to set out on their long canoe journeys to the fur country, she and her nuns, and the inmates of the hospital who were well enough, might be seen all working together, finishing and packing the goods. She developed business with the churches. She made altar cloths, vestments, candles, wafers. Further revenues came when women of means in the town, in widowhood and in their later years, asked to enter the Hôpital Général as boarders.

Madame d'Youville also developed the farms of the order to high levels of production. She sold the farm at Chambly as being relatively unproductive and too involved in legal disputes; she bought the seigneury of Châteauguay. She regularly visited the Châteauguay farm, as well as the one at Pointe St. Charles. To visit Châteauguay she had to go by cart along the rough road to Lachine and cross Lake St. Louis by canoe. Soon the farms were not only providing what the hospital needed; she was selling eggs, chickens, ducks, butter, lard, cereals, feathers, animal skins, wood. She also bought tobacco leaf, prepared the tobacco for use and sold it. If anyone with a trade was admitted to the hospital, she used his skill as far as he might be able to serve. The hospital had its tailor, its baker, its shoemaker, even an occasional mason. She conducted a cartage business. Tradition even has it that she operated a ferry service between Montreal and Longueuil.

At the same time as revenue was coming in from all these sources, Mother d'Youville practiced and imposed strict economy. The Grey Nuns, having no time to knit stockings for themselves, wore strips of cloth wound round their legs. Their pocket handkerchiefs were bits of cotton left over from their needlework.

Efficiency in production, economy in use—this combination financed the charity that excluded no need.

The appearance of Mother d'Youville is difficult to reconstruct. She would never allow her portrait to be painted. "If they insist on having my portrait," she would say, "they can have it only when I am dead." A portrait was painted after her death. Death, age, illness had all altered her features. Little impression was left of how she had appeared in the active years of her life.

Evidence suggests Mother d'Youville was a large woman. Even when a girl of twelve at the Ursuline Convent she could have passed for fifteen. Her presence could be awesome. Her son said she was both loved and feared. One day a drunken soldier called at the Hôpital Général, a pistol in his hand. His mistress was among the "fallen girls" being cared for by Mother d'Youville in the "Jericho." He told the porter he had come to shoot the Mother Superior if she would not release the girl at once. The porter ran to Mother d'Youville and begged her to hide herself; she might be killed. She strode to the door. She faced the soldier. He turned and ran without a word.

The Grey Nuns both loved and feared her. They knew her kindness, especially at the hour of the day when they gathered about her and she talked with them. While she knew that virtue must be firm and disciplined, she knew recreation was needed too. She would send her nuns on holidays to the community's farms. She encouraged gaiety and romping in the open air.

In matters of duty, however, she would yield to no compromise. She had to be obeyed. A novice, Sister Célaron, working in the laundry, insisted on lifting a heavy tub of wet washing. She was disobeying instructions. The sisters had been told to do nothing that might injure their health. If something heavy had to be lifted, they were to ask for help. Sister Célaron ruptured herself internally. Everything possible was done to nurse her back to health, but her illness grew worse. From her deathbed she made one last request. Her novitiate was practically completed. She asked to be permitted to take her vows, make her profession and become one of the Grey Nuns before she died. Mother d'Youville refused. Discipline had to be upheld.

The refusal of Mother d'Youville to grant the wish of the dying novice involved her in a quarrel. Sister Célaron's mother, a widow, lived as a boarder at the Hôpital Général. She denounced Mother d'Youville for her hard heart and spread the story into the town. Some of the cliques and coteries always opposed to Mother d'Youville were almost stirred up to renew their persecutions. Mother d'Youville paid no attention to the clamor. In the end she was approached by the girl's mother. She humbly asked to be admitted to the Grey Nuns in her daughter's place. Mother d'Youville, believing her to be a woman of "uncommon virtue," despite the storm she had aroused, consented. The dead novice's mother pronounced her vows as a nun in 1771—the last nun admitted by Mother d'Youville before her own death later in the same year.

The severity of her rule was seen in another instance. She happened to hear loud voices as she came into one of the rooms of the hospital. The voices were hushed the moment she entered. She demanded to know what was going on. A nun confessed that she has just been telling another nun what she thought of her. Mother d'Youville ordered her to perform immediate penance: she was then and there to kiss the feet of every nun in the room. The offending nun at once obeyed, though some of the nuns tried to spare her the humiliation. Mother d'Youville had acted on her principle that efficient charity is impossible without effective discipline.

Among Mother d'Youville's talents was a strange power of prophecy. Repeatedly she foretold events. One day, in the recreation hour at the hospital, with the sisters round about her, she suddenly pointed to Sister Thérèse-Gèneviève Coutlée. Her tone was serious and confident as she said: "She is the one who will be the last to die. She will outlive us all." The prophecy was fulfilled. Sister Coutlée outlived all those present on that April day in 1766. She did not die until July, 1821.

A grandniece of Mother d'Youville recalled the time when she and other members of the family had visited the Grey Nuns. They were then only young children. Mother d'Youville tapped one of the little boys on the shoulder, and said: "You will die a priest, my little man." And to one of the girls she said: "As for you, my little girl, you are going to die among the Grey Nuns." The boy, Jean-François Sabrevois de Bleury, was ordained a priest in 1790. He died as the Curé of the parish of St. Charles de Lachenaie. The girl, Charlotte de Labroquerie, married, but was widowed. Her house at Boucherville was destroyed by fire in 1843. Then in her seventies, she sought shelter with the Grey Nuns. She died in their hospital in St. Hyacinthe (a house of the Grey Nuns not established until long after Mother d'Youville's death).

Mother d'Youville prophesied her own death. Hers had been a long illness. On the afternoon of December 23, 1771, she was visited by her niece, Madame Porlier Bénac. Her niece offered to sit up with her that night. "Oh! tonight I shall be no more!" said Mother d'Youville, in the same distinct, matter-of-fact tone she always used in making a prophecy. Her remark was surprising. That day, and for several days before, nothing in her condition seemed to give cause for alarm. Yet that evening, toward half-past eight, she suffered another stroke of apoplexy and died.

Today Place d'Youville recalls the area of the old Hôpital Général. Running south from this square is Normant Street, named after the Sulpician priest, Louis Normant de Faradon, who supported her in her work and defended her from her enemies. On the east side of Normant Street, a little below Place d'Youville, is a long range of stone buildings. In the center is one said to be the original Hôpital Général of the Charon Brothers. This is the hospital Mother d'Youville took over and renovated. It was gutted in the fire of 1765, but is believed to have been rebuilt within the old walls. A window is still pointed out as being that of the room where Madame d'Youville died in 1771.

Part Two

Americans' Montreal

SKETCHBOOK

John Collins

ETHAN ALLEN
HOUSE

EIGHT

The Man George Washington Did Not Admire: Ethan Allen

ON THE MORNING of September 24, 1775, Montreal "was thrown into the utmost Confusion." Some of the officials went so far as to take refuge on ships in the river. An invading force of the American Revolution—commanded by the Vermonter, Ethan Allen—had crossed the St. Lawrence in the night and landed at Longue Pointe. Already they were mobilized in the fields, ready to attack the town.

The Governor, Sir Guy Carleton, learned the news about nine o'clock in the morning and ordered the drummers to sound the alarm in the streets. The volunteers turned out under arms on the old parade ground, the Champ de Mars. He said they were "all the old Gentlemen & better sort of Citizens English & Canadian," and "some of the lower Classes followed their Example."

Carleton addressed them. His words were brief and pointed: The town was in danger. The people must join the regular soldiers to fight off the enemy. The response, in general, was loyal; and loyalty was reinforced by the fear that the Yankee invaders might plunder the town after they had captured it. But disloyalty showed itself also. Many of the merchants and traders who had come up to Montreal from the colonies to the south did not hide their sympathy with the Revolution. When the volunteers were asked to step forward, the revolutionary sympathizers stepped forward too—but "turned off the contrary way."

The little army Sir Guy Carleton was able to muster for the defense of Montreal was oddly assorted: some regular troops, some volunteers among the British settlers (including a number of Guy Johnson's rangers), some French Canadians, a few Indians. They all moved out of town by way of the eastern gate. When they came into the open fields they saw that Ethan Allen had ranged his men with a frontiersman's knowledge. They were well placed behind trees and buildings and in the bed of a small stream. The battle soon opened.

Ethan Allen and his Green Mountain Boys were, in a sense, a pack of outlaws. They had come together in a struggle against Cadwallader Colden, the Lieutenant Governor of New York. The area that was to become the state of Vermont, where Allen and his Green Mountain Boys lived, was part of New York, and Lieutenant Governor Colden was trying hard to upset the old land claims of the Vermont settlers, arguing that their claims were no longer valid. Allen was chosen the colonel of this private regiment, pledged to defend the lands of the settlers against interference. It was a rugged, efficient regiment, in terms of frontier fighting. A reward was offered by the New York Assembly for Allen's arrest. The Lieutenant Governor threatened to drive him and his men back into "the green mountains." And so they came to be known as the Green Mountain Boys.

At the outbreak of the American Revolution the Green

Mountain Boys were seen in a new light. They were a fine fighting force, already in being and close to the frontier. Congress was recommended to make use of them by William Gilliland, a friend of Allen's and a man of some importance, as the owners of lands, sawmills and gristmills. He explained that the Green Mountain Boys "might prove immediately servicable to the common cause . . . These men being excellent wood rangers, and particularly acquainted in the wilderness of Lake Champlain, would in all likelihood, be more servicable in these parts than treble their number of others not having these advantages, especially if left under the direction of their present enterprising and heroick commander, Mr. Allen."

Ethan Allen, however, with his impudent independence, was viewed with misgiving, notably by Major-General Philip Schuyler, the commander of the forces of the Revolution in the region of Lake Champlain and Lake George. "I am apprehensive of disagreeable consequences arising from Mr. Allen's imprudence. I always dreaded his impatience of subordination," he said, "and it was not until after a solemn promise made me in the presence of several officers, that he would demean himself with propriety, that I would permit him to attend the army . . ."

Ethan Allen disregarded military propriety from the start. His first maneuver was against Fort Ticonderoga, practically an outpost of Montreal, as it stood on a promontory at the southern end of Lake Champlain, guarding the approach to Canada by way of the Richelieu Valley. Benedict Arnold appeared on the scene, claiming superior rank. The Green Mountain Boys threatened to arrest him. After quarreling over the command, Allen and Arnold reached a compromise, though Arnold found himself performing minor duties, while Allen led the attack. Allen's audacity achieved surprise. He burst into Fort Ticonderoga, ran up the stairs to the commandant's room and pounded on the door with the pommel of his sword.

"Come out here this instant, you damned old rat, or I'll sacrifice the whole garrison!" he shouted. The sleepy-eyed commandant, holding his breeches in one hand, opened the door.

"Give up the fort immediately!" Allen ordered.

"By what authority do you demand it?" asked the bewildered British officer.

Allen roared: "In the name of the Great Jehovah and the Continental Congress!" The commandant put on his dressing gown and paraded his disarmed garrison as prisoners of war.

Allen's spectacular achievement in seizing Fort Ticonderoga without the loss of any of his men brought him the thanks of Congress. He was already changing from the uneasy role of outlaw to the more comfortable status of hero. If he could add Montreal to Ticonderoga, no traces of the oulaw would remain; he would be the hero complete and beyond challenge. "The Key is ours," he wrote to the New York Congress. ". . . I will lay my life on it, that with fifteen hundred men, and a proper train of artillery, I will take Montreal."

Allen with a small mixed party was sent northward on a reconnaissance expedition. He was only to feel out the ground. But he held a council of war on the South Shore of the St. Lawrence opposite Montreal, with Major John Brown, an old friend and an officer in the Revolutionary forces. Brown proposed an attack on Montreal without waiting for permission from the higher command, and without waiting for reinforcements. Allen, without hesitation, agreed. Already he had considered Montreal an easy prey. He would snatch it up in the same way he had snatched Ticonderoga.

He and Brown agreed on their strategy. Allen and his men were to cross the St. Lawrence from Longueuil; Brown and his men would cross from Laprairie. By attacking east and west, they would divide the defending forces. Brown, when ready, would give three loud huzzas. Allen and his men would reply with a cheer. Then they would both move forward to the assault.

Allen crossed in the night from Longueuil to Longue Pointe with about 120 men—American militiamen and French Canadian recruits. For some reason (never fully explained) Major John Brown failed to cross the river from Laprairie. No loud huzzas were heard from the west. Allen and his men were left to meet unaided Sir Guy Carleton's oncoming force from Montreal. He decided to fight it out as best he could and hope for a swift victory. As the battle was in open fields, it would be won by the side that might be able to outflank the other. Allen seems to have maneuvered first, sending out his flanks to protect his position. But the Canadians he had recruited had a change of heart once the bullets began to fly. Many deserted. His two flanks collapsed. Left with only a small core, he still fought hard. His enemies admitted that his "banditti" made a "pretty smart" fight; Allen "conducted himself in the action with great valor."

In a last attempt at escape he tried to lead his men back toward the river. It was a futile move. The canoes in which he had crossed during the night had already been destroyed by his enemies. He had retreated out of range of most of the regulars, but the volunteers and the Indians were closing in upon him. He was now running. A British officer, Peter Johnson, was running after him. The officer fired, but missed. Allen fired back, but missed also. He kept running. He was afraid, if taken prisoner, that he might be killed on the spot.

Allen and the British officer, both running, shouted to each other. Allen wanted to know what would happen if he and his men surrendered: would he "be treated with honor," and would his men be assured of quarter? The officer, still chasing him, shouted back that no prisoners would be killed. Allen halted. He ordered his men to ground their arms. The officer told Allen to advance toward him. Allen approached him and gave up his sword.

In frontier warfare, however, officers could not always control their Indian allies. Half a minute after Peter Johnson had received Allen's sword an Indian came running up. In his narrative Allen wrote: ". . . a savage, part of whose head was shaved, being almost naked and painted, with feathers intermixed with the hair of the other side of his head, came running to me with an incredible swiftness; he seemed to advance with more than mortal speed; as he approached near me, his hellish visage was beyond all description; snakes' eyes appear innocent in comparison to his; his features extorted; malice, death, murder, and the wrath of devils and damned spirits are the emblems of his countenance . . ." Ethan Allen, very tall and strong, seized a nearby British officer who was very small. He picked up the officer and held him as a shield, while the Indian scouted around with his gun, watching his chance to fire.

Allen was as nimble as the Indian. Wherever the Indian moved, Allen swung round and faced him, still holding up the officer in front of him; his danger was Allen's security. Another Indian was running up. Allen, with his human shield, could not hope to face two enemies at once. But he did his best, twisting this way and that, swinging the little officer with him. Help came. A French Canadian, who had lost one eye, hurried up and took his part against the Indians. Then came an Irishman with fixed bayonet, shouting that he would kill every Indian in sight.

Allen was saved. But it had been a near thing. His relief at having escaped "from so awful a death" composed his mind. Even imprisonment seemed a happy prospect, all the more so because the officers who had gathered around him said nothing to make him feel humiliation. Now "great civility and politeness" prevailed. The officers said they were happy to see

Colonel Allen. He said he would rather have seen them in the camp of General Montgomery, the American commander.

They walked together through the fields toward the town, a pleasant, almost cheerful group. In his account Allen wrote: ". . . as I walked to the town, which was, I should guess, more than two miles, a British officer walking at my right hand, and one of the French noblesse at my left; the latter of which, in the action had his eyebrow carried away by a glancing shot, but was nevertheless very merry and facetious, and no abuse was offered me . . ."

In the barracks at Montreal on that September day in 1775, the British officer, Brigadier-General Robert Prescott, was awaiting the arrival of the American prisoner. General Prescott was a choleric, impulsive man in any case. Nothing was more likely to stir his bad temper than the sight of Ethan Allen. Not only was Ethan Allen a rebel against King George III: he had, with insolence, captured Fort Ticonderoga while His Majesty's garrison slept. The extent of Allen's victory at Ticonderoga had been the extent of the humiliation of the British soldiers and their officers.

When Ethan Allen was led into the barrack square in Montreal, General Prescott glared at him. He demanded his name. Allen told him. He was then asked if he was that Colonel Allen who took Ticonderoga. Allen said he was the very man. The general could no longer hold back his anger. He shook his cane over Allen's head, shouting "many hard names," the name "rebel" frequently, and worked himself into a rage. Allen, the independent frontiersman, was not having any of this sort of treatment. "I told him," he says, "he would not do well to cane me, for I was not accustomed to it, and shook my fist at him." If the general struck, said Allen, his fist would finish him off. Anything might have happened between the two angry men, but one of the British officers, Captain M'Cloud, pulled the general by the skirt of his jacket and whispered in his ear. Later M'Cloud told Allen what he had said: it would be inconsistent with a general's honor to strike a prisoner.

By now General Prescott was so angry that he would be reasonable in one way only to become unreasonable in another. He ordered a sergeant to come forward with his men with fixed bayonets. They would shoot to death thirteen of the Canadians who had fought with Allen and been captured. The Canadians were wringing their hands and saying their prayers, expecting to be shot dead at any moment. Allen then made the dramatic gesture. He stepped between the Canadians and the fixed bayonets and opened the clothes at his chest. If the general was so thirsty for blood, said Allen, let him thrust the bayonets into his heart, but let the Canadians be spared; for he, as commander of the expedition against Montreal, was the sole cause of their taking up arms. Allen, a shrewd Yankee, admits he did not expect to be killed; he was only outmaneuvering General Prescott. The next few minutes were tense, nonetheless. Allen pictured the scene:

"The guard, in the meantime, rolling their eye-balls from the General to me, as though impatiently waiting his dread commands to sheath their bayonets in my heart; I could, however, plainly discern, that he was in a suspense and quandry about the matter: This gave me additional hopes of succeeding; for my design was not to die, but to save the Canadians by a finesse. The general stood a minute, when he made me the following reply; 'I will not execute you now; but you shall grace a halter at Tyburn, God damn you.'"

Ethan Allen was hustled aboard a ship-of-war in the river in front of the town. He was handcuffed; heavy irons were fixed to his legs. A bar eight feet long was attached to the leg irons, and so placed that he could lie only on his back. He proved hard, difficult, defiant even in chains. With his teeth he twisted off the nail that went through the mortice of the bar in his handcuff. The nail had to be replaced with a padlock.

No chances were taken that a rebel as enterprising as Allen might escape. He was taken overseas to Falmouth and securely imprisoned in Pendennis Castle. He might well have been hanged for treason at Tyburn, as General Prescott had hoped he would be, but a difficulty stood in the way. In the meanwhile General Prescott had been taken prisoner by the rebels. Allen himself could not have devised a situation more clever: if he were to be hangd, the general might be hanged also. At the end of 1776 Allen was taken from Pendennis Castle to New York (still held by the British) and paroled. In 1778 he was exchanged for a British officer, Colonel Archibald Campbell.

The madcap attempt by Ethan Allen to capture Montreal was viewed by General George Washington without admiration. To him it was only the freakishness of an irresponsible adventurer. He hoped Allen's failure, disgraceful and inevitable, would hold in check any similar impulses. "His misfortune," said Washington, "will, I hope, teach a lesson in prudence and subordination to others who may be ambitious to outshine their general officers, and, regardless of order and duty, rush into enterprises which have unfavorable effects on the public, and are destructive to themselves."

Ethan Allen has a memorial in Montreal in the Ethan Allen House. It is a venerable stone farmhouse. It used to stand on Notre Dame Street East. Tradition had it that Ethan Allen surrendered nearby, even in the house itself. The setting had become incongruous. Oil refineries had been built on three sides of it, with an iron foundry across the street. To save it from demolition, the house was lifted from its foundations in June, 1970 and towed intact to Mercier Park, at Notre Dame and Mercier Streets. There it stands today as the Ethan Allen House, even though its connection with Ethan Allen's battle, flight and surrender has been obscured by time.

John Collins SKETCHBOOK

NOTRE DAME
and
McGILL STREET—

NINE

The American Who Captured Montreal:
Richard Montgomery

AT FIVE O'CLOCK in the afternoon of November 11, 1775, a little group, worried and depressed, gathered on the Montreal waterfront. The scene was bleak. An eyewitness said it "was like the saddest of graveside partings." Sir Guy Carleton, the Governor, was leaving—in a hurry. Munitions, baggage, official papers had just been loaded on three armed sloops in the river. Sir Guy had ordered all the cannon in Montreal be spiked and rendered useless. His one hope was that he was not leaving too late--that he might not be caught on his way down the river.

Only the evening before, an American army of invasion, commanded by Major-General Richard Montgomery, having comandeered boats along the South Shore, crossed nearer to Montreal—to St. Paul's Island (now Nuns' Island). Sir Guy Carleton had decided Montreal could not be defended. His plan was to slip through to Quebec, hold out there for the winter and trust that reinforcements would arrive by sea in the spring.

Sir Guy had made a hard, realistic decision. He was leaving Montreal at the mercy of the incoming troops of the American Revolution. Some of the Montreal merchants had gone to the waterfront to speak to the Governor before he left. They asked him what they ought to do. His reply, if scarcely comforting, at least did not restrict them. He told them to do as they saw fit.

The seizure of Montreal was part of General George Washington's plan to draw all Canada away from British rule. He doubted that the American colonies, now that they had asserted their independence, could ever know security so long as the huge land mass of Canada hung over them to the north. Sooner or later, he believed, the British Government would use Canada as a base of operations to regain its old colonies.

The Continental Congress, then sitting in Philadelphia, authorized the invasion of Canada by two expeditions. One, under Colonel Benedict Arnold, was to advance through the forests of Maine into the forests of Canada and emerge before Quebec. The other, under Major-General Richard Montgomery, was to come up by way of Lake Champlain and the Richelieu and move on to Montreal. When Montreal had been taken, Montgomery was to descend the St. Lawrence to join forces with Benedict Arnold. Together they would take Quebec.

The path northward to Montreal was obstructed by three outposts. In origin they were old French forts, built to resist English invasions. The first of them, Fort Ticonderoga, had already been captured for the Revolution by Ethan Allen and his Green Mountain Boys. Two more remained: the fort at St. Johns on the Richelieu, twenty-seven miles southeast of Montreal; and Fort Chambly, only sixteen miles from Montreal, beside a rapids on the west shore of the Richelieu.

The success of Montgomery's invasion depended on the prompt capture of St. Johns. If the fort held out till winter came, he would be compelled to give up and turn back. His volunteers, without heavy clothing, were not equipped for a winter campaign. In any case, they had enlisted only for a few months' service. By winter the time would be up; they would be ready to go home.

For Sir Guy Carleton, as the defender of Canada, St. Johns was equally important. He had been left to defend Canada with less than a thousand regular soldiers. He had sent urgently for reinforcements. None had come, none were to be expected until spring. His few regular soldiers had to be scattered on essential duties here and there. He had taken the chance of committing the greater number of them to St. Johns. If St. Johns could hold out, his judgment would be confirmed. If St. Johns fell, he would have lost both an outpost of Montreal and most of his professional troops. He had reasonable grounds for hoping he might block Montgomery at St. Johns. The fort might seem to have few natural advantages of position; it lay in flat country. Yet it had earthworks, not impressive to look at, but well suited to absorb bombardment. It was fairly well provided with cannon and ammunition. In Major Preston of the 26th Regiment it had a resolute commandant.

General Montgomery laid siege to St. Johns about the middle of September. He bombarded the fort day after day. His fire was returned. One of Montgomery's men wrote: "We have Cannon and Shott for Breakfast & Dinner, & Shells at Night for Supper." Both sides, however, were able to shelter themselves. Montgomery came to realize that he was not winning the siege, or was not winning it in time.

His troubles went much further. He commanded troops oddly assorted, opinionated, impudent, undisciplined. They were volunteers—amateur soldiers, most of them without uniforms and carrying muskets of various sorts. He had little control over them. They were independent Yankees. They had enlisted for a few months not to fight for a king but for themselves. It was not easy to expect subordination to authority in a cause based on self-assertion and a rebellious spirit. The men were willing to consider his commands. Whether they would obey them or not was their own decision. "The privates are all generals," complained Montgomery. And again he deplored "the want of subordination and discipline . . . my unstable authority over Troops of different Colonies, the insufficiency of the military law, and my own want of power to enforce it, weak as it is." He had discovered that the common cause of liberty had not overcome the prejudices of regionalism. Most of his troops were New Englanders. They looked askance at him because he was from New York. In a private letter to his wife he wrote: "Could I with decency, leave the army in its present situation, I would not serve an hour longer."

He had still another discouragement: the wretched terrain of his encampment. The land around the fort was low-lying, water-logged. It was "drowned land." Men by the hundred sickened in the wet and the cold. They were afflicted by malarial fevers, rheumatism, dysentery.

Finally, munitions and supplies were short. The British Major Preston, shut up in St. Johns, seemed to have more and better guns and more gunpowder. Montgomery appealed to Congress. Few munitions arrived; Congress had other obligations to consider.

Sir Guy Carleton was beginning to hope that he might be able to save Montreal after all. But fortune suddenly swung in Montgomery's favor. General Montgomery had sent a few hundred of his troops, and a few small cannon, to attack Fort Chambly. That stone fort would be the next obstacle on his way to Montreal. He scarcely expected to capture it; he was only testing its strength. To the astonishment of the Americans, and in strange contrast to St. Johns, Fort Chambly was surrendered at once. This, in itself, would have been a useful victory. But what made it the turning point in that autumn's campaign was the failure of Fort Chambly's commandant, the Honorable Major Stopford (the son of an English peer) to destroy the stores. The Americans came into sudden possession of munitions and supplies, which included 124 barrels of gunpowder, some good cannon, 6,564 musket cartridges, 150 stand of French arms, 288 barrels of good provisions.

With these new resources Montgomery became able to tighten the pressure on St. Johns. He gained in strength just at the time when Major Preston's resources were running out. Casualties inside the fort were increasing. Food was scarce; the garrison had to be put on half-rations. Shoes were worn out; some soldiers had to tear the tails from their jackets to wrap the cloth around their feet.

The situation of Governor Carleton was painfully embarrassed. Many thought it strange that the Governor sat in Montreal and did nothing when only twenty-seven miles away to the southeast the garrison at St. Johns, at his orders, was fighting for its life. But Sir Guy was still reluctant to make any move. He doubted that the mixed, poorly trained and uncertain force he could raise would encounter anything but defeat. In the end, however, he had to make a gesture. He mobilized on Ile Ste. Hélène a small force of about seven or eight hundred men. Only about 130 were regular troops. About eighty were Indians. The rest were the untried militiamen.

On October 30 Governor Carleton put out with his men from Ile Ste. Hélène. There were thirty-five to forty boats; one boat had a cannon. An American force, about 350 strong, had taken up its position on the South Shore of the river at Longueuil. Carleton would first have to land and defeat them. As his boats moved along the shore the Americans opened fire. Among them were Green Mountain Boys from Vermont. All were superb sharpshooters. The Americans also opened fire on the boats with a cannon, supplied with captured gunpowder from Fort Chambly. Under this telling fire the men in the boats panicked. They pulled away from the shore in disorder, carrying off some forty or fifty dead and as many wounded. On the extreme right some of Carleton's militiamen (one of them a hairdresser in civilian life) had landed on the shore. They hoped to make a bridgehead. Reinforcements, they expected, would soon back them up. But the other boats were pulling away.

Sir Guy probably deplored the whole affair. He may well have wished he had kept to his natural prudence, stayed in Montreal and done nothing. As the boats were hurrying away from the Longueuil shore the man in charge of the one cannon turned to the Governor. "What shall I do?" he asked. "Go and have supper in town," was the Governor's disgruntled reply.

It is just possible that Major Preston could have kept up the defense of St. Johns if he could only have believed help was on the way. News of the fall of Fort Chambly had been a blow to morale. Now General Montgomery took care Major Preston would learn that Carleton's half-hearted attempt to go to his rescue had been defeated. Major Preston despaired of any help ever coming to him. He surrendered the fort. Its half-starved, shell-shaken garrison marched out, by Montgomery's agreement, with the full honors of war. When the officers had laid down their arms, Montgomery said: "Brave men like you deserve an exception to the rules of war; let the officers and volunteers take back their swords! "But he made certain that Montreal should know St. Johns had fallen. He sent one of his soldiers to Sir Guy Carleton with the disheartening news.

In Governor Carleton's opinion the fall of St. Johns meant the inevitable fall of Montreal. He had no confidence that

Montreal could be defended. The fortifications, erected in the French Régime, were never strong. They were crumbling with neglect. He had only a handful of regular troops. He doubted that the militia would now take the chances of loyalty. He understood their position. He could hardly blame them for trying to secure their interests as best they could, by neutrality or worse. "I cannot blame these poor People for securing themselves," he remarked, "as they see Multitudes of the Enemy at hand, and no Succour from any Part." Treason and treachery already were evident. In Montreal many merchants from the colonies to the south were an active fifth column, eager to see Montgomery arrive. One night every English-speaking volunteer on guard lost the flint from his musket. None could explain how it had happened. Carleton realized that the fate of Canada would be decided, not in Montreal, but in Quebec. He made ready to leave.

On November 10 General Montgomery marched his men from St. Johns to the shore of the St. Lawrence opposite Montreal. The roads had always been bad. Now rain turned them to mud. Then snow fell in the mud. It was black slush all the way. The men struggled through it, "mid-leg" deep. When they reached the St. Lawrence they were benumbed. But they could see the winking lights of Montreal over the water.

On the Sunday morning of November 12 word reached Montreal that the American forces were beginning to land on the Island of Montreal at Pointe St. Charles. The bells were ringing; Montrealers were on their way to church. Solemn groups began to form in the streets. A few of the fiercer Tories felt that they still ought to put up a fight. But the general hopelessness of their situation was in the end acknowledged.

Four deputies were chosen to represent the citizens of Montreal. They went out to see Montgomery. They blustered. Why, they demanded to know, had he come against Montreal, armed as he was? Montgomery told them that he came as a friend, to bring them the blessings of independence and true liberty. The deputies commanded him to come no nearer. Perfectly sure of himself, Montgomery replied that his men were cold and needed shelter. Then and there he sent fifty of them into the houses of the Récollet Suburb—the suburb just outside the Récollet Gate, at what today is the corner of Notre Dame Street and McGill. He then told the deputies to draw up terms of capitulation. He gave them four hours to do it.

The deputies realized that bluster had gained them nothing, and disconsolately they went back to the town. Terms of capitulation were drawn up. The deputies tried to be reasonable but they also tried to get as many concessions as they could. The document was signed by twelve prominent citizens, six French and six English. Among the English signatures was that of the fur trader, James McGill, later to be the founder of McGill University.

The deputies went out again into the Récollet Suburbs and laid their terms of capitulation before General Montgomery. He began by telling them there was one thing they must keep clear in their minds. They had no power to arrange a formal capitulation of Montreal. He was not disposed to bargain with them, for he knew well they had nothing to bargain with. "The city of Montreal," he pointed out, "having neither ammunition, artillery, troops, nor provisions, and having not in their power to fulfill one article of the treaty, can claim no title to a capitulation." He was, however, disposed to be generous, while emphasizing that he was being generous on principle, not by necessity. He would not grant them all they asked, but he granted much. The people of Montreal would be secure in their property; they would have religious freedom; they would not be called upon to take up arms against the Crown or to contribute to the costs of the American invasion; trade would be extended and protected (though probably not with the mother country). He also made the important concession that the terms he had sanctioned would be binding on his successors in command.

Concessions were the prelude to occupation. He concluded the terms of surrender with the words: "Tomorrow morning, at nine o'clock, the continental troops shall take possession by the Récollet Gate. The proper officers must attend with the keys of all public stores, upon the Quarter-Master-General, at nine o'clock . . ."

The Monday morning of November 13, 1775, was bitter. Winter had come early, with snow and gales. The streets of Montreal were "stiffened with cold." That morning, through the old Récollet Gate, General Richard Montgomery led the soldiers of the American Revolution into Montreal. They marched along Notre Dame Street to the barracks, which the retreating British troops had abandoned.

On that icy day Montrealers caught their first glimpse of the commander of the American invasion. He was tall and slender, "well-limbed" and "genteel, easy, graceful, manly." The defects were baldness on the top of the head, and a handsome face spoiled by being "much pock-marked." His military bearing was evident: "His air and manner designated the real soldier."

The military bearing was to be expected, for Richard Montgomery was a real soldier. Through sixteen years he had served as a commissioned officer in the British Army. His genteel, easy, graceful manner was also to be expected, for he was the well-bred aristocrat. He came of one of the prominent families of Ireland; he had studied at Trinity College, Dublin. After he had settled in New York, he married Janet Livingston, daughter of Judge Robert Livingston. His wife's family was as prominent in New York as his had been in Ireland.

As a man who had served in a professional, disciplined army, and who had been accustomed to the society of gentlemen, Richard Montgomery reacted with distaste, even with disgust, at the raw, contentious, insolent insubordination of the officers and men of his Revolutionary army in Montreal. When he made ready to move on to Quebec he found many among his troops were not disposed to accompany him. Some argued that their term of enlistment had expired. Others claimed to be ill. Generally their spirit was turbulent, even mutinous. All the troubles with undisciplined troops Montgomery had experienced during the siege of St. Johns recurred in Montreal, and with even more defiant insolence. His subordinates criticized him to his face.

Montgomery confided his difficulty to his superior officer, Major-General Philip Schuyler: "An affair happened yesterday," he wrote on November 24, "which had very near sent me home. A number of officers presumed to remonstrate against the indulgence I had given some of the king's troops. Such an insult I could not bear, and immediately resigned. To-day they qualified it by such an apology, as put it in my power to resume the command." He wondered whether General Schuyler would be prepared to take his place in Montreal. "Will not your health permit you to reside in Montreal this winter?" he asked; "I must go home, if I walk by the side of the lake. I am weary of power, and totally want that patience and temper so requisite for such a command."

Montgomery believed that much of the disordered state of the Revolutionary army would be set right if only its officers were gentlemen: "I wish some method could be fallen upon for engaging *gentlemen* to serve. A point of honor and more knowledge of the world, to be found in that class of men, would greatly reform discipline, and render the troops much more tractable."

Before coming to America, Montgomery had belonged to the Whig Party. He was a liberal and a reformist. His wife's family were leaders in the movement towards political independence for the colonies. His marriage had brought him under the Livingstons' influence. He had gone the whole way to revolution. He had the revolutionary sentiments. "The will of an oppressed people," he declared, "compelled to choose between liberty and slavery must be obeyed." Soon after the outbreak of the American Revolution he was elected to the provincial Congress and appointed Brigadier-General.

A shadow of reluctance, however, hovered at times over his decision. Perhaps, more than most Revolutionary officers, he felt the sadness of it all, and the irony. After sixteen years as an officer serving the Crown, he was now fighting against soldiers in the same red uniform he himself had once worn. Just before he left his home in New York to serve in the campaign against Canada, he sat long with his wife, musing on the turn of fate. Suddenly, in a voice "strangely awesome," he expressed a conflict of emotions. " 'Tis a mad world, my masters!" he said. "I once thought so, now I know it."

While General Montgomery was having troubles with his troops in Montreal, Governor Carleton was having troubles of his own in trying to escape from Montreal to Quebec. Contrary winds retarded his ships. One of them went aground. By the time all were afloat and under sail, the Americans had gone ahead of him and threatened the passage of the river with batteries on the shore. A French Canadian, Captain Jean-Baptiste Bouchette, agreed to take him through by night in a whaleboat. Sir Guy Carleton changed from his uniform into the homespun clothes of the country. He went over the side of his ship at night, with Bouchette, one other officer and a sergeant. They rowed with oars muffled. The danger point was Berthier. The Americans were encamped on both shores of the river. Their bivouac fires flared across the water. From the whaleboat Sir Guy could hear clearly the sentinels' calls on shore and the barking of dogs. They put the oars aside. Lying flat in the boat, they paddled with their hands. The boat drifted by like a log in the damp darkness. Governor Carleton got through to Quebec. The loyal inhabitants greeted him with "unspeakable joy."

In Montreal the headquarters of General Montgomery and his staff had been set up in one of the better houses in town. It was Jean Legrand's big stone house on the southeast corner of Notre Dame and St. Peter Streets, later known as the "Forretier House," and demolished in 1940. Here Montgomery wrote to his wife: "I am summoning all my virtue against the legion of females soliciting for husbands, brothers and sons taken prisoners." He also told his wife of Carleton's escape: "The Governor has escaped—the more's the pity." But the ships in which he had at first tried to get away surrendered to the Americans. Montgomery gained their munitions and stores. In these ships he sailed for Quebec with the troops he was able to mobilize.

At Quebec his troops were joined with those of Benedict Arnold. The city was besieged. But Montgomery soon realized that a siege would not be enough: Carleton might hold out until spring. Montgomery could do little or nothing to prevent the arrival of British reinforcements by sea, once the ice was out of the river. He knew he must attack Quebec. The only question was to fix the time. His decision was forced: the term of service of many of his volunteers expired at the end of December.

Montgomery gave his orders to attack in a blizzard in the early morning of December 31. He planned a two-pronged assault on Quebec's Lower Town. Colonel Arnold was to advance by way of Sault-au-Matelot. Montgomery would lead his men along the road that came in from the west, beneath the great cliff. Arnold attacked with boldness and dash, but was beaten back. Montgomery's men, advancing below the cliff, could scarcely raise their heads; a gale was driving the snow horizontally into their faces. Plunging through the drifts, battered by the gusts, they struggled round the base of Cape Diamond. The post at Près-de-Ville lay ahead; it defended the first street into the Lower Town.

The post was manned that night by about thirty Canadian militiamen and fifteen English sailors. They allowed the Americans to come within thirty or forty paces, then fired all six cannon and a shower of musket balls. There was a swirl and struggle of dimly seen figures in the snow. Then a movement of wild retreat.

In the morning the defenders went out to inspect the effects of their firing. Snow had drifted over the bodies—all except part of a left arm, still erect. There they uncovered the body of General Montgomery. It was much distorted; the knees were drawn up toward the head. It was "hard frozen."

JOHN COLLINS SKETCHBOOK

CHATEAU
DE
RAMEZAY

TEN

The Ruler of a Testy Winter:
David Wooster

FOR ONE WINTER—the winter of 1775-76—Montreal was ruled by a testy old American, Brigadier-General David Wooster. He was dull, abrasive, impulsive, blundering. He had the town in "great confusion and irregularity." He was a hearty, bluff old fellow, full of tedious tales of his thirty years of military service. He was generally crude (though a graduate of Yale) and at times shrewd.

Wooster was appointed to command Montreal after the town had been seized in November, 1775, by Major-General Richard Montgomery, and Montgomery had gone on to join Colonel Benedict Arnold in the siege of Quebec. From his headquarters in the Château de Ramezay (the old stone building still standing on Notre Dame Street) General Wooster ruled Montreal in the name of Congress. In him great authority resided. For that one winter Montreal was American-held and governed for the American Revolution.

The appointment of General Wooster was a calamity. The post in Montreal was subtle and sensitive; it called for the diplomat's touch. The commander should not be a tyrant, but a man of good will, a seeker after cooperation. Congress did not wish to give the impression that it was invading Canada as conqueror. It wished its troops to come as liberators. They had entered Canada to free its people from the British yoke, to invite them to join the other colonies of North America in the grand cause of independence. This appeal for cooperation was to be made particularly to the French Canadians. It would be their opportunity to throw off British rule, to be free of all monarchs.

When David Wooster arrived, the hope of having a diplomatic commander in Montreal sagged. An American Congressman, Silas Deane, wrote in despair to his wife: ". . . when Wooster was appointed, I washed my hands of the consequences, by declaring him in my Opinion, totally unequal to the Service."

His doubts were soon confirmed. Wooster had brought all his old prejudices with him. Among them was an antipathy to the Roman Catholic Church. He soon became aware that the Roman Catholic clergy in Montreal were exerting all their influence against the Americans and the Revolution. Their bishop, Mgr. Jean-Olivier Briand, had called upon Roman Catholics to be grateful for the singular security the British Government had given the French Canadians and their church. He appealed to them to join in repelling the invading enemy. "The Clergy," complained Wooster, "refuse absolution to all who have shown themselves our Friends and Preach Damnation to all those that will not take up Arms against us."

Wooster only made worse a difficult situation. When General Montgomery had been the American commander in Montreal he had been well aware that the Church was working against him. But he chose to ignore it, hoping that the passing of time and a conciliatory attitude might bring the clergy to see colonial independence in a new light. General Wooster had no such patience. He turned against the principal religious authority in Montreal, M. Etienne de Montgolfier, Superior of the Sulpicians and also Vicar General. He sent James Price, one of the most rabid supporters of the Revolution in Montreal, to see M. de Montgolfier at the Sulpician Seminary (the same building, Montreal's oldest, still standing on Place d'Armes, just to the west of Notre Dame Church). Price demanded that new instructions be issued to the clergy. Montgolfier refused. General Wooster then declared he would send the Vicar General, together with some of his clergy, into exile in the American colonies to the south. Mrs. Price interceded. The Vicar General and his priests were spared the indignity of being dragged away. But they lived uneasily. They never knew what Wooster might do next. One account says that he closed all Roman Catholic churches on Christmas Eve to prevent the traditional celebration of Midnight Mass.

In his bumbling way, however, General Wooster gave the priests a powerful weapon to use against him. He sent a dispatch to Congress expressing his poor opinion of French Canadians as a whole. "There is," he said, "but little confidence to be placed in the Canadians; they are but a small remove from the savages." A copy of this dispatch fell into British hands. The British passed it on to M. de Montgolfier in Montreal. He let it be known to the priests; the priests spread it through the parishes. Wooster's dispatch, they said, disclosed what these American "liberators" really thought of the French Canadian people.

General Wooster not only tried to coerce the clergy; he saw Tory conspirators on every side. He was determined to take drastic measures against them. He sent forty sleds crowded with protesting Tories to Albany. It was a harsh measure, especially in a bitter winter. What was worse, the population of

Montreal was thrown into anxiety. These forty Tories had been charged with no specific crimes. Wooster accused them only of "ungenerous conduct." When accusations so imprecise were considered sufficient cause for sending citizens into exile, who could feel safe?

A delegation went to see Wooster, to protest. He cut them short. "I regard the whole lot of you as enemies and rascals," he told them. Judge John Fraser, of the Court of Common Pleas, sent General Wooster a letter of remonstrance. The letter was carefully phrased—restrained and respectful. The reply was savage. Wooster acknowledged the judge's "insolent letter." The judge, he said, justly merited a felon's chains—a set of iron ornaments. He was told, as soon as he received this reply, to make ready to be taken, under escort, to the fort at Chambly, "there to remain in close abode till further orders." Judge Fraser was confined in the fort for five weeks. Then he was deported to Albany. When he arrived he found that no "particular charge" had been laid against him. In the meantime, the judge's wife, though in delicate health, was under guard in Montreal.

Terror settled down over Montreal. The harsh, erratic, crude old man in the Château de Ramezay was unpredictable. He was acting on vigorous whims. He ordered the people not to discuss the affairs of the Americans—not even to mention them. A notice was nailed to all church doors. Anyone might be "severely punished, imprisoned and even transported from the province" if even "suspected" of acting against the Americans.

It was not enough for General Wooster to quarrel with everybody about him in Montreal; he quarreled also with his superior officers in the army of the Revolution. When the Revolution broke out, he was the oldest general to be appointed by Congress. He was already sixty-four. Few officers in the American army could have had a longer record of military service; it went back to 1741. The trouble was that he thought length of service, and experience in old wars, should count for more than the military abilities of younger men. He hated, with his seniority in service, to be placed in subordinate positions to others younger than himself. He was piqued from the start when Congress appointed so many to the rank of major-general, while assigning him the invidiously inferior rank of brigadier-general.

When sent into Canada, Wooster had as his superior officer Major-General Philip Schuyler in New York, the commander of the northern front. He began quarreling with Schuyler at once. Animosity was eased for a while when Major-General Richard Montgomery came upon the scene. With tact and forbearance Montgomery acted as a buffer between Wooster and Schuyler. When Montgomery was killed in the assault on Quebec, Wooster resumed his fight with Schuyler. When Schuyler sent him instructions from New York, Wooster replied that he would do as he saw fit, as he, being in Canada, was in a better position to decide what was needed for the "internal regulation of the Army" and "the immediate safety of the country."

Nor did Wooster content himself with writing abrupt, defiant letters to Schuyler. He went over the head of his superior officer; his complaints against Schuyler were sent at times straight to Congress. "I know of no reason under Heaven," he told Congress, "why he should treat me thus cavalierly, but merely to indulge his capricious humour, which, in the course of the last year, he has dealt out very liberally." General Schuyler was finding Wooster unbearably insolent. "Either he or I must immediately quit this department," he declared. Neither of them did quit, or was required to do so. This running quarrel between the two commanders, becoming known, undermined discipline among the troops—a discipline already miserable enough.

Yet David Wooster, for all his prickly ways, was confronted

with desperate harassments that those farther away did not understand. As the American commander in Montreal he had only about 500 troops in a large, restless area. He was surrounded by enemies, and their hostility was increasing because the Americans had to seize what they could not pay for. Congress had left Wooster with little "hard money." Nothing but hard money mattered in Canada; for the paper money of Congress was rejected as worthless and would not be accepted in payment for anything. Wooster's position in Montreal was sustained by funds provided by the Montreal merchant of Revolutionary sentiments, James Price. But Price's resources were running out.

General Wooster was faced with a new and still bigger dilemma when General Montgomery was killed. Wooster then became the highest-ranking American officer in all Canada. What ought he to do now? Remain in Montreal? Or go on to command the siege of Quebec?

From Quebec came pressing appeals from Benedict Arnold. "For God's sake," cried Arnold, "order as many men down as you can possibly spare, consistent with the safety of Montreal." Wooster realized he was in a "very critical and dangerous situation." To send troops from Montreal to strengthen the forces before Quebec might so weaken Montreal that it would fall into British hands. This would be a double disaster. Montreal would be lost, and the American troops at Quebec would be cut off from their line of retreat up the St. Lawrence. Montreal, he believed, "must be saved for a retreat." The narrow mind of David Wooster had a certain hard realism at its core. He did not take exalted, romantic views. He saw clearly that no amount of patriotic fervor would bring victory to the Americans in Canada. The game was up. If Congress actually expected Quebec to be captured, or even the siege to be maintained, it must send more men and more cash. He was convinced Congress had no intention of sending either. As for himself, he had no desire to become a futile victim. If Montreal was weakened, he and the other Americans there might "perhaps, all be sacrificed."

At first he sent Arnold what limited help he could but stayed in Montreal. As the days passed he came to realize his decision, sound as he felt it to be, would place him in an extremely unfavorable light. Quebec was still the main field of action, the heart of the struggle. It would certainly appear odd if the highest-ranking American officer in Canada did nothing more than linger on the line of retreat. Eventually he appeared at Quebec.

At once he resented the presence of Benedict Arnold. He refused even to consult Arnold about his plans. Arnold soon saw the hopelessness of trying to serve under a commanding officer so difficult, so quarrelsome, so quirky. He had hurt his leg when a horse fell on it. This injury offered a sufficient pretext. He suggested that he withdraw to Montreal. Wooster, he said, "very readily granted me leave of absence."

General Wooster was puttering about Quebec when a fresh blow struck his self-importance. On March 6, 1776, Congress appointed a new officer to command all the American forces in Canada. He was John Thomas, who was raised to the rank of major-general before he left. Wooster seethed with resentment, still an inferior brigadier-general. He would stay in Canada no longer, he said. When Thomas arrived, and decided on retreat, Wooster hurried away with all his baggage. But a turn of fate was to bring Wooster up again to be the highest-ranking officer in Canada. Smallpox scourged the retreating Americans. Thomas fell ill of it. Wooster was back in his old command.

Meanwhile, however, Congress, in a last effort to save the disintegrating American position in Canada, had sent northward a special commission headed by Benjamin Franklin. The commissioners arrived too late to make any hopeful recommendations. But one recommendation they made was emphatic: "General Wooster is, in our opinion, unfit—totally unfit—to command your army and conduct the war . . . His stay in the colony is unnecessary, and even prejudicial to our affairs. We would therefore humbly advise his recall."

Congress acted promptly on the suggestion. Wooster was pulled out of Canada. He left protesting this decisive humiliation. He demanded a Congressional inquiry into his conduct. A committee of Congress acquitted him of anything censurable; it made a nice distinction between incompetence and guilt. But Wooster was transferred from the regular army to the Connecticut militia.

David Wooster saw one last action. The British invaded Connecticut from the sea in 1777. They moved inland twenty-three miles, to burn the Congressional army stores at Danbury. As they retreated old Wooster, then in his sixty-eighth year, led 200 Connecticut militiamen to harass their rear guard. He was pressing his attack with spirit and effect. Then his men wavered. He rode up to cheer them on. A musket ball brought him down from his horse. He lived only long enough for his wife and son to hurry to him from New Haven.

General George Washington had once remarked: "General Wooster, I am informed, is not of such activity as to press through difficulties." It had been true. But he had shown a burst of activity at the very end.

Congress voted him a monument as a defender of American liberties. But this monument was never put up. Congress had begun to hesitate, for it could scarcely forget that it had to recall General David Wooster from Canada as "unfit—totally unfit." Wooster's irascible despotism as the American ruler in Montreal in the winter of 1775-76 had effectively destroyed confidence in George Washington's appeal to Canadians: "Come then, my brethern, unite with us in an indissoluble union, let us run together to the same goal." Few in Montreal wanted to run anywhere with David Wooster in the winter of 1775-76.

SKETCHBOOK

John Collins

RUE BONSECOURS

DU CALVET HOUSE

ELEVEN

The Great Diplomat
Who Failed:
Benjamin Franklin

BENJAMIN FRANKLIN WAS an aging, ailing man when he set
out for Montreal in the early, icy spring of 1776. He had gone
only part of the way when he began to doubt whether he would
live to arrive. When he reached Saratoga and found it under
six inches of snow, he wrote a farewell letter to Josiah Quincy:
"I am here on my way to Canada, detained by the present
state of the lakes, in which the unthawed ice obstructs navigation. I begin to apprehend that I have undertaken a fatigue
that at my time of life may prove too much for me; so I sit
down to write to a few friends by way of farewell."

Franklin's reluctance to undertake the journey to Montreal
had been overcome by his sense of duty. The invasion of Canada by the forces of the American Revolution, after its early
successes, was in desperation. The American soldiers were
ragged, unpaid, demoralized; the prestige of Congress in Canada was sinking and falling apart; even the people who might

have been friendly and helpful were growing more and more skeptical, aloof or hostile. Something had to be done, and done at once, to give new leadership to the American invaders in Canada; and diplomacy was needed to bring Canadians to realize the advantages of independence. The very fact that such a mission might be almost too late gave it all the greater urgency; for it might be the last chance to make Canada the fourteenth colony of the American Revolution.

Benjamin Franklin had brought the obligation upon himself by recommending such a mission. On February 14 he had reported to Congress as the head of its foreign affairs committee. The report, written in his own hand, said that the French Canadian noblesse and clergy, to secure their own interests, had turned the French Canadian people against the Revolution. Agents should be sent by Congress to Canada to explain the revolutionary principles more clearly and to persuade French Canadians that liberty would mean more to them than submission to arbitrary authorities.

When Congress agreed with Franklin's report, it turned to him to undertake the mission. He was the most persuasive diplomat of the Revolution. He, if anyone, could save the situation in Canada. Franklin realized the difficulty of refusal. If Canada were lost to the Revolution, speculation would never cease over what might have happened if he had gone there. He agreed to go, though it might cost him his life. He was seventy years of age. Among other ailments, he suffered cruelly from gout. He resigned from Congress' Committee of Safety and from the Assembly. "It would be a happiness for me," he explained, "if I could serve the public duly in all these stations; but, aged as I am, I feel myself unequal to so much business and on that account think it my duty to decline a part of it." If he felt unequal to so much Congressional business, he felt even more unequal to journeying through ice and snow to Canada to bring order out of chaos. But he went, writing along the route his farewell letters to his friends.

For his mission to Montreal, Congress clothed Franklin with immense authority—with almost absolute powers. He was to be the arbiter of military and civil affairs alike. His terms of reference were in the spirit of his own report to Congress. Canadians were to be diplomatically convinced that the Americans had invaded their soil only to set them free. They were to be given the liberty to set up any form of government as would, in their judgment, be most likely to promote their happiness. He was to assure them, in the strongest terms, that it was the earnest desire of the Americans to adopt them into the union as a sister colony.

Franklin was not sent alone to Canada. He was to head a commission. One of the commissioners serving under him would be Samuel Chase. As a supporter of the American Revolution Samuel Chase had been prompt and bold. When elected a member of the Maryland legislature in the old colonial days, he led the opposition to the royal governor. When riots broke out over the Stamp Act, he gloried in playing a conspicuous part. Naturally, he was sent as a delegate to the first Continental Congress in 1774. He even anticipated the Declaration of Independence by making one of his own, when he declared that "by the God in heaven he owed no allegiance to the king of Great Britain." When Congress selected commissioners to accompany Franklin to Montreal it could have every confidence in Samuel Chase. And he readily agreed to go.

The second commissioner was Charles Carroll Carollton, whose signature, like that of Samuel Chase, is on the Declaration of Independence. (He used to add "of Carrollton" to his name to distinguish himself from his father "of Annapolis.") Charles Carroll's qualifications for the mission had been outlined by John Adams (who was to succeed George Washington as President of the United States). Adams described Charles Carroll as "a gentleman of independent fortune, perhaps the largest in America . . . educated in some university in France, though a native of America; of great abilities and learning, complete master of the French language, and a professor of the Roman Catholic religion, yet a warm, a firm, a zealous supporter of the rights of America, in whose cause he has hazarded his all."

These were the commissioners. To strengthen the mission still further, Congress appointed, as an associate or auxiliary, a Jesuit priest, Father Carroll (Charles Carroll's cousin). John Adams looked upon the appointment of Father Carroll as a "master stroke." As a priest he could devote his time on the mission influencing the Roman Catholic clergy of Montreal to view the Revolution in a more favorable light. His qualifications were impressive: a Jesuit of learning and noble appearance trained in subtle debate and suave manners, with an education in France and (like his cousin) a fluent knowledge of French.

Congress also appointed a military associate: a Baron de Woedtke, once a high officer in the army of Frederick the Great. He had left Prussia after a falling-out with the Emperor and offered his services to Congress. He was given a field commission with the rank of brigadier-general. The Baron was also fluent in French.

Franklin and his fellow commissioners had a rough journey to Montreal. Soon after they had set out from New York on April 2 and were sailing up the Hudson they were caught in a squall that nearly drove them on the rocks. The mainsail was split and took a day to repair. At another stage they were in flatboats, thrusting their way through drifting ice. They went ashore from time to time to warm themselves at a fire and cook their meals. At night Franklin slept aboard a flatboat, with no protection but an awning. When they traveled by wagon, they were bumped and jolted over deeply rutted roads.

"The roads at this season of the year are generally bad," wrote Charles Carroll in his diary, "but now worse than ever, owing to the great number of wagons employed in carrying the baggage of regiments . . ."

On April 27, twenty-five days after leaving New York, they reached St. Johns on the Richelieu. All were cold, hungry and tired, but Montreal was now only twenty-seven miles away. French Canadian carriages—calèches with their enormous two wheels—had been ordered from Montreal. "I never traveled through worse roads, or in worse carriages," complained Charles Carroll. When three or four miles from Laprairie they began to catch glimpses of Montreal. When they came to the South Shore of the St. Lawrence at Laprairie itself they stood and gazed across the river. "At *La Prairie*," wrote Charles Carroll in his diary, "the view of the town and the river, and the island of Montreal . . . form a beautiful prospect."

When they landed at Montreal they were received at the waterfront, "in the most polite and friendly manner," by Benedict Arnold, by then a brigadier-general and Montreal's commander. Arnold conducted them to his headquarters in the Château de Ramezay on Notre Dame Street, while the cannon in the citadel thundered a salute. Father John Carroll, in a letter to his mother, described Benedict Arnold's hospitality: "At the general's house we were served with a glass of wine, while people were crowding in to pay their compliments; which ceremony being over, we were shown another apartment, and unexpectedly, met in it a large number of ladies, most of them French. After drinking tea, and sitting sometime, we went to an elegant supper, which was followed with the singing of the ladies which proved very agreeable, and would have been more so if we had not been so much fatigued with our journey." At the end of the evening's entertainment, with its "decent mirth," General Arnold conducted them to their lodgings in the splendid nearby house of Thomas Walker, one of the Revolution's most implacable supporters in Montreal.

The next day Benjamin Franklin got down to business, even though he had also to receive visitors and dine "with a large company." He attended a council of war in the Château de Ramezay and began to form his opinions of the American prospects in Canada. The main problem appeared immediately: the Americans in Canada had no cash and they could expect to do nothing without it. The troops could not be disciplined while they were not being paid. Recruits among the Canadians were unlikely so long as they had no assurance of being paid either.

Nor could the Americans purchase supplies. They had to seize what they needed, more or less with violence. They were looked upon as robbers, and hated as robbers always are. They had come into Canada as liberators; they were lingering as oppressors. Congress in Canada had no status. Its paper money, based on its credit, was laughed at. Franklin gave an example. The Americans in Montreal had trouble even arranging for the carriages to bring him and his commissioners from St. Johns. Nobody would accept an American dollar bill. Nothing could be done until someone friendly to the cause was willing to exchange the bill for silver.

The commissioners tried to borrow. But they could raise funds neither on the public credit nor on their own. Franklin advanced £353 of his personal gold. It was only a trifle compared to the needs. The commissioners sent an appeal to Congress to send £20,000 with the "utmost despatch." And they added: "With this supply, and a little success, it may be possible to regain the affections of the people, to attach them firmly to our cause, and induce them to accept a free Government, perhaps to enter the Union." Congress tried to respond. But its treasury held less than one-twelfth of the amount the commissioners in Montreal were requesting.

Franklin realized that neither his personal prestige nor his authority from Congress meant anything in Montreal in the absence of hard cash. The people had expected him to arrive with a large sum in silver and gold. When they came to understand that he had come with nothing more substantial than prestige and authority, he found himself left with little of either.

The commissioners were in trouble in another way. They tried to undo some of the harm done during the winter, when Brigadier-General David Wooster had commanded Montreal in the name of Congress. Wooster, ruling by harshness and oppression, had given a poor idea of the benefits of liberty—benefits the invading Americans were supposed to bring to the people in Canada. The commissioners felt obliged to improve the American image. They brought about the release of some of the prominent Montreal Tories sent by Wooster into exile in Albany.

This policy of tolerance and reconciliation infuriated the small group in Montreal that had come out early and openly for the Revolution and had risked everything in doing so. They charged the commissioners with showing more concern for Tories than for the "true sons of Liberty." The commissioners replied that "they could not do Evil that good might ensue." It was "a substantial wrong" to tear a man away from his wife and family and exile him a hundred miles away from his home, and not for any defined charge but only because he happened (like many others) to belong to the wrong side. They added that "a cause that can't support itself upon the principles of Liberty is not worth pursuing." And they expanded their policy of clemency, permitting the Montreal traders to renew communications with their posts to the west, and releasing from Fort Chambly the militia officers confined there by General Wooster for refusing to resign their commissions.

Every easement of penalties and restrictions extended by the commissioners to the Tories only provoked a wilder rage in the pro-Revolutionary patriots in Montreal. They were in no mood to see justice done to their opponents on abstract principles at the very time when the struggle for Canada had reached a crisis. They charged the commissioners with taking "advice of the Tories." The commissioners retorted that they took counsel of nobody but themselves, "that they themselves were equal to the purposes of their Embassy & if they had not pleased their friends, they had pleased themselves & nobody had a right to call their doings into question." This assertion of superior authority was countered among the supporters of the Revolution in Canada who had become officers in the American forces. In Montreal some of them pulled out their commissions, trampled them under their feet and declared they would never serve under such treacherous leaders. In St. Johns an officer damned Samuel Chase to his face. When Chase prayed him to accept an important command, he said that "he would not fire another Gun for the Congress, *till their Officers & Soldiers were put on an Equal footing with their Enemies.*"

Meanwhile, Benjamin Franklin's Jesuit associate, Father John Carroll, had set about his task of persuading the Roman Catholic clergy of Montreal that their future would be best secured under an independent and republican form of government. But Father Carroll found the doors closed against him. The Roman Catholic Bishop, Msgr. Jean-Olivier Briand, had warned his clergy to have nothing to do with this revolutionary from the south. The only door opened to him was in the house of the Jesuits on the north side of Notre Dame Street (on land now occupied by the eastern end of the Old

Court House and La Place Vauquelin). At least once he dined with the Jesuits, though conversation at the table was said to be only social and general. The Vicar-General of Montreal, M. Etienne Montgolfier, relaxed the probibition against him sufficiently to allow him to say Mass in the Jesuits' chapel.

Father Carroll, however, had not come north to Montreal to engage in casual table talk or to say Mass. He was impatient to get down to political discussions. But these discussions, if they were to take place at all, would have to take place in secret. Arrangements were made to hold them in a garden. That garden may still be seen. It is back of the huge stone house on the northeast corner of St. Paul Street and Bonsecours. The spot was chosen in that spring of 1776 because the owner of that house, Pierre du Calvet, was a cryptic revolutionary—a devious man who was privately supporting the Americans while trying to preserve an appearance of loyalty to the British.

In Pierre du Calvet's garden Father Carroll had his meeting with some of Montreal's Roman Catholic clergy and presented his arguments to them. But he soon heard a rebuttal that frustrated even all his debating skills. He was told that by the Quebec Act of 1774 the British Government had granted to the Roman Catholics all their essential rights and privileges. Could they expect as much from the uncertainties of a revolutionary movement? Nor could they forget that the first Continental Congress in 1774, on the very brink of the Revolution, had utterly condemned the Quebec Act, calling it "impolitic, unjust, and cruel, as well as unconstitutional, and most dangerous and destructive of American rights." Why should the Catholics of Montreal believe that the leaders of the Revolution had changed their minds in only two years' time?

They recalled other facts to Father Carroll's attention. In many of the colonies to the south it was not safe even to harbor a Roman Catholic. Only in Maryland and Pennsylvania were Catholics tolerated; they had full rights only in Pennsylvania. Nor did Montreal Catholics have to look to the colonies to the south for instances of persecution. They had experienced religious persecution in their own town during the last winter, when General Wooster had railed against the Church and even tried to intimidate the principal clergy, threatening to send them into exile.

Father Carroll still did his best to suggest that Congress was to be trusted and that Catholic rights would be guaranteed. But he realized that his secret conversations in Pierre du Calvet's garden had failed. His conscience was beginning to trouble him. He doubted that he would be morally justified in urging people toward revolution if they seemed reasonably satisfied with their existing government. He was also surprised by the extent of the consideration shown the Roman Catholics in Montreal by the British authorities. They had gone so far as actually to provide "a military escort to accompany the grand procession on the festival of Corpus Christi."

Benjamin Franklin soon decided to get out of Montreal. He had been sent by Congress on a hopeless mission. He would have remained if he felt anything could be accomplished, but he had reached the point of despair. In his conclusions the other commissioners totally agreed. Charles Carroll of Carrollton and Samuel Chase had been busy moving about, examining defenses, holding military discussions. All they had to recommend was that certain points near Montreal might be strengthened to assure the American retreat.

On May 1, 1776, Franklin and his fellow-commissioners sent their first report to Congress. They had been in Montreal only two days. But it was long enough to realize that Congress commanded no confidence among the people. There was a "general apprehension that the Americans would be driven out of Canada as soon as the King's troops arrived."

Canadians had come "to consider the Congress as bankrupt, and their cause as desperate."

If the first report of May 1 was gloomy, the second report, of May 6, was final. It urged that failure be recognized. "You will see . . . that your commissioners themselves," this report emphasized, "are in a critical and most irksome situation, pestered hourly with demands great and small that they cannot answer, in a place where our cause has a majority of enemies, the garrison weak, and a greater would, without money, increase our difficulties. In short if money cannot be had to support your army here with honor . . . instead of being hated by the people, we report it, as our firm and unanimous opinion, that it is better immediately to withdraw it."

The end was at hand. While Franklin and his colleagues were writing their report in the Château de Ramezay in Montreal, a squadron of the Royal Navy, headed by *H.M.S. Surprise*, was sailing up the St. Lawrence to Quebec. On May 10 word reached Montreal that five ships of war had reached Quebec already and fifteen others were in the river. The American troops had given up the siege; they were in disorderly retreat toward Montreal. The commissioners passed the news on to General Philip Schuyler in New York. "We are afraid," they told Schuyler, "it will not be in our power to render our country any further service in this colony."

Franklin had reasons of his own for wishing to stay no longer. His health was deteriorating. Boils tormented him; his legs were swelling; he feared it might be dropsy. On May 11 he suddenly decided to leave. Father Carroll went with him, to look after him. Slowly he made his way to Albany, then to New York. His illness lay heavily upon him; he was worn out and in pain. Samuel Chase and Charles Carroll stayed in Canada a few weeks longer. They held councils of war with "the generals and field officers." But these councils were concerned mainly with disposing "matters so as to make an orderly retreat out of Canada." On June 1 they left St. Johns and headed south. They were interviewed by General George Washington. Far removed from Canada, Washington had no real understanding of what conditions there were like. After he had talked to Chase and Carroll he remarked to John Hancock: "Their account . . . cannot possibly surprise you more than it has me."

Benjamin Franklin recovered from the exhaustion of his futile mission to Montreal. He came to look upon it with a certain wry amusement. "Canada," he would say, "where I was a piece of a Governor (and I think a very good one) for a Fortnight."

Yet Benjamin Franklin's mission to Montreal was not altogether fruitless. There were incidental results. It led to the establishment to the craft of printing in Montreal, and it influenced the appointment of the first Roman Catholic bishop in the United States.

When Franklin was sent north to Montreal in the spring of 1776 Congress had instructed him "to establish a free press and to give direction for the publication of such pieces as may be of service to the cause of the United Colonies." But Montreal had no press and no printer. Congress had to provide him with both. The printer selected was Fleury Mesplet. He was a Frenchman, of revolutionary principles, who had left his own country to set up his press in London's Covent Garden. He apparently arranged an interview with Franklin, then in London as agent for a number of the American colonies. Franklin is said to have advised Mesplet to settle in Philadelphia and even to have given him a letter of recommendation. In Philadelphia, from 1774 to 1776, Congress awarded him three contracts for printing, in French, revolutionary appeals to the French inhabitants of Canada.

When Franklin's commission was about to leave for Montreal, Congress appointed a committee to inquire into Mesplet's qualifications to go with it, as the printer of "such pieces" as might be of service to its influence. One of the three members of this committee was Franklin himself. Mesplet was approved.

On March 18, 1776, Mesplet set out from Philadelphia, his press and all his other belongings loaded in five wagons. When he reached Lake George they were loaded on to five bateaux. The boatmen decided to run the rapids to Chambly to save a longer haul from St. Johns. But it was spring, and high water. The bateaux were nearly swamped. Most of his fine paper, and his wife's clothes and his own, were ruined. He reached Montreal on May 6. It was too late. Franklin and his fellow-commissioners had already given up and were making ready to get out. Mesplet did no printing for them. He found himself abandoned, for he could not join the commissioners in their flight. Traveling with a printing press was not easy, as he had realized in his journey from Philadelphia. Nor was he likely to find anyone to accept payment in American currency. In any case, he may not have been eager to leave. He may have felt more comfortable in Montreal, a town mostly French-speaking, than in English-speaking Philadelphia. He had made a flying visit to Quebec and Montreal early in 1775 and may, even then, have had some intention of settling in a French environment.

When the British forces came back to Montreal, Mesplet was thrown into prison. Twenty-six days later he was released. He seemed harmless and might prove useful in a town with no other printer. He had set up his press on Capitale Street—the lane running from St. Sulpice Street (then called St. Joseph) to St. François-Xavier. His press was busy. Mesplet turned out Montreal's first books (including the first illustrated book in Canada) and its first pamphlets, commercial printing and newspaper. This newspaper, begun in 1778 as *La gazette du commerce et littéraire*, was so abusive of the judges that it was suspended and Mesplet was imprisoned. After his release, he revived his paper in 1785, in a more prudent spirit, as *The Montreal Gazette*.

If Fleury Mesplet was made Montreal's first printer as an offshoot of Franklin's Montreal mission, so was Father John Carroll led (at least in part) to become the first Roman Catholic bishop in the United States.

Father Carroll had been a source of aid and comfort to Franklin. Franklin had found him a singularly agreeable companion—intellectually interesting and gifted as a conversationalist. Far more than this, as Franklin was an aging invalid, too old and too ill to have undertaken the journey to Montreal, he appreciated Father Carroll's attentiveness in smoothing the problems of difficult travel. When he reached New York on the way home, Franklin wrote: "I find I grow daily more feeble, and I think I could hardly have got along so far but for Mr. Carroll's friendly assistance and tender care of me."

In the years that followed, Franklin lost no opportunity to recommend Father Carroll to the Roman Catholic authorities, especially while representing the American colonies in Paris. His recommendations were not without their effect. The Roman Catholic Church was planning to set up its first ecclesiastical organization in the United States. The first bishop would have to be a man of extraordinary tact and wisdom. Recommendations for Father Carroll from someone as eminent in the new United States as Benjamin Franklin, and with so high a reputation for sound judgment, powerfully strengthened Father Carroll's claims for the office. On July 1, 1784, Franklin wrote in his private diary: "The pope's nuncio called, and acquainted me that the pope had, on my recommendation, appointed Mr. John Carroll superior of the Catholic clergy in America, with many powers of bishop; and that, probably, he would be made a bishop . . ."

The appointment of Father Carroll as Bishop of Baltimore

came in 1789. As the first Roman Catholic Bishop he laid the foundations of the church in the new nation. He held the first synod. He drew up the first rules of ecclesiastical administration. He set up Catholic schools and colleges. He welcomed many of the religious orders to begin work in the United States. In 1808 he was appointed archbishop. His huge diocese of Baltimore was then divided into the four new dioceses of Boston, New York, Philadelphia and Kentucky. He virtually nominated the bishops and supervised their administration. He reconciled many differing and often conflicting national traditions. Before his death he had entrenched the Roman Catholic Church as a truly American branch of the universal church.

Yet the far-reaching influence of Archbishop John Carroll on the church history of the United States might never have been felt if he had not come to Montreal with Benjamin Franklin on the mission that failed in 1776.

John Collins SKETCHBOOK

RECEPTION ROOM
CHATEAU DE RAMEZAY

TWELVE

The Last American to Command Montreal:
Benedict Arnold

BENEDICT ARNOLD WAS the last American to command Montreal. He commanded at an anxious time. The forces of the American Revolution would soon be retreating from their siege of Quebec. They would be falling back on Montreal. The town was their corridor of escape toward the Richelieu River and Lake Champlain. Benedict Arnold's responsibility was to keep that corridor open. If the British were able to retake Montreal, the American forces would be cut off and lost. The chief threat would come from the west: the British might come down from the upper St. Lawrence. Nothing could stop them from descending on Montreal except Benedict Arnold and the few American soldiers assigned to him.

In leaving Montreal in Benedict Arnold's hands the American leaders could not have done better. Though Arnold was to be the archtraitor of the American Revolution, he was in 1776 one of its boldest and most competent commanders. He was daring enough to attempt anything, a man of incredible will power and stamina. He was to be audacious even in his treachery, when he plotted with the British to surrender West Point, the key to the Hudson. His courage, however, was strangely mingled with jealousy, grievance, avarice, corruption. Of all the figures that loom out of the history of the American Revolution, his is the most Shakespearean. His life had all the drama of inner conflict. He could be hero or traitor. All depended on which of the passions prevailed as they fought inside him. The cause of the Revolution had no braver man, none more unstable, none more capable of planned deception.

Arnold was described by John Joseph Henry, one of the American officers who served under him in Canada: "Our commander, Arnold, was of a remarkable character. He was brave, even to temerity; was beloved by the soldiery, perhaps for that quality only. He possessed great powers of persuasion, was complaisant; but, withal, sordidly avaricious. Arnold was a short, handsome man, of a florid complexion, stoutly made, and forty years old at least." (Obviously, he appeared considerably older than he was; for at this time, during his invasion of Canada, he was thirty-four to thirty-five years of age.)

Benedict Arnold's "great powers of persuasion" influenced the decision of General George Washington, when he was planning a two-pronged invasion of Canada by the Revolutionary troops. While Major-General Richard Montgomery was advancing against Montreal, by way of Lake Champlain, another expedition would advance from the seacoast of Maine through the wilderness to Quebec. Arnold persuaded Washington to give him the command of the invasion's second prong.

The autumn chill had already set in when Arnold plunged into the wilderness with about eleven hundred men. The settlements were few and meager. Then they ceased. He and his men were moving far away from any help in food or shelter.

They made portage after portage. Their boats began to leak; some broke apart and had to be left behind. They went through bog and freezing slime. They slept in the frost in wet clothing. Provisions were lost; little was left but flour and salt pork. The number of men in his expedition dwindled. Some deserted; some sickened; some died. At times they seemed to be moving by inches. At the Great Carrying Place they pulled and struggled forward; for a fortnight they were in sight of Mount Bigelow.

Never could they have come through without Arnold's massive, furious will power. By November 8 he led them from the Chaudière to Point Lévis, in full view of Quebec. They were starved, battered, torn. But with about 700 men he had arrived. Even his enemies had to admire his courage. "Surely a miracle must have been wrought in their favor," wrote an inhabitant of Quebec. "It is an undertaking above the common race of men in this debauched age. They have travelled through woods and bogs, and over precipices, for the space of one hundred and twenty miles, attended with every inconvenience and difficulty, to be surmounted only by men of indefatigable zeal and industry."

After his desperately successful thrust through the wilderness, the command of Montreal was an ironic anticlimax for Benedict Arnold. But all real hope of seizing Quebec was lost in the assault in the blizzard of December 31, 1775. With Montgomery killed and Arnold wounded, and the American troops unpaid and demoralized, another assault on Quebec became unrealistic. Every day brought springtime nearer, and springtime would bring a British fleet into the St. Lawrence. Arnold was appointed to command Montreal and make sure a way of retreat would be kept open.

In his headquarters in the old Château de Ramezay on Notre Dame Street the commander waited for messages. One came to him from the upper St. Lawrence to the west—from

the Cedars. There he had sent 400 men under Major Butterfield to entrench themselves beside the rapids between Lake
St. Francis and Lake St. Louis. A British force under Captain
Forster had come down the river from Ogdensburg (then
called Oswegatchie). It had 300-400 Indians, with about thirty-
five regular soldiers and 100 Canadian volunteers. Forster
scared the Americans. They had better surrender, he warned.
If they did not, and he had to attack them, some of his Indians
might be killed. If they were killed, he might be unable to
control what the other Indians would do in revenge. Major
Butterfield's nerve had been shaken. He put up only a brief
fight. Soon he surrendered on the condition that he and
his men would be protected from the cruelty of the Indians.

Word had reached Benedict Arnold in Montreal that his
American detachment at the Cedars was being attacked. He
at once sent nearly a hundred more soldiers as reinforcements.
He made ready to come himself. The reinforcements under
Major Sherburne got no farther than Vaudreuil (then called
Quinze Chiens). There they encountered a British party sent
on by Captain Forster. They skirmished, with a few casualties.
Then Major Sherburne surrendered.

Arnold had lost altogether some 500 men. Captain Forster
was exhilarated. He decided at once to move against Arnold
in Montreal. He crossed to the Island of Montreal from
Vaudreuil. He came down to Pointe Claire, where 500 volunteers joined him. Then he marched for Lachine, only nine
miles from Montreal itself.

For the first time Captain Forster was up against Benedict
Arnold. In the crisis Arnold was showing all his resolute
energy. He came up to Lachine with a hundred men, and
looked about for a position to defend. His eye fell upon a
heavy stone barn or storehouse. He gave rapid orders to dig
entrenchments round about it. Meanwhile more of his troops
arrived. He was ready to clash with Forster.

On the Friday evening of May 24, 1776, the drums of the advancing British could be heard. They were only a league away. Arnold's aide-de-camp, Captain James Wilkinson, was writing at midnight: "We shall be attacked within six hours. The morning dawns—that morning big with fate of a few, a handful of brave fellows." But Captain Forster, advancing down the road to Lachine, heard disturbing rumors. Arnold's "handful of brave fellows" had been magnified by reports into a powerful army, equipped with formidable artillery and strongly fortified. With only his few soldiers and his mob of Indians he decided he would do well to retreat.

Once he heard that Captain Forster was in retreat, Benedict Arnold was after him. Arnold led his men along the lakeshore road, and then on to Fort Senneville—the old fort still standing in lonely, picturesque ruins, where the branch of the Ottawa, known as the Rivière des Prairies, turns to the north of the Island of Montreal. As they approached the fort they could see Forster's men crossing the river to the Vaudreuil side. Arnold still hoped to recover the 500 American prisoners in Captain Forster's hands. But he could not cross the river in pursuit. His bateaux, laden with baggage and provisions, were still being brought slowly up the rapids at Ile Perrot. He sent several messages downstream, pressing for speed.

About five o'clock in the evening the bateaux arrived. Arnold had baggage and provisions tossed ashore. He rushed his men aboard. No delay was allowed for system or rank. They pulled out into the river. But it was growing late. The slanting sun, shining out of a clear evening sky, blinded them. When they neared the shore Captain Forster opened fire with two brass cannon. The light began to fail. Arnold could not see the shore clearly; it was all strange ground. He decided to row back to the Montreal side. He would attack the next day.

Arnold held a council of war with his officers. His plan was to go a few miles up the Ottawa. He would come down by land. Captain Forster would be taken by surprise. Some of his officers differed with him. His chief opponent was Moses Hazen, a fighter of much experience. The plan, he said, might be bold but it was mad. They would be advancing against Indians. And Indians would be the last in the world to be taken by surprise. Arnold was not a man to bear opposition easily. He and Hazen exchanged rough words. At midnight the council broke up. Later Arnold insisted it had been unanimous, which probably meant he had insisted on having his own way.

At two o'clock in the morning a British officer, Lieutenant Parke, arrived under a flag of truce. He was conducted to Arnold's headquarters. He said that Major Sherburne (the commander of the American reinforcements captured by Captain Forster at Vaudreuil) had negotiated an agreement. Captain Forster would release the American prisoners in exchange for British prisoners held by the Americans. Arnold, after demanding and receiving certain amendments, agreed and signed. Congress was later to repudiate Arnold's signature. But at the time it had seemed to him the best way of assuring that the prisoners would not be massacred by Forster's Indians.

A truce of three days was set for the transfer of the prisoners. As soon as the truce was up, Arnold moved against Captain Forster. But Forster had taken advantage of the truce to retreat up the river. He had escaped while the prisoners were being delivered. Arnold, however, was not without satisfaction. He had at least driven the British off, after they had come within nine miles of Montreal. He returned to his headquarters in the Chêteau de Ramezay, to be ready for the next alarm. It came about five o'clock in the evening of June 15, 1776.

The Americans had given up the siege of Quebec. They were retreating rapidly up the St. Lawrence toward Montreal. They were a dishevelled, ragged lot, "broken, disheartened . . .

without discipline and altogether reducd to live from hand to mouth . . ." Arnold had sent his aide-de-camp, Captain Wilkinson, with dispatches for the American commander, Major-General John Sullivan. He believed Sullivan must be at Sorel. Wilkinson found to his horror that the retreat had gone much farther upstream. The advancing British were already at Varennes. And Varennes was only eighteen miles from Montreal. He had to get the news to Arnold as quickly as he could. Near Varennes he stole a horse outside a mill. He rode it bareback, at a gallop, to Longueuil. At the point of his sword he forced a French Canadian to help him launch a canoe. From the Montreal waterfront he ran to the Château de Ramezay.

The news astounded Benedict Arnold. He had had no idea the British could be so near. The further defense of Montreal would be futile. His duty now was to manage the retreat out of Montreal. He acted promptly. He assembled a fleet of bateaux. He took with him his garrison of 300 men, and also took away the sick and the baggage. His sordid avarice appeared even in the excited haste of retreat. Into the bateaux he also loaded the valuable goods he had seized for his own advantage from the Montreal merchants.

At Longueuil he set out with a procession of carts. Progress was slow. He feared attack. His aide-de-camp was sent to find General Sullivan and ask for reinforcements to protect the retreat. Captain Wilkinson went riding about the countryside, but could find no one in command. The American army had really fallen apart. Men "overwhelmed with fatigue, lay scattered in disorder over the plain and buried in sleep," without a single sentinel to watch for their safety.

Somehow General Sullivan was able to rally his men and bring them, in confused order, to St. Johns. Benedict Arnold was already there, waiting to supervise the embarkation. Whatever artillery and military stores the Americans still had with them were loaded into a flotilla of boats. The troops went aboard. Only Arnold remained ashore with his aide-de-camp. They rode to reconnoiter the British advance. They found the British coming on fast. They turned their horses round and rode back to the boats. Arnold removed the saddle and trappings and tossed them into a boat. He drew his pistol and shot his horse dead. He ordered Captain Wilkinson to do the same. Wilkinson, reluctantly, obeyed.

The sun was setting. Arnold ordered the crew aboard and Wilkinson also. Refusing all help, he himself pushed the boat off from the shore and jumped into it. He had secured the retreat; he was the last to leave. The boats were scarcely beyond gunshot when the British burst into St. Johns.

John Collins SKETCHBOOK

PLACE
VAUQUELIN

THIRTEEN

"Good God! This is Murder!":
Thomas Walker

"GOOD GOD!" CRIED Mrs. Walker. "This is murder!"

She had sat down to supper with her husband in the hall of their house in Montreal. It was the evening of December 6, 1764, at half-past eight. She remembered the hour exactly. She had looked at her watch and said it was time to go to supper. The cloth had been laid on the table in the hall. But her husband had not been well. She had tried to persuade him to stay and eat his supper in the parlor. They had spent fifteen minutes discussing this and other matters. Then they had gone into the hall for supper.

The front doors of the house led into the hall. This was no doubt the reason why she thought it might be drafty on that December night and had recommended the cosier warmth of the parlor. Actually the house had two front doors. One was flush with the street. The second, a door with glass, was inside, at the head of a few steps. Thomas Walker seated himself at the hall table, his back to the doors. They had scarcely begun their supper when the latch of the outer door was rattled loudly. Someone was in a hurry to get in. Mrs. Walker had no apprehension; she thought some French Canadians, who had seen her husband on business the day before, had come back. "Entrez," she called out.

She heard the outer door being opened. Then, through the glass of the inner door, she saw a crowd of men rising on the steps. They looked ghastly. Some had blackened their faces; others had covered their faced with crepe. The inner door gave way. They burst into the hall. It was then that she cried out: "Good God! This is murder!"

Thomas Walker kept his guns in his bedroom, and he had many of them. The way to the bedroom lay through the parlor. He tried to fight his way to it. Someone struck him a blow from behind; he thought it was from a broadsword. But he struggled forward to the end of the parlor, near the bedroom door, battered and wounded all the way. At the door he was confronted by two men. They had got their first and blocked the way. He was jumped upon and forced away from the door to a window. In the scuffle he became entangled with the curtains. This, he believed, saved his life. It prevented them from dashing out his brains against the wall.

Walker fainted, with fifty-two wounds. As he swayed back into consciousness, he heard someone shouting: "Let me at him. I will despatch the villain with my sword!" He tried to throw himself at the man who had spoken. Another wild, confused struggle began. He felt himself being carried toward the fireplace, to be tossed among the burning logs. Walker, fighting for his life, twisted himself free. He sprang away from the fireplace. A weight came down on his head. He had been struck (so the surgeons later deduced) with a tomahawk. He sank to the floor. Someone kneeled beside him. Now he feared his throat was to be cut. He turned his head to his shoulder. When he tried to protect his throat with his hand, a finger was cut to the bone. The knife then sliced off part of an ear. His last impression was of somebody saying, "The villain is dead!" Somebody else added: "Damn him, we have done for him!" A third man said something more, but Walker's senses gave way; he could never recall what it was.

The attack on Thomas Walker had been swift, vicious, brief. Mrs. Walker had escaped to a cowshed in the yard. She came back, she said, in four minutes "to Mr. Walker whom the Ruffians had left in a very deplorable situation."

The brutal assault on Thomas Walker, merchant and magistrate, on that December evening in 1764 was not a mystery. He had provoked the officers of the garrison. The officers had retaliated. It was all part of the seething, heaving emotions that foretold the approach of the American Revolution. The army represented the Establishment. Thomas Walker, and others like him, represented the self-assertive, contentious, independent spirit that was challenging authority. They were of a type described by the Governor, General James Murray, as "the licentious fanaticks trading here."

Thomas Walker, born in England in 1718, came to Boston about 1752. Readily and naturally he responded to the revolutionary mood then rapidly developing in Boston. In 1763 he came north to Montreal. There he, and other merchants from New England, adopted a hard line toward the French Canadians. Their attitude was that the French Canadians ought to be suppressed or expelled. The Canadian colony should be made as much like the New England colonies as possible. All vestiges of the French Régime must be swept away. The trade and administration of Canada should pass into the hands of the English-speaking settlers.

These New England traders at once came into conflict with Governor James Murray. He believed the French Canadians to be "perhaps the bravest and the best race upon the

Globe." He urged that they be guaranteed the rights of their language, law and religion, and bound to England by bonds of enlightened toleration. "I glory in having been accused of warmth and firmness in my protecting the King's Canadian Subjects," he wrote to Lord Shelburne in 1767, "and in doing the utmost in my Power to gain to my Royal Master the affection of that Brave, hardy people."

Governor Murray was in a difficult position. He had to appoint magistrates from among the prominent citizens. He could not overlook the New England merchants in Montreal. Something had to be done to placate them. Walker's claim to be a magistrate was high; he was one of the richer citizens, with a reputed fortune of £10,000. The Governor took his chances; he made a magistrate of Walker. Trouble began at once. Walker saw in his office a means of baiting the army.

Montreal at that time had no barracks. Officers and soldiers of the garrison were billeted in the houses of the citizens. An exemption, however, had been granted to all magistrates. In November, 1764, Captain Payne of the 28th Regiment was assigned to rooms in a Montreal house. It so happened that one of the magistrates rented rooms in that some house. During the first night in his new billet Captain Payne was startled from sleep. The magistrate was ordering him out of the house. Captain Payne ignored him. Only about an hour later a constable arrived with a warrant. The captain was placed under arrest. He was marched off through the streets to prison like a common criminal.

Captain Payne was eventually released on a writ of habeas corpus, but the garrison had been outraged. The law had been twisted against one of its officers. It was true that no officer or soldier could legally be billeted in a house owned or leased by a magistrate. But it was straining the law deliberately to claim that no one could be billeted in a house where a magistrate happened to rent rooms.

Thomas Walker relished this way of tormenting the garrison. He was the magistrate who had signed the warrant for Captain Payne's arrest. Other officers found themselves subjected to indignities—indignities that the magistrates, led by Walker, condoned or arranged. Complaints became so serious that Governor Murray sent word to Walker to come to Quebec to make explanations. Only two days before he was to leave for Quebec he was assaulted and beaten in his house and left disfigured for life.

The attack on Thomas Walker was a sensation. He had succeeded, at cruel cost to himself, in his aim to set the civilians in Montreal against the military. The citizens were irked by the practice of billeting officers or soldiers in their houses. Now the feeling spread that no citizen was safe. If a citizen so prominent as Thomas Walker could be attacked and mutilated in his own house, what could other citizens expect? Fear of the military became hysterical. Montrealers would not go out into the streets without weapons for self-defense. They "never went to dinner or to their homes without pistols before them." Whenever a soldier came into a shop the shopkeeper would snatch up a pistol left handy on the counter. He would keep the soldier covered until he left, to prevent any outrage.

Walker had not only succeeded in poisoning relations between citizens and garrison; he had also brought the Governor into trouble. The British Government took a serious view of what had happened to Walker. The Secretary of State wrote to Governor Murray that "such treatment is a disgrace to all government." The Governor and the Attorney-General came down posthaste from Quebec. The Governor offered a reward of 200 guineas for the apprehension of Walker's assailants. Walker himself offered 100 more.

Walker came to rest his case largely on the declaration of George Magovok, a former soldier of the 28th Regiment. Mogovok went before Chief Justice William Hey. He swore an affidavit that a number of persons, whom he named, "feloniously and of malice aforethought" had cut off part of the ear of Thomas Walker "with an intention in so doing to disfigure" him. The persons named were arrested. After long legal maneuverings, some were never charged; others, though charged, were never brought to trial. Walker himself was partly responsible for the failure to proceed. He was insolent and overbearing. He quarreled with the Grand Jury and with the Chief Justice, and at times refused to cooperate.

One trial, however, did take place. A captain of the 44th Regiment, Daniel Disney, was charged with taking part in the assault that ended in Walker's disfigurement. The Disney trial was held in a courtroom fitted up in the residence of the Jesuits on Notre Dame Street—a site now covered by the "Old Court House" beside Place Vauquelin.

Thomas Walker had made a grave error in putting faith in George Magovok. Chief Justice Hey perceived that Magovok gave his testimony "not without a manifest confusion in his countenance and a trembling in his voice common to those who have a consciousness that they are telling untruly, and a fear of being detected." In the cross-examination Magovok so often contradicted himself, or tried to rearrange what he had previously said, that the Chief Justice felt compelled to set his testimony aside. He instructed the jury to disregard it.

Thomas Walker and his wife both testified that they had recognized Captain Disney among the assailants on the night of December 6, even though all the assailants were in disguise. But an alibi was produced in the Captain's defense. A number of very respectable witnesses swore that the captain, at the time of the assault on Walker, had been at the house of Dr. William Robertson. That evening Dr. Robertson was giving a party. Many were present. Captain Disney had danced with Madame Landrief till suppertime. He had not left Dr. Robertson's house until he was sent for by General Ralph Burton after the town was in an uproar over what had happened to Walker. The witnesses "spoke all very positively to his being present the whole time and the impossibility that he could be absent for 5 minutes without their knowing it." The jury withdrew for an hour. It returned to court with a verdict of "not guilty."

Yet no one doubted that the army had attacked and disfigured Walker. Governor Murray, in a letter to London, wrote that in Walker's parlor "was left a regimental hat" and "a bayonet of the 28th Regiment." Moreover, though at least twenty men were involved in the assault, and though the alarm was soon given, and though Montreal was a garrison town with many guards and sentries, no prompt arrests had been made.

Thomas Walker was not a man to be intimidated. The attack in his house and the loss of part of an ear did not discourage or silence him. He became all the more vehement in his criticism of British authority, all the more determined to make Canada part of an independent North America. He entered into correspondence with leaders in the New England colonies who were moving toward an open break with the Crown.

In 1774 Walker's voice was heard louder than ever. The Quebec Act gave him his chance to thrust himself forward as the champion of English rights in Montreal against the domination of the French. Though General James Murray was no longer Governor, the Quebec Act embodied his aims. It guaranteed to the French inhabitants the rights of their language, religion and civil laws. English colonists saw in the Quebec Act the frustration of all their ambitions to draw Quebec into their own pattern of life. The New Englanders in Montreal, with their revolutionary tendencies, saw that the act would draw the French Canadians away from joining them in declaring independence of the Crown. Frustration expressed itself in vandalism. One morning the bust of King George III in Place d'Armes was found to have undergone a shocking transformation. Its white marble face had been painted black; a mitre stood on its head; a rosary of potatoes hung about its neck. Suspended from the bust was a placard: "Behold the Pope of Canada and the English sot!"

Walker was calling upon the English merchants of Montreal to fall in with the merchants of New England and to begin the active consideration of independence. In the spring of 1775 a Continental Congress was to be held in Philadelphia to make plans for the future. A meeting of merchants took place in Montreal to consider representation at the Congress. The meeting was regarded with anxiety by Murray's successor as Governor—Sir Guy Carleton. Carleton wrote: "Walker, a great Republican, harangued the meeting . . . moved a Committee of Observation . . . and two delegates to the Continental Congress." The Montreal merchants hesitated. Their loyalties were divided and confused. But eventually a merchant, James Price, was sent to Philadelphia as an informal representative.

Walker was working for revolution, secretly and openly. He was in clandestine correspondence with Benedict Arnold. And he thought nothing of declaring openly in the marketplace: "Blood will wash off the stains with which the Ministers have soiled the Constitution. We must have blood, and then in a few years everything will be set right." Revolutionary talk, before a revolution, was straining the limits of free speech. It became intolerable in Montreal after the Revolution had broken out in New England. Walker was visiting Repentigny and Chambly, telling the French Canadians that the "Bostonians" were coming and they would do well to join them.

Sir Guy Carleton could wait no longer; he had to remove Thomas Walker. He spoke to Mrs. Walker. He told her (so she said) "many severe things in very soft & Polite terms." He told her that her husband would have to quit the colony.

"He *must* go," he said. "You may stay and take care of his affairs, & you shall be protected." Mrs. Walker protested: "Your Excellency knows that Mr. Walker's dealings are very extensive, so much so that *I* could by no means undertake to superintend them." The Governor, however, was insistent. But the Walkers refused to take him seriously. Thomas Walker said he would go if the Governor was prepared to indemnify him for the loss of his business and properties. Sir Guy, of course, could not comply. He was left facing Walker's insolent defiance of his order. The Walkers were confident the Americans would soon invade Canada and capture Montreal. They would then come into their own; it would be the Governor who would be scurrying away.

Sir Guy Carleton had to take action. He arranged for a warrant to be issued for Thomas Walker's arrest. The carrying out of the arrest was entrusted to Major-General Robert Prescott. This was the same General Prescott who had dealt with Ethan Allen, the American adventurer who had tried to capture Montreal a few weeks before. He organized a posse to go after Walker. Walker's determined courage was not underestimated. Prescott realized that Walker might have to be smoked out of his house. The captain commanding the posse was equipped with a bag of pitch and oakum.

On the evening of October 5, 1775, Mr. and Mrs. Walker were sitting together in their comfortable farmhouse on their country property at l'Assomption, very much as they had been sitting together in their house in Montreal on that December evening nearly eleven years earlier. Suddenly the dogs barked wildly. "Go and see what it is," Walker told a servant. The servant reported: "Some men are rowing up the stream as if the devil was in them!" But several hours passed. Nothing happened. Walker may have concluded that it was all a false alarm. Meanwhile the main body of General Prescott's posse was arriving by the road. It was a sizable group: about twenty regular soldiers and some French Canadian volunteers. About two or three o'clock in the morning, when Walker and his wife were in their nightclothes, the posse attacked. His door was smashed with an axe. The men rushed in, yelling like Indians.

Walker showed his expected courage. He threw on a waistcoat and a coat, slipped a brace of pistols into his pockets, caught up a short rifle and stood at the head of the stairs leading to the attic, where Mrs. Walker had taken refuge. He fired twice. He heard screams and feet scrambling to get out.

Walker was ready to defend his house like a fortress. But now he smelled smoke. The posse had set fire to his house at the four corners. The pitch and oakum gave the flames a rapid start. His wife screamed: "We shall both be burned to death! Shoot me!" Walker laid down his weapons. He carried his wife to the window. He held her by the shoulders, while she lowered herself as far as she could, clinging to the windowsill. She was crying: "Mercy! Quarter!" The soldiers below set up a ladder; they brought her down to the ground. Walker still tried to hold out. But the floor was burning under his feet. He had to surrender. Walker and his wife stood in bare feet in the mud, in the October night-wind. They looked on while the posse plundered whatever it could, and shivered until she was given a coat, and he a coverlet. In this odd-appearing dress they were taken to Montreal. Walker was paraded before General Prescott.

In September the general had bellowed at the captured Ethan Allen and called him "many hard names." He now bellowed at Thomas Walker: "You're a traitor and a villain, you scoundrel, to betray your country!" Walker demanded to know what crime he had committed. Prescott roared back: "Your crime is high treason and rebellion; and we will show you what military justice is. Give that poor unhappy man a straw bed in No. 4 in the barracks!"

For thirty-three days and nights Thomas Walker lay in solitary confinement on his hard mattress, with heavy irons on hands and legs. Then General Prescott did with him exactly what he had done with Ethan Allen: he took him out to an armed schooner in the river and imprisoned him in the hold. But Walker's imprisonment did not last long. When an American army of invasion was advancing on Montreal, Sir Guy Carleton abandoned the town to make his stand at Quebec, and set sail with a flotilla of eleven vessels. One of them was the armed sloop where Walker lay. The Americans, however, had gone ahead of them. They set up batteries to prevent the flotilla from getting through. Though Carleton himself slipped by in the night in a whaleboat, the flotilla, then commanded by General Prescott, surrendered. The tables had been turned. Walker was now free; Prescott was the prisoner.

Though Thomas Walker was now free, he brooded much and bitterly on all he had suffered in the cause of colonial independence. He viewed himself as a martyr. And he felt strongly that Congress should recompense him generously. In the late winter of 1776 he set out for Philadelphia, laden with his grievances. Perhaps Walker's abrasive, overbearing manner was counterproductive, and Congress, with many demands to meet and an inadequate treasury, was not disposed to be generous. Walker produced a receipt for "fifty half johannes equal to 400 dollars." This was a loan he had made to Brigadier-General David Wooster, the American commander of Montreal, in the winter of 1775-76. Congress paid him back. But Walker was not satisfied. He wanted interest as well. Congress refused. It was so far in arrears in payments to its army officers that paying interest might result in "an enormous Debt." It wanted to set no precedent in Walker's case.

Walker felt he had been shabbily treated. He had a further dissatisfaction. He wanted Congress to deal severely with General Prescott. He related all he had suffered at Prescott's hands.

But to his great surprise he found that the general, on account of alleged ill health, had been released from close confinement. He had been lodged in the best tavern in Philadelphia. He was walking or riding at large. He was even "feasting with gentlemen of the first rank in the province, and keeping a levee for the reception of the grandees." The general, though having his choleric moods, had also his social graces. He had adapted himself readily to the role of prisoner and gentleman.

Thomas Walker was disgusted. It was too much for him to bear. In gloomy bitterness he turned back to Montreal. Meager consolation awaited him there. The American grip on Canada was loosening. Everything might be lost. Only one hope remained. Benjamin Franklin, with sweeping powers, was coming to Montreal as the Commissioner of Congress. This great man, so shrewd and wise, might yet save Canada for the Revolution. Thomas Walker made one last gesture. He received Franklin and his fellow-commissioners into his house, And one of the commissioners, Charles Carroll, declared it to be "the best built, and perhaps the best furnished in this town."

Then came the final blow. After less than two weeks in Montreal, Franklin announced he was getting out—getting out because he was convinced the situation was hopeless. The Walkers saw their own hopes crumbling. They turned on Franklin, with their bad tempers, their sharp tongues. Walker accused him of betraying his trust. Mrs. Walker went further: she said he was governed by the Tories.

Pelted by taunts and charges, Benjamin Franklin's philosophic calm almost gave way. He recognized, nevertheless, that he was obligated to the Walkers for their hospitality. What was far more important, he recognized that they were victims of their loyalty to the Revolution. He took measures to protect Mrs. Walker. On the day he decided to leave Montreal he drew up a document, now preserved in the museum at the Château de Ramezay. It was an attempt to provide "safe conduct" for Mrs. Walker out of the country, asking that "every civility" be shown to "facilitate her on her way to Philadelphia." Franklin signed it himself, together with the other two commissioners.

Actually, Franklin did more for Mrs. Walker. He took her with him when he left. "We continued our care of her, however," he wrote, "and landed her safe in Albany, with her three wagon loads of baggage, *brought thither without putting her to any expense*, and parted civilly though coldly." Thomas Walker had joined them at Saratoga. Franklin had again to endure their united venom. He said that "*they both took such liberties in taunting at our conduct in Canada, that it came almost to a quarrel.*" And then he added: "*I think they both have an excellent talent at making themselves enemies, and I believe, live where they will, they will never be long without them.*"

George Washington shared Benjamin Franklin's feeling that Thomas Walker, for all his sufferings and services for the Revolution, was an almost intolerable ally, and unlikely to win friends for the cause. Washington remarked that "it is natural enough that Mr. Walker's resentment should be up for the wrongs he has suffered; it is incident to humanity, but yet the passions of an individual ought never to prevail so far as to injure the state."

Thomas Walker spent the rest of his life harassing Congress. He never ceased to insist on compensation for his losses and ordeals and patriotism. His petition for redress on March 28, 1776, had been "considered and left undetermined." It remained undetermined until he died in 1788—a man frustrated, indignant, vindictive, stubborn to the end.

Part Three

Adventures and Ordeals

SKETCHBOOK

John Collins

MILL STREET —
ENTRANCE TO THE
HARBOR

FOURTEEN

Murder Among Gentlemen:
The Duel

HOW DID DUELING in Montreal end?

It was part of the life of Montreal for some two centuries. It was part of higher social custom, the code of gentlemen. Many considered it was an indispensable guarantee of civilization. Once the duel went, they feared, the sense of honor would go with it and the right to take personal action to redress personal wrongs.

The Canadian duelist, Major John Richardson, in a book published in Montreal, defended the duel as "the good old fashion, instituted in the days of chivalry." He deplored the tendency of a matter-of-fact, commercially minded society to discountenance it. He thought a man "must be debased indeed" to suffer passively under an insult to himself or to those he was bound to protect. Yet how was redress to be had in such private grievances except in the duel? The duel, with all its civilized regulations, was the natural and legitimate means of satisfying injured feelings. Suppress the duel, he warned, and men of spirit would be compelled to seek redress in more brutal and less admirable ways—"with the secret pistol or the bowie knife."

Critics of the duel might suggest that it was a poor means of righting wrongs. The injured party, who challenged his offender, might himself be the one to be maimed or killed. But those who upheld dueling had their reply: a man must have a pitifully weak sense of his status as a gentleman if he were afraid to risk his life to defend his honor.

Dueling began in Montreal under the French Régime. It continued under the British Régime, but with one important change: pistols were substituted for swords. Perhaps this change increased the possibility that the parties might be reconciled at the last minute. The solemnity of the ritual, when a duel was to be fought with pistols, had a sobering effect: the measuring of the ground, the opening of the case containing the pistols, the procedure of loading. If reconciliation was possible, it was likely to be brought about by negotiations between the seconds during the interval of preparation.

The history of dueling in Montreal is not marked with as many tragedies as might be expected. Considering the risks when fire was exchanged between two men at short range, fatal duels were remarkably rare. Evidently the parties to a duel fired to wound, rather than to kill. In many instances (perhaps in most) fire was exchanged without injury to either party. There may be an inference here that many duels were only a performance, an obeisance to social custom. Were such duels not fought, some imputation might linger that the sense of honor had not been sufficiently sensitive. An exchange of fire, even if no one was hit, was generally accepted as sufficient proof that honor had not been neglected.

Only rarely did the duelists go on to exchange a second fire, or more. Certainly the drawing of blood, even if only in a superficial wound, was usually the signal that the duel was over. This did not mean that all such duels were merely pretense and play-acting. The serious possibility was always there. If any duelist wished to fire to kill, he had the social privilege to do it. When anyone went to fight a duel he could never be certain of the outcome, even if he knew that most duels were something of a formality.

Montreal was appalled when someone was killed on the dueling ground. The news reverberated through the town, and lingered on for generations as a tale that is told. Statistics are difficult to establish, but it would seem that from 1760 onward only two deaths resulted. A few other duels could have ended fatally. The antagonists had faced each other in a rage, knowing well they might be killed and were determined to kill. But even in these desperate cases the duelists, though mercilessly wounded, still recovered.

The fiercest of such duels was fought on the Sunday morning of April 11, 1819. It took place on the customary dueling ground of the time—beside the old stone mill on Windmill Point. The mill was just beyond the Lachine Canal, not far from Black's Bridge. The name lingers not only in Windmill Point, but in Mill Street and in the name Windmill Basin in the nearby Montreal waterfront. One of the opponents was Dr. William Caldwell, a veteran of the Peninsular War and one of the original doctors of the Montreal General Hospital and McGill's Medical Faculty. The other duelist was Michael O'Sullivan, a veteran of the War of 1812, a lawyer and the member for Huntingdon in the Legislative Assembly of Lower Canada.

The dispute had arisen over the proposal to establish the Montreal General Hospital. A delegation from Montreal (John Molson was among its members) had gone to Quebec to petition the Assembly for a grant. Michael O'Sullivan had opposed the grant in a debate in the Assembly. His speech, full of ridicule and satire, was directed mostly against the Montreal doctors sponsoring the project. The outcome of his speech was the indefinite postponement of any consideration of the petition.

Angry with frustration, Dr. Caldwell wrote a letter to the editor of the *Canadian Courant*. It was a vigorous, reasonable letter. But at the end of his long argument he lost self-control. He charged O'Sullivan with want of personal courage. Not long ago, he implied, O'Sullivan had been insulted and provoked to such an extent that he ought to have sent a challenge to a duel. But he had done nothing. The letter to the *Canadian Courant* had been anonymous. O'Sullivan demanded that the editor tell him who had written it. The editor abandoned his professional confidence; he divulged the name. Dr. Caldwell was challenged. He responded at once.

The duel near the Windmill on that April Sunday morning was fought with extraordinary ferocity. Five times they exchanged fire. O'Sullivan was twice wounded. But the duel went on. On the fifth exchange O'Sullivan staggered and sank to the ground, a bullet in his chest. Dr. Caldwell's arm had been shattered. He might have fared worse. Another of the bullets fired by O'Sullivan had ripped the doctor's coat and vest, close to his neck.

Though this vicious duel was not fatal, it may have shortened the life of Michael O'Sullivan. For days he hovered between life and death. The surgeons were puzzled. The procedure of probing out the bullet might kill him. In the end they decided to leave it where it was. O'Sullivan's recovery was far from complete. Life for him was troubled and painful. By force of will be progressed in the law. In 1838 he was appointed Chief Justice of the Court of King's Bench in Montreal. He presided on the bench for only one term—the February term of 1839. On March 7 he died. The autopsy disclosed Dr. Caldwell's bullet of 1819 lying right against the middle of O'Sullivan's spine.

Terrible as O'Sullivan's wound had been, his encounter with Dr. Caldwell can hardly be reckoned among Montreal's fatal duels. A fatal duel has to be strictly defined as death on the field itself, or within a few days, and directly attributable to the exchange of fire. The two fatal duels after 1760 were widely separated: the first was fought in 1795; the second in 1838.

The first took place near the same spot in the early morning of March 24, 1795. The opponents were the nineteen-year-old Lieutenant Samuel Lester Holland and Captain Shoedde. Both were officers of the 60th Regiment. Tradition has it that they quareled over some indiscretion committed by Lieutenant Holland at a ball at the governor's residence in Quebec. Tradition also has it that Lieutenant Holland's father, Major Samuel Jan Holland, surveyor-general of the British colonies north of Virginia, had equipped his son. He handed him a pair of pistols given to him while serving under General James Wolfe. "Samuel, my boy," he said, "here are the weapons which my beloved friend, General Wolfe, presented to me on the day of his death. Use them to keep the old family name without stain."

While these details are only tradition, the facts of the duel itself were reported on March 30 in a Quebec paper, *The Times*. The procedure, in one way, was unusual. Fire was not discharged simultaneously, at a given signal. One of the duelists was given the opportunity to fire first. It was a considerable opportunity; for he might kill or incapacitate his opponent without being fired on himself. A copper was tossed. It favored Captain Shoedde. He fired first, at ten paces. His bullet struck young Holland "immediately under the short rib." He nearly fell, but "recovering himself immediately, and though mortally wounded," he returned the fire. Captain Shoedde's right arm was broken in two places.

Lieutenant Holland was carried back to the town, to a bed in Sullivan's Coffee House. He died, after seventeen hours of pain and fever. Major Samuel Holland came from Quebec. When he viewed the body he is said to have groaned that the pistols he had given his son should have been the means of ending his life. The body was taken to Holland House, on Major Holland's huge estate of 700 acres at Quebec. There it was buried in the grounds under a lone fir, known to later generations as the Holland Tree. When Major Holland died in 1801 he was buried at his son's side. When the property was sold, provision was made in the deeds that the burial ground would be "for ever sacred and inviolable." In later changes of ownership the provision was omitted. The gravestones were broken, the graves obscured. They were rediscovered in 1957. A special cadastre was made, designating this burial ground as a separate and distinct civic lot (53A-1). It is now just off de Callières Street, about halfway between Holland Avenue and Ernest Gagnon Avenue in Quebec.

It would seem that forty-three years were to pass before another fatal duel took place in Montreal. In the meantime many nonfatal duels were fought. They involved some of the principal citizens. Simon McTavish (whose name survives in McTavish Street) fought in one of them.

McTavish could be described as the most prominent Montreal citizen of his day, and probably the richest—the head of the great North West Company, which was rivaling even the Hudson's Bay Company itself in the struggle for the fur trade of the interior. McTavish fought his duel with Dr. Robert Jones. The bullet from the doctor's pistol entered McTavish "a little above the groin and lodged near the skin in the back." It was easily extracted by a surgeon. McTavish quickly recovered.

Many a duel in Montreal was fought by a lawyer, some even between lawyers. Several of these dueling lawyers later became judges. All of which shows that dueling was commonly regarded as outside the law, in the sense of being above it and not governed by it. It is true that after a fatal duel a coroner's inquest had to be held. But these inquests failed to name the guilty party.

Such an inquest was held in 1838, after the last fatal duel in Montreal. In this duel a lawyer, Robert Sweeny, had killed an officer of the garrison, Major Henry John Warde. At the inquest a medical doctor, Dr. Aaron Hart David, was present. In front of the jurors he opened the body. The track made by the bullet was carefully traced. At one point the doctor introduced his finger into an opening and brought out fragments of the shattered vertebrae. There was no doubt how Major Warde had died. Nor was there the slightest doubt who had killed him. The parties to the duel were well known. The newspapers had even published their names. They had been identified by witnesses at the inquest. Yet the verdict of the coroner's jury read: "We are of the opinion that the late Major Henry John Warde came to his death, in consequence of a gun shot wound inflicted by some person unknown in a duel this morning."

But the days when dueling held its assured social status, and was placed by social custom above the law, were close to an end. That fatal duel of 1838, and the popularity of Major Warde in town, had produced a revulsion of public feeling. The practice of dueling was now being challenged—challenged by public opinion. So far from being regarded, as it had for centuries, as a guarantee of civilization, it became branded as a relic of barbarism.

The duel that made such a difference was fought a little after five o'clock in the morning of May 22, 1838. By this time the old dueling ground near the Windmill had been abandoned; increasing commercial activity at the port had destroyed the needed privacy. Duels were now being fought several miles to the west, on a race course near the river. A race course at dawn seemed certain to be deserted. The site had an added advantage: a country, or sportsmen's inn, named the Pavilion, stood nearby. Here a wounded duelist could be readily carried, for bed and care. The location of this dueling ground today is near the northwest corner of La Salle Boulevard and Church Avenue in Verdun.

On that May dawn in 1838 the race course was not as deserted as had been expected. A French Canadian farmer, J. B. Lanouette, was walking across a neighboring field, on his way to begin the day's plowing. He saw four men close to the grandstand of the race course. The light of day was just beginning to stream over the area. He was surprised to see four strangers about at that early hour. When he was some "four acres" from them, he saw two of the men taking up their positions to fight a duel. When he was within "two and a half acres" he heard the commands: "Ready! Fire!" One pistol was discharged. One of the duelists leaped two or three feet into the air, then dropped over backward.

Lanouette came up to the wounded man. He saw him die. He was ordered off the ground. At first he refused to go away. Before he finally went he turned to the surviving duelist. "That's a bad way to begin the day," he said. The man he spoke to made no reply. He threw his pistol to the ground and began to sob. The other two men knelt beside the body. They felt the dead man's chest. They "appeared deeply agitated and grieved."

The sobbing, the agitation and the grieving spread from the field in Verdun over Montreal. The town was shocked. The man who had leaped two or three feet into the air and fallen over backwards had been killed by one of his best friends. He and Robert Sweeny had been seen walking together only the day before. They were in their usual good humor. Something had happened that evening—some dispute about Robert Sweeny's wonderfully attractive wife, Charlotte.

Sweeny had come down to the officers' mess of the Royal Regiment, where Warde was dining with his brother officers. They were celebrating good news: Warde was to be promoted from major to lieutenant-colonel. Angry words were exchanged between Sweeny and Warde. Sweeny issued a challenge for five o'clock the next morning.

To Montreal the duel was an appalling tragedy because both duelists were prominent in the town's society; both were exceptionally well liked. Major Warde had many attractions: a bachelor of "magnificent physique and kindly manners," a man with a record of daring and enterprise in battle. His challenger, Robert Sweeny, was a member of a "good family" in the north of Ireland. As well as a lawyer, he was splendid horseman and a captain in the volunteer cavalry, and the author of a book of light, amorous verse in the modish manner of Thomas Moore. Mrs. Sweeny, an American girl from Vermont, had been "brought up . . . in all the courtly graces and accomplishments that marked the higher classes." In later years, after she had remarried and became Lady Rose and was living in England, she shone even in the sparkling society the Prince of Wales (to be King Edward VII) had gathered about him. A member of that coterie, Sir Algernon West, was to remark that Lady Rose "of all the women I ever knew was the brightest and most witty."

Any death in a duel would have been startling. But this was a society tragedy. It was, in an instant, not only the talk of the town but the town's grief. The horror of dueling was brought home as never before. Montrealers read in the papers the harrowing details. The body of Major Warde had been carried to the Pavilion. The inn was locked. They pounded the door till someone was roused. They carried the body in. A trestle was set up. As they were laying the body on it a bullet fell from the left arm. It rolled across the floor.

Montreal's sorrow is pictured in the diary kept by Abraham Joseph, the Quebec merchant. On May 23, 1838, he wrote: "Today's steamboat put us in possession of very melancholy news, which has caused a gloom in Montreal. Major Warde of the Royals, was shot in a duel . . . Poor Warde never spoke after the shot was fired. He jumped some height and fell dead. Thus ends the life of a splendid man and a brave soldier."

Then, on May 26, Abraham Joseph wrote in his diary: "Maj. Warde's funeral took place in Montreal, Friday 25th inst. He was buried with military honors, all the officers in the garrison attended as mourners. The Royal Regiment preceded the body and were the firing party. They marched with arms reversed. The body was followed by his horse, with boots reversed, etc., etc. An immense body of civilians attended the funeral, sorrow was pictured on everyone's countenance."

Public sorrow in Montreal soon turned to public anger. The duel, accepted for generations as part of a gentleman's code and a social protection, was now condemned as a moral wrong, a blot on society. Warde's death was held up as an example of what must never be allowed to happen again. The sudden new way of looking at duels was expressed in a poem written and published in Montreal a few days after Major Warde's funeral:

>   . . . *would that beneath*
> *The cold earth with thee, might for ever sleep,*
> *That cruel law of custom, which doth keep*
> *Man's better nature down—and doth make the hands*
> *Which should be—yea, oft have, in social bands,*
> *Been linked together—draw each other's blood!*
> *Thus might thy much regretted death do good;*
> *And as in life, thou others did incite*
> *To deeds of bravery, and actions bright,*
> *Thou also might'st in death a warning be,*
> *A useful lesson to humanity . . .*

The clergy of Montreal, in the wake of the Warde tragedy, took a firm stand. They would henceforth treat duelists as moral outcasts. The Reverend William Taylor of the United Secession Church preached an unrelenting sermon against the old custom. He denounced it as brutal, absurd, intolerable. His thirty-three-page sermon was widely circulated, widely approved. The Roman Catholic Bishop of Montreal, Msgr. Jean-Jacques Lartigue, made a public demonstration of his abhorrence. It happened in 1838 that the Fête Dieu, with the Corpus Christi Procession, came on the first Sunday after Warde's funeral. On that Sunday afternoon the bishop was to carry the Host through the streets around the cathedral, which stood on St. Denis Street, a little above St. Catherine. Arrangements had been made to have the Montreal Volunteer Rifles line the streets as a guard of honor. The bishop, horrified at Warde's death in a duel, made a request to Captain De Bleury, commanding officer of the Volunteer Rifles. He asked that Lieutenant Leclere should not be present at the sacred ceremony. His reason: the lieutenant had recently been concerned in a duel. Captain De Bleury made a spirited reply. He informed the bishop that the reason given for excluding Lieutenant Leclere was unfortunate, for he, the captain, had also once been concerned in a duel. He refused to make an invidious distinction between the lieutenant and himself. The bishop, however, held his ground. The result was that the Montreal Volunteer Rifles did not appear to line the route of the Corpus Christi Procession. To Bishop Lartigue their absence was not undesirable. It served to make public that any Roman Catholic who fought a duel, or had any part in its arrangements, would risk the condemnation of the Church.

The climate of public opinion in Montreal had changed abruptly. Hitherto a challenge to a duel could scarcely be rejected without the danger of losing the reputation of a gentleman. Now it could be rejected on the grounds of moral principle and as a duty to society. Men in public life were able to state openly that they would never appear on a dueling ground. Francis Hincks, prominent in politics and journalism, was one of them. "For my own part," he declared in the 1840's, "nothing would induce me to take part in such a barbarous practice."

In 1848 the journalist, Pierre Blanchet, went so far as to publish in his paper a rejection of a challenge. In the columns of *l'Avenir* he had attacked the new Montreal coroner, Charles-Joseph Coursol. Feeling insulted, Coursol sent a friend to Blanchet to arrange a duel. Blanchet would have nothing to do with him. Instead, on July 22, 1848 he announced his reply in the paper:

"You can tell Mr. Coursol that I regard the duel as a savage and barbarous act which belongs to those who, not having reason on their side, wish to have recourse to brutal force; that I am, and that I have always been, opposed to the brutal madness of the duel, which violates reason and dishonors society; that, in consequence, I will not name a friend to act as second to settle the affair; that, moreover, I may remark how strange it is that a public official appointed to carry out the laws and preserve the peace and social order, should himself be the first to set a scandalous example of violence and disorder; that the laws are there to protect Mr. Coursol if I have gone beyond the limits of the freedom of the press ... But that I utterly scorn and reject the duel as the means of settling this affair."

Dueling declined further in Montreal when the British War Office amended the Articles of War in 1844. Officers of the army were encouraged to settle their differences without having recourse to pistols. The amended articles declared it to be "suitable to the character of honourable men to apologize and offer redress for wrong or insult committed, and equally so for the party aggrieved to accept, frankly and cordially, explanation and apologies for the same." The change was important for Montreal as one of the garrison towns of the

British Empire, where military men often set the social tone.

Though duels continued to be fought by civilians in Montreal, they were becoming fewer. They had to be more furtive, for the police might interfere. In 1848 the police prevented a duel between George Etienne Cartier and Joseph Doutre. Cartier had objected to an attack made on himself in 1848 by *l'Avenir*. Joseph Doutre, unlike Blanchet, was ready to accept a challenge. The duelists met on the ground, prepared to proceed. But the police appeared. Cartier and Doutre were told to go home and report the next morning at the magistrate's court, to answer a charge of disturbing the peace. The police, it was said, had been summoned by Cartier's brother. A duel (harmless, as it turned out) was fought later. But Cartier and Doutre had to go as far away as Chambly to be free of the police.

Duels, however, were bound to fade, now that they were no longer sanctioned by public opinion or supported by social custom. They were rapidly becoming old-fashioned, peculiar, anomalous. By the 1860's they had come to be regarded with satirical amusement. *The Montreal Gazette* in 1864 carried an item headed "THE AGE OF CHIVALRY":

"It is reported that a person in town received a challenge on Friday to fight a duel and that he answered the hostile message by promptly showing its bearer out of doors. It remains to be seen what steps the challenger will take to vindicate his outraged feelings. The disputants had better sip the coffee and leave the pistols out of sight."

Dueling could continue only so long as it was chivalrous and gentlemanly, an affair of courage and honor. Once it had become merely ridiculous, its day was done.

John Collins

SKETCHBOOK

OLD
HUDSON BAY
HOUSE — LACHINE

FIFTEEN

Citizens of the Wilderness:
The Voyageurs

EVERY YEAR, AT the end of April, hundreds of French Canadian voyageurs gathered in and about the Old Market in Montreal (now La Place Royale). They seemed a lighthearted lot, without a care in the world. Thomas Storrow Brown had seen them when he came to Montreal, a boy of fifteen, in 1818. In the Old Market, he said, "they spent a few days drinking and fighting, nobody interfering in it, as it was all among themselves and good natured, for even the fighting was without ill will, only to give proofs of strength and endurance. Rare sport was it for the boys to see the whole square filled with these people—a dozen fights going on at the same time—fresh men stepping into the ring, as the vanquished, in their blood, were led off—all as gay as if it were merely a dance."

At that time of the year a festival also took place nine miles west of Montreal, on the waterfront at Lachine—the starting point for the Northwest. There the voyageurs invited all their friends and spent all their money. Liquor flowed like water. Every evening they had a dance. Each voyageur told a story about his adventures in the Indian country. Everything they said was bigger than life, and wilder. It was a common saying that no voyageur ever saw a little wolf. They shouted and boasted and everybody laughed and reveled and roared.

When the great brigades of "Montreal Canoes" put out from Lachine for the wilderness, the voyageurs left with a song. Hugh Gray, residing in Canada about 1807, went to Lachine to see a brigade depart. To him they seemed a remarkably cheerful lot of men: "They strike off, singing a song peculiar to themselves, called the *Voyageur Song*: one man takes the lead, and all the others join in a chorus. It is extremely pleasing to see people who are toiling hard, display such marks of good humour and contentment . . ."

Yet all this jollity was being shown by men who were journeying into danger or death. A number of them would never come back. They were reminded of imminent death at every rapids along the route. On the shore a little cluster of crosses stood under the trees. Some would be old, askew, in decay; others would be straight and new. Some crosses marked the graves where voyageurs lay buried. Others would be in memory of those whose bodies had been carried away by the river and never found.

Such doomful reminders brought a momentary hush and awe. The voyageurs prayed—some in piety, some in superstition. Nobody scoffed at prayer. All were touched by dread. These shuddering prayers on the rivers were described by Daniel Williams Harmon, a partner in the North West Company. When he set out as a young clerk on his first journey up the Ottawa by canoe, he wrote in his journal on May 23, 1800:

"The Canadian Voyagers, when they leave one stream to go up or down another, have a custom of pulling off their hats, and making the sign of the cross, upon which one in each canoe, or at least, in each brigade, repeats a short prayer. The same ceremonies are observed by them, whenever they pass a a place, where any one has been interred, and a cross has been erected. Those, therefore, who are in the habit of voyaging this way, are obliged to say their prayers more frequently perhaps, than when at home; for at almost every rapid which we have passed, since we left Montreal, we have seen a number of crosses erected; and at one, I counted no less than thirty!"

A journey so dangerous gave intense meaning to the last church the voyageurs saw before plunging into the wilderness. The Roman Catholic church at St. Ann's (now Ste. Anne de Bellevue), near the western tip of the Island of Montreal, was "the church of the voyageurs." At the rapids of St. Ann they had to go ashore to make a portage, carrying part of their cargo, or all of it, on their backs. Here they might pause for a last prayer before the altar, and to make an offering at the shrine of St. Ann. As they set out on their journey they could see the steeple and hear the bell. St. Ann was chosen by the voyageurs as their patron saint.

The craving for security in a hazardous life kept the thought of the church at St. Ann's in the minds of the voyageurs even 2,000 miles away. A story is told by Sir John Franklin, later celebrated for his voyages into the Arctic and the mystery of his disappearance. In 1825-26 he was exploring the Mackenzie River. One of his French Canadian voyageurs was so anxious to make another offering at the shrine of St. Ann on the Island of Montreal "that when on the most northern coast of America, not less than two thousand miles from the spot, he requested an advance of wages, that an additional offering might be transmitted, by the hands of a friend, to the shrine of his tutelar Saint."

Overseas visitors on the waterfront at Lachine were astonished that men would travel far, and run risks, in "one of the most frail conveyances you can imagine." Even the big Montreal Canoes, used in carrying the heavy freight of the fur trade, were nothing but bark, stretched on a light wood frame, a sort of skeleton. A thin layer of wood, sometimes split cedar, was used as flooring. A thick coat of spruce or pine gum was laid over the seams. Yet such frail canoes could carry a cargo of three tons. The added weight of crew and any passengers, and all their baggage and gear, might raise the weight to four tons. They were so weighted down when fully laden that the water would rise within six inches of their gunwales. Yet these were the canoes that had to pass through rapids and confront the waves, almost ocean-like, of Lake Superior.

The tremendous canoe journeys of the voyageurs, from Lachine to Grand Portage on the north shore of Lake Superior, were nothing more than the routines of the fur trade. They began every year in May, as soon as the rivers were free of ice. Every journey, however, with its hardships and hazards, its challenge and struggle, was an epic in itself.

A Hudson's Bay Company officer, Robert Michael Ballantyne, had an eye for the drama and could easily imagine what the excitement must have been in the days of the North West Company, when a brigade of canoes from Lachine came into sight and hearing of Grand Portage. "No one who has not experienced it," he wrote, "can form an adequate idea of the thrilling effect the passing of these brigades must have had upon a stranger. I have seen four canoes sweep round a promontory suddenly, and burst upon my view, while at the same moment the wild romantic song of the *voyageurs*, as they plied their brisk paddles, struck upon my ear; and I have felt thrilling enthusiasm on witnessing such a scene. What, then, must have been the feelings of those who had spent a long, dreary winter in the wild North-West, far removed from the bustle and excitement of the civilized world, when thirty or forty of these picturesque canoes burst unexpectedly upon them, half shrouded in the spray that flew from the bright vermilion paddles; while the men, who had overcome difficulties and dangers innumerable during a long voyage through the wilderness ... sang, with all the force of three hundred manly voices, one of their lively airs, which, rising and falling faintly in the distance as it was borne, first lightly on the breeze, and then more steadily as they approached, swelled out in the rich tones of many a mellow voice, and burst at last into a long enthusiastic shout of joy!"

The voyageur's day knew little leisure. It was hard, insistent work from dawn to dusk. The pauses for breakfast and lunch were brief, only a few minutes. Nor did many stay up late around the campfire by night. Fatigue, and day after day of early rising, sent most soon to sleep.

The canoes, even when heavy-laden, had to be moved fast. Voyageurs were expected to strike the water with their paddles forty or fifty times a minute. Sir George Simpson, as Governor of the Hudson's Bay Company in Canada, exacted an even higher standard: he required sixty strokes of the paddle every minute. Using a light canoe, he would travel at times ninety to a hundred miles a day. Even the heavy canoes—the Montreal Canoes—could outdistance any boat. Isaac Weld, visiting Lower Canada at the end of the 18th century, wrote: "It is wonderful to see with what velocity a few skillful men with paddles can take on one of these canoes of a size suitable to their number. In a few minutes they would leave the best moulded keel boat, conducted by a similar number of men with oars, far behind."

The voyageurs paused at regular intervals to light their pipes and take a brief rest. Soon they would be back to their paddles, refreshed. The progress of a canoe could be reckoned by these pauses for pipe-lighting. "Trois pipes" was estimated to be twelve miles.

Sir George Simpson always tightened the regime a little more than usual. He raised camp and started the day's journey at two or three o'clock in the morning. They went ashore for breakfast about eight o'clock, after five or six hours' paddling. Breakfast was hurried; the canoes were soon on their way again. The midday meal came at one o'clock in the afternoon. It lasted eight to ten minutes. Sir George had a servant cut off for him a slice of something cold and pour him a glass of wine. At eight o'clock in the evening they put ashore for supper, after about fifteen to sixteen hours of hard travel.

The exertion of paddling at the required rate ceased at the portages, only to be replaced by the even greater exertions of carrying the canoe and its freight. Portages, made necessary wherever a river became unnavigable, were often frequent. They varied in length. At one point in the Hudson's Bay Company's territories was the longest portage of all: it stretched over twelve miles. Many portages were several miles long. Even where a portage was short, it might be beside a rough and dangerous river, where one brief portage after another had to be made. On a stretch of the Winnipeg River ten portages had to be carried out in one day. None was more than a quarter of a mile; several were only a few yards. Yet the voyageurs found them tedious. The canoe had to be unloaded and reloaded several times to travel a mile.

In making a portage each voyageur had to carry a heavy weight. Archibald MacDonald, Chief Factor of the Hudson's Bay Company, said that the ordinary load was 180 pounds. The voyageur bore it in two pieces. One was made to fit into the small of the back. The second, often some bag-shaped thing, or a barrel, or a box, rested in the hollow between the shoulderblades. Part of the weight was borne by a band stretched across the forehead. When a voyageur raised this weight and set out on the portage he started off at a bound, short but quick. He went forward at a trot, legs and body

178

slightly bent. The pace was kept up, even on rough ground or uphill.

No complaints were made against these burdens. Voyageurs prided themselves on their strength. Even the smallest man would refuse to take less than his 180 pounds. He would be disgraced if he confessed that he was unable to carry as much as the others. Some lusty voyageurs gave proof of strength by taking on added weights. One Hudson's Bay voyageur was reputed to have carried 600 pounds.

Carrying the canoes over the portage was another feat of dogged strength. The Montreal Canoes from Lachine weighed about 600 pounds. They were turned upside down and carried by four men: two near the bow, two near the stern. An officer of the Royal Engineers, writing about his traveling experiences in the 1830's, made a quaint comparison, in describing the half-run of the voyageurs with a canoe at a portage. "The pace they go at," he wrote, "resembles that used by sedan-chairmen, but it is quicker."

Along the canoe routes the voyageurs suffered many discomforts. Rain often soaked them to the skin. Their blankets, once wet after a rainy night, had to be quickly rolled for the next day's journey. They might not have a chance to spread them out in the sun long enough to dry, and had often to sleep the next night, or for several nights, under blankets still wet or damp.

It might seem that the life of the voyageur—comfortless, harsh, full of risk and labor—would hold few attractions. Yet it was a life many French Canadians preferred above all others. Once they had known it, they were unlikely to settle on a farm and exchange the paddle for the hoe. The Scottish traveler, John M. Duncan, visiting Lachine in the autumn of 1818, remarked: "The toils and privations of a life so spent must be very great; yet the Canadians in this neighbourhood prefer it to every other, and the villages are so filled with the families of voyageurs, that in the summer months there are scarcely any inhabitants to be found in them but women and children."

When it came to hiring voyageurs, Montreal was the center. In all North America no finer voyageurs were to be found. John Jacob Astor realized this in 1810. He was then planning to set up his post, Astoria, at the mouth of the Columbia and reach out for the fur trade of the Pacific. He knew that the North West Company of Montreal was also reaching for the Pacific trade. In this rivalry the North West Company had an advantage over him in having in Montreal the best of the voyageurs. Astor sent his agents north to hire Montreal voyageurs for his own expedition. The first contingent was to be taken from New York in his ship *Tonquin*, round Cape Horn to the Columbia River.

The jaunty, carefree vitality of the Montreal voyageurs was seen in the way they arrived at New York. They decided to give New Yorkers a spectacle, and they succeeded. Washington Irving described their arrival: "An instance of the buoyant temperament and the professional pride of these people was furnished in the gay and braggart style in which they arrived at New York to join the enterprise. They were determined to regale and astonish the people of the 'States' with the sight of a Canadian boat and a Canadian crew. They accordingly fitted up a large but light bark canoe, such as is used in the fur trade; transported it in a wagon from the banks of the St. Lawrence to the shores of Lake Champlain; traversed the lake in it, from end to end; hoisted it again in a wagon and wheeled it off to Lansingburg, and there launched it upon the waters of the Hudson. Down this river they plied their course merrily on a fine summer's day, making its banks resound for the first time with their old French boat songs; passing by the villages with whoop and halloo, so as to make the honest Dutch farmers mistake them for a crew of savages. In this way they swept in full song and with regular flourish of the paddle, round New York, in a still summer evening, to the wonder and admiration of its inhabitants, who had never before witnessed on their waters, a nautical apparition of the kind."

As Washington Irving had observed, the French Canadian voyageurs were vivacious, lively, full of good humor. Daniel Harmon found them "rarely subject to depression of spirits, of long continuance, even when in circumstances the most adverse." They used to set out from Lachine with "heavy hearts and weeping eyes," because they were leaving family and friends behind. But in only a little while they had become "very merry." They might be disgruntled when roused at dawn or earlier. In the morning mists they paddled in silence. But the rising sun would start them singing a river song, and soon they were paddling cheerfully. Their songs were to them what sea chanteys were to sailors.

Voyageurs had their ugly side. The savagery of the wilderness could come to the surface. They were quickly angry, prompt to fight. But there was "a complaisance and kindness beneath all this." They might lose their tempers, but they bore few grudges. They were conspicuous for a natural courtesy, and were "exceedingly obliging to strangers."

Dr. W. George Beers of Montreal had seen them coming back to civilization from the wilderness: "Their arrival at Lachine, nine miles from Montreal . . . is a time of great excitement. The wild picturesque appearance of the men, and the distance they have come, awakens a sympathy for them, and hundreds will go out from town to see them. Their appearance in the city is very odd. They go along the streets, either gaping and staring at everything, in such haste and excitement that they run against people and stumble over little obstructions. They . . . roar aloud with laughter at the extensiveness of the ladies' hoops, and the peculiarity of their hats,

&c.; look in the windows at the jumble of new things, to them, and have hearty laughs at what they consider the absurdities and curiosities of city people."

The voyageurs were a race apart—distinct from their friends and relations who stayed at home. When they returned to Montreal, they returned as strangers, as aliens almost, astonished by what they saw, and contemptuous of it. The world of the voyageur was the wilderness. He needed or envied no other.

Zahn Collins SKETCHBOOK

THE IRISH STONE

SIXTEEN

The Huge, Rugged, Uneven Boulder:
The Irish Stone

IT IS A huge, rugged, uneven boulder. It came out of the bed of the St. Lawrence River. Raised on its end, it stands ten feet high. Weather and more than a century's grime have made it almost black. It looms up, massive and solemn, and broods mysteriously at night. It stands in a grassy island on Bridge Street, near the entrance to Victoria Bridge. Heavy traffic thuds by on both sides. The spot is scarcely peaceful. Yet the boulder stands to guard the bones of thousands of Irish immigrants buried there and nearby. Anyone who crosses through the Bridge Street traffic and comes close to the boulder may look up at it and read the words:

TO
PRESERVE FROM DESECRATION
THE REMAINS OF 6000 IMMIGRANTS
WHO DIED OF SHIP FEVER
A.D. 1847-48

THIS STONE
IS ERECTED BY THE WORKMEN OF
MESSRS. PETO, BRASSEY AND BETTS
EMPLOYED IN THE CONSTRUCTION
OF THE
VICTORIA BRIDGE
A.D. 1859

The workmen had been unearthing bones as they dug the approaches to the new bridge. They had been disturbing the dead. And when they heard the story of how these poor people had died, they wished to do something to preserve their bones from further desecration. This great boulder, taken from the bed of the river in laying one of the piers of the bridge, seemed a natural monument. In their own way they paid their tribute to the dead. The "Irish Stone," the simplest of Montreal's monuments, is in many ways the most impressive.

The "ship fever" given as the cause of death was actually the typhus. It went under other common names, such as "hospital fever" or "jail fever." It was defined as "essentially a fever of the poor, ill-fed, and badly housed." The Irish immigrants were natural victims. They were suffering from poverty; they were half-starved by the failure of the potato crop; and, long ill-housed where they had lived, they were housed more miserably still as they crowded into Ireland's port towns to await ships to North America. The typhus came to be known among the Irish as "ship fever" because so many fell ill on the voyage over the Atlantic. Some of these immigrants must have had the typhus when they came aboard, for one of the insidious characteristics of the disease is a period of incubation, without symptoms, lasting as long as twelve days. Some rapacious shipowners ordered captains to set sail though cases of typhus had already been reported among the passengers. Even if a ship had left Ireland with no known sick aboard, the disease might break out among those who already had it in them, though they had sailed without symptoms. On the long journey over the ocean "ship fever" spread rapidly; the ships provided the very overcrowding and ill feeding that favored the disease.

In the spring of 1847 Dr. Michael McCulloch of McGill's Medical Faculty made an ominous report to Montreal's Board of Health. He said that "in passing along the wharf at the upper end of the harbour in the afternoon he noticed several sick persons who had been there several days and among them one very dangerous case of fever." Ship after ship was arriving. Thousands were coming ashore. More and more came sick with typhus.

Something had to be done quickly. The immigrants had to be given shelter, but they had to be kept near the waterfront to prevent their coming into the city and spreading the infection. The Mayor of Montreal, John Easton Mills, was also President of the Immigration Commission. He gave orders for the hasty building of temporary wooden sheds at Pointe St. Charles. These were to serve as hospitals. At first three sheds were considered enough; more were added, as the need spread. In the end twenty-two sheds had to be set up. They were dotted over a long distance, apparently from the shore of the river to a line somewhere east of Bridge Street. These temporary hospitals were soon horrible. The sick were crowded in; no proper care could be provided. The sick, the dying, even the dead were lying together. In the courtyards between the "fever sheds" coffins of different sizes were stacked. To make things worse, Montreal had a summer of "Calcutta heat."

On June 17, 1847, news reached the Grey Nunnery that hundreds of Irish immigrants were dying untended in the sheds by the waterfront. The Superior of the Grey Nuns was Mother McMullen. She went out to see for herself what the situation was, taking Sister Sainte-Croix with her. They went into the sheds. The horrors appalled them. The Mother

Superior at once drew up a report and sent it to the Emigrant Agent. She asked permission to have her nuns care for the sick in the sheds. The Emigrant Agent readily consented. She was authorized to act as she thought best.

Mother McMullen went into the room at the convent where the sisters, young and old, had gathered for the recreation hour. It was the customary free and happy hour of the day. She heard the lively conversation, the laughter coming from one group or another. When she entered the room the sisters, as usual, stood to receive her. She took her seat in the circle. After a pause, she is reported to have addressed them in these words: "Sisters, I have seen a sight to-day that I shall never forget. I went to Point St. Charles and found hundreds of sick and dying huddled together. The stench emanating from them is too great for even the strongest constitution. The atmosphere is impregnated with it, and the air filled with the groans of the sufferers. Death is there in its most appalling aspect. Those who thus cry aloud in their agony are strangers, but their hands are outstretched for relief. Sisters, the plague is contagious." At this point she is said to have broken down. When she had recovered her voice, she added simply: "In sending you there I am signing your death warrant, but you are free to accept or refuse."

A few minutes' silence followed while the nuns could recall their vows. When they were admitted to the order they had heard, on the altar steps, the bishop asking them: "Have you considered attentively and reflected seriously on the step you are now going to take? That, from this time forth, your life must be one of sacrifice, even of death, if the glory of God or the good of your neighbor requires it?" And they, taking their vow, had answered: "Yes, My Lord; and I am willing to undertake the task with God's help." Their vow was now being put to the ultimate test. The nuns all got up and stood before the Superior. Together they said, in a sort of chorus,

"I am ready." Mother McMullen chose eight of her nuns. The next morning they went to Pointe St. Charles.

What they saw was described by one of them: "I nearly fainted when I approached the entrance to this sepulchre. The stench suffocated me. I saw a number of beings with distorted features and discolored bodies lying heaped together on the ground looking like so many corpses. I knew not what to do. I could not advance without treading on one or another of the helpless creatures in my way. While in this perplexity, I was recalled to action by seeing the frantic efforts of a poor man trying to extricate himself from among the prostrate crowd, his features expressing at the same time an intensity of horror. Stepping with precaution, placing first one foot and then the other where a space could be found, I managed to get near the patient ... We set to work quickly. Clearing a small passage, we first carried out the dead bodies, and then, after strewing the floor with straw, we replaced thereon the living who soon had to be removed in their turn."

When more immigrants arrived and more fever sheds were built Sister McMullen called for more sisters to serve. Until the 24th of June no sickness was reported among them. The long incubation period of typhus was hiding the symptoms. But on the 24th two of the sisters did not respond to the matins bell. Day by day, more fell ill, until thirty of the convent's forty professed nuns were at the point of death. When the Grey Nuns could no longer carry on their work at the sheds, their place was taken by the Sisters of Providence. Soon after, Bishop Bourget gave the sisters of the Hôtel Dieu permission to leave their cloister and join the work among the immigrants. But the Grey Nuns had withdrawn only long enough to restore the sisters who were sick and bury the seven who had died. By September they had again taken their places at the sheds. A glimpse of the nuns at work was given by a visitor, William Weir. To him "the saddest sight" was "to see the nuns, at the risk of their own lives, carrying the sick women and children in their arms from the ships to the ambulances to be taken to the sheds."

Clergymen were also risking their lives at the sheds. For the Roman Catholic clergy the risks were the greatest. Their duty was to hear the confessions of the desperately ill and the dying. Hearing confessions in the crowded sheds, where two or three people might be lying in one bed, meant that the ear of the priest had to be kept close to the mouth of the penitent, if the duty of receiving the confession in honorable confidence was to be carried out. The priests did not shrink from a procedure so dangerous and revolting. Many caught the contagion from the gasping breath of the dying. The losses among the English-speaking priests in Montreal were so heavy that a call for help was sent to New York—to the Jesuits at Fordham. They responded at once. A band of Fordham Jesuits came up to Montreal and went to work in the sheds.

Though most of the Irish immigrants were Roman Catholics, the Anglican clergy of the city were in the sheds, to give any help they could. Among them was the Reverend Mark Willoughby, the first Rector of Trinity Anglican Church (now Trinity Memorial). He went to the sheds himself and organized in his congregation a band of workers. Willoughby contracted typhus. He was nursed by Captain Maximilian Montagu Hammond of the Rifle Brigade in the British garrison. "His attendance on the sick emigrants almost passes belief," said Captain Hammond. "He furnished them with milk and other comforts which he distributed with his own hands, passing from bed to bed, irrespective of race or creed . . ." He died on July 15, 1847, aged fifty-one.

In the group organized by the Reverend Mark Willoughby to serve in the sheds was a lieutenant formerly with the Royal Navy—Lieutenant Lloyd. (Some of the old accounts give his rank as captain, but lieutenant was carved on his gravestone.)

He was staying in Montreal with Mark Willoughby. Captain Hammond said that Lieutenant Lloyd "was the life of our little band; full of love, and faith, and zeal for the cause of God ... Soon after the arrival of the emigrants he became deeply interested in their pitiable condition, and used to spend whole days at the sheds, administering food and medicine, listening to their tale of sorrow, and giving advice and assistance, as it lay in his power. For some weeks he continued exerting himself indefatigably in this manner, until at last he himself caught the fever, and was laid upon a bed of sickness, from which he never rose."

Lieutenant Lloyd, Captain Hammond and others used to meet regularly for prayer meetings and to sing hymns together. One day they were sitting round the fire, after having just sung Isaac Watts' hymn, "Not all the blood of beasts." Lieutenant Lloyd said to Captain Hammond: "I have a curious fancy concerning that hymn. I should like it sung by six young men as they lower me into the grave." Captain Hammond remembered that request. Six young men sang that hymn as Lieutenant Lloyd was buried in the military cemetery on the Papineau Road.

Mayor Mills himself became a victim. He was an American from Leland, Massachusetts, who had come up to Montreal, where he became bilingual, prosperous, charitable and popular. As Mayor he modified the anger of Montrealers who were demanding to know why these immigrants were being allowed to land, bringing the typhus with them. Indignation meetings were held on the Champ de Mars. Anger mounted when a ship arrived with sick tenants from the Irish estates of the British Foreign Secretary, Lord Palmerston. Rumors went about that a mob of outraged citizens might descend on Pointe St. Charles to toss the fever sheds into the river.

Mayor Mills not only urged restraint upon the citizens, but became a voluntary nurse in the sheds. He contracted the typhus and died on November 12, 1847. The Montreal *Herald* commented on his death: "His office, indeed, might seem to call for his attention to the general administration of the sheds; but nothing less than the benevolence of a feeling heart could have prompted his personal and assiduous visitations at the bedside of the diseased and dying." And the Governor-General, the Earl of Elgin, wrote in his dispatch to Earl Grey, the Secretary of State for the Colonies: "This day the Mayor of Montreal died, a very estimable man who did much for the immigrants—and to whose firmness and philanthropy we chiefly owe it that the Immigrant sheds were not tossed into the river by the people of the Town during the summer. He has fallen a victim to his zeal . . ."

Death in the sheds broke up the immigrant families. Separation was swift and startling. A Montrealer, J. W. Shaw, described two such cases: "I wrote a letter for a man to his friends in Hamilton. By this means I got acquainted with his family. Next day he told me that his wife having a headache he had taken her to the . . . Hospital. On the following day I saw that he was troubled, and asked for his wife, presuming that she was worse. 'Oh,' he said, 'she's trenched.' I soon learned what this meant—that she was dead and buried. Only some twenty-six hours had elapsed since he had taken her there.

"A young man and his sister came out in our ship. He had been a teacher in Ireland. He prized his sister dearly. He had found lodgings at the Tanneries [St. Henri], a suburb of Montreal. His sister fell sick and as orders were strict that the sick should be removed immediately, he took her off to the sheds. Lest she might be deprived of any delicacy she might fancy he gave her two sovereigns, and had her take a silk dress with her that she might return to her lodgings in a few days looking neat and respectable. On the third day afterwards he called at the sheds. Not a relic of his dear sister, money, clothes or any belongings were ever forthcoming. Poor fellow, I felt for him, indeed."

The victims of the typhus in the immigrant sheds were not only those who died. The living victims were the children, the orphans left when their dead parents had been carried away to the burial trenches. As one account reads: "Children were counted by hundreds . . . the infant taken from its dead mother's breast, or from the arms of some older one trying in vain to still its cries, the creeping baby shrieking for the father and mother who would nevermore respond to that call, and older ones sobbing and frantically trying to escape to search for parents already beneath the sod. This scene in the children's shed was beyond description, adding a new pang in the agony of the expiring father or mother."

The Grey Nuns took over the care of many orphans. The St. Patrick's Orphan Asylum of Montreal, opened in 1846, had been given into their charge. The Roman Catholic Bishop of Montreal, Msgr. Ignace Bourget, did all he could to find homes for the orphans. He appealed to the country people. They came from all the surrounding parishes. Each family adopted one or two.

As for the dead, the workmen building Victoria Bridge, many of them immigrants, chose as the monument the great stone from the river—a stone then lying by the side of the railway track. The spot was visited in 1870 by an Irish priest, Father M. B. Buckley, who was in North America collecting money to build the cathedral at Cork. All the modern changes that have since altered the appearance of the area round about the stone had not yet obliterated the marks of the tragedy. "I came down with Father Hogan," this visitor from Ireland wrote, "to see the spot where so many of my fellow-countrymen so miserably perished. There was the desolate spot, enclosed by a fragile paling—there the numerous mounds—and, above all, in the centre, an enormous stone ... . May God have mercy on their souls!"

The workmen who had set up that enormous stone had intended it to stand on the spot forever—"while grass grows and water flows." But it had been set up in an awkward position. Montreal grew; use of the Victoria Bridge increased. To practical minds, the "Irish Stone" seemed a block in the path of progress. In 1900 the Grand Trunk Railway decided to shift the stone several streets away. It would be set up in St. Patrick Square. The railway consulted nobody; it made no public announcement. About nine o'clock in the morning of December 21, 1900, it simply hauled up the "Irish Stone" with a big steam derrick. It ran the stone on a flatcar along the track on St. Patrick Street and deposited it in a corner of St. Patrick Square.

The Grand Trunk had hoped controversy would be avoided by moving quickly and quietly. It was not long in realizing its mistake. The Irish community was in an uproar. It demanded that the monument be restored immediately to its original and rightful place. The railway, claiming that public convenience was on its side, refused to give in to a sentimental clamor. It was hesitant, however, to go ahead with its plans to run tracks over the spot where the monument had previously stood. Years went by in inconclusive controversy. In 1910 the Grand Trunk decided to proceed. It made a formal application to the Board of Railway Commissioners. It asked for the right to expropriate the old site. The purpose would be the improvement of the approach to Victoria Bridge.

The Board of Railway Commissioners announced its decision in 1911. The Irish case had been strengthened by evidence that the old site actually belonged to the Anglican Bishop of Montreal. This fact made the Grand Trunk a trespasser. Thomas Brassey, one of the firm of contractors who built Victoria Bridge, had conveyed the monument and its site to the Anglican Bishop of Montreal. It was not really a sale, but a matter of trust. A nominal sum of five dollars was all that was paid. Monument and land were to be held as a trust by the Bishop of Montreal and his successors forever. The Board took this legal fact into consideration. But, at the same time, it reached a compromise between sentiment and utility. The land was reduced to a quarter of its original size. The stone was to be shifted about fifteen feet to the east from where it had at first stood. The Bishop of Montreal (at that time Right Reverend John C. Farthing) sold the land to the Grand Trunk. The railway assumed responsibility for its perpetual maintenance.

With this compromise the issue remained settled for half a century. Then Montreal began to make plans for Expo '67. Bridge Street needed to be widened and straightened. Once more the "Irish Stone" was said to be standing in the path of progress. In September, 1965, City Council was asked to vote funds for the changes to Bridge Street. Councillors Kenneth McKenna and John Lynch-Staunton spoke up in defense of the stone. It was sacred in the eyes of the Irish community, they insisted; it must not be disturbed. The Chairman of Montreal's Executive Committee, Lucien Saulnier, had a suggestion to make: let the Irish community form a committee and offer recommendations. The committee was formed; consultations with the civic administration took place. At the meeting of City Council on June 21, 1966, Lucien Saulnier announced that Montreal's planning and public works department had worked out a solution. The "Irish Stone" would remain unmoved. Bridge Street would be changed instead. It would pass on either side of a central dividing mall. On this mall the stone would stand, with its site extended at both ends.

Over the years the "Irish Stone" has not only marked a grave site; it has been the gathering place of bones unearthed nearby. Burials evidently took place over a wide area. Whenever bones have been dug up, they have all been buried close to the old stone. Every time these bones are found (said the Irish Ambassador, John Hearne, when some were unearthed in 1942), they have been "a voice arising from the old clay."

John Collins SKETCHBOOK

SLEIGHS ON MOUNT ROYAL

SEVENTEEN

Winter Cheerfulness
and Muffins:
The Sleighs

SEVERE AND SNOWY weather was welcomed in Old Montreal. It brought good sleighing conditions. A mild winter, with thin snowfall, meant poor roads, hard travel. A writer of 1833 said: "Nor must it be forgotten that the severity of cold is productive of its advantages. By the consolidation of the snow, the worst roads are converted into the best . . . Indeed, a mild winter is regarded as a great calamity by the Canadians . . ."

A snowy winter, and good roads for the sleighs, were all the more welcome because winter, until about the middle of the 19th century, was one long holiday. The business of Montreal depended on the port. When the river froze and the port was closed, Montrealers and the people of the countryside round about had little to do except to enjoy themselves until spring. Those who went out in their sleighs went mostly on visits to one another for "frolic and jollity." Isaac Weld pictured the cheerful scene as he had known it in the closing years of the 18th century:

"Winter in Canada is the season of general amusement. The clear frosty weather no sooner commences, than all thoughts about business are laid aside, and every one devotes himself to pleasure. The inhabitants meet in convivial parties at each other's houses, and pass the day with music, dancing, card-playing, and every social entertainment that can beguile the time. At Montreal, in particular . . . it appears then as if the town were inhabited but by one large family."

The sleighs kept at hand for prompt and ready traveling were often the carioles. These sleighs, carrying two passengers and the driver, were small, simple, cheap. Usually they were drawn by one horse. If two horses were used, they were harnessed one in front of the other; the track in the roads might be too narrow for them to go abreast. Carioles had very low runners; they seemed almost to travel on their bottoms. They were shaped in different styles, from the plainest to the handsomest. But, by and large, the cariole was not an elegant sleigh, made to impress the onlooker. It was meant to be handy, fast, serviceable—an easy means of getting about.

Carioles had cheerfulness. Cornelius Krieghoff caught it in his winter scenes. They were all the more cheerful because those traveling in them were generally going to some pleasure, or returning from it. They even made a cheerful noise, with bells ringing from the harness or horns blown to give warning. Even the horns, from the gaiety of the passengers, had a party-like sound. Isaac Weld felt this cheerfulness when he wrote: "The rapidity of the motion, and the sound of these bells and horns, appears to be very conducive to cheerfulness, for you seldom see a dull face . . ."

It might seem that traveling by open sleigh in winter— however cheerful the bells, swift the motion or convivial the purpose—would chill the passenger to the bone. But Canadians then knew how to dress for the weather; they could make sleigh travel comfortable. The Irish visitor, Edward Allen Talbot, about 1819, wrote of the careful preparations for a trip by cariole and how effective they were:

"On taking an excursion in this vehicle, the Canadians are very warmly clothed; for they wrap themselves up in bear and buffalo skins. Persons of both sexes draw coarse yarn hose over their shoes and stockings, and cover their hands with doeskin gloves, lined with wool. They also wear fur-caps and top-coats. The back of the sleigh is generally lined with bear skins; and a buffalo hide, retaining its fur, covers the travellers from their feet to their waists. Thus equipped, they bid defiance to the most severe weather, and often travel ten or fifteen miles without a stoppage for refreshment or any other purpose."

Not only Canadians, hardened by the cold of many winters, could travel by open sleigh without discomfort. Old Countrymen, once they had learned how to keep themselves warm, found they suffered less from the cold than in England. One of these was Right Reverend Ashton Oxenden, who came from his "sweet Kentish rectory" in 1869 to become the Anglican Bishop of Montreal. "We have sometimes been out at night in an open sleigh," he discovered, "when the thermometer has been considerably below zero, without feeling it so much as on an ordinary cold night in England."

Traveling by sleigh took a person out into the open; he came to see the loveliness of the winter landscape and to enjoy it. Moving out among the snow-covered fields in an open sleigh was not unlike putting out to sea: the traveler was made aware of the vastness of the sky. Old narratives describe how daybreak, sundown and night each had a wintry splendor of its own.

Robert Michael Ballantyne, of the Hudson's Bay Company, described the daybreak experience in January, 1846, when he set out from Lachine for Montreal on the first stage of a sleigh journey to Tadoussac: "The stars shone brightly as we glided over the crunching snow, and the sleigh-bells tinkled merrily as our horse sped over the deserted road. Groups of white cottages, and solitary gigantic trees, flew past us, looking, in the uncertain light, like large snow-drifts ... In silence we glided on our way, till the distant lights of Montreal awakened us from our reveries, and we met at intervals a solitary pedestrian, or a sleigh-load of laughing, fur-encompassed faces, returning from an evening party ...

"The lamps were still burning as we left the city, although the first streaks of dawn illumined the eastern sky."

To drive westward on a late winter's afternoon, facing "the cauldron of the setting sun," was a very different experience. An officer of the Commissariat service in the British garrison wrote his description of a January twilight, as he traveled by sleigh near the St. Lawrence in the 1820's: "As evening came on, the glowing tints which suffused the bleak landscape were particularly beautiful,—such as a winter sunset in Canada can alone produce. The glaring sun became magnified as he touched the horizon. A deep fiery red was reflected from bright tin spires, and blazed from the glass windows of the scattered white houses in the distance. The snow sparkled with purple and varying prismatic colours; while large fragments of ice, scattered here and there, completed a picture of winter in all its intensity."

Those who went by sleigh in the night saw winter in still another form of majesty. As they traveled under the stars, or by the light of the moon, the vast white snow reflected the lights of the sky. The sportsman, John J. Rowan, writing in the 1870's, found in Canada a night brightness unknown in England:

"The nights in this country are lighter than in England, and owing to the clearness of the atmosphere, the moon and stars are much brighter. A still cold Canadian winter's night is one of the things to be seen . . . The stars then appear little higher than the tree-tops, and the flashes of the aurora borealis in the north are like spectres flitting about in the distance; the smooth surface of the snow reflects the light of the moon and of the stars, so that it is possible to read small print; the silence is most profound . . ."

In Montreal those who lived by standards of sophistication had to have elegant sleighs and elegant horses. Sleighing as an expression of opulence increased as the 19th century advanced and Montreal moved into greater and greater prosperity. "Perhaps nowhere outside of the Russian capital," said a writer of 1881, "are to be seen better constructed or more comfortable sleighs than in Montreal. There is no end to the variety of shape, each according to its owner's fancy, while robes of the finest furs complete the outfit . . . and how our noble animals enjoy the Winter season when the roads are hard and dry and the air bracing. You see them prancing along in their handsome harness trappings . . . There is no need for the whip, the music of the bells is inspiriting to the animal as it is pleasing to the occupants of the sleigh, who sit embowered in luxurious robes. Every afternoon from Christmas day to the end of March our principal streets are made lively and gay by the gorgeous turnouts of 'Uppertendom.' "

This parade of elegance in the principal streets of Montreal, while it adorned the winter season, was not typical of sleighing. Most of the sleighs in Montreal, even more in the countryside, were still the plain, rough little carioles, or the larger, boxlike berlines. They were drawn by plain, rough little horses.

These hardy little horses were not the well-groomed animals of Montreal's "Uppertendom." They were the working animals. They never felt the currying comb; their curled and matted hair added to their quaintness. In winter, when their hair was heaviest and most unkempt, and they had been heated in a long drive, icicles seemed to hang all over them. The long icicles from their noses made some visitors think they looked like funny little elephants.

The unkempt Canadian horses could be left standing in Montreal's streets without shelter in cold, snow and wind. "You will see them brought from the country in the coldest weather," an English visitor noticed, "and left standing in the open air without covering, for hours together, while their owners are transacting their business, or drinking in a public house; and they seem not to be the worse for it." Their owners would come out, "rushing with one consent," when the time came to go home. They would jump into the sleighs, seize their whips, and immediately the horses, standing a moment before in the cold, and perhaps white with snow, would start off "at top speed." Such little horses, ungainly, with narrow chests, and only about fourteen hands high, were scarcely racers. They moved without grace in "a kind of amble, between a trot and a canter." Yet French Canadian drivers often raced them on the roads. Such are the impromptu races, with challenges and betting, shouts and whip flourishes, in Henri Julien's long series of lively sketches.

The officers stationed with the British garrison in Montreal took up sleighing as the only way of entering into the social pleasures of a Canadian winter. Their sleighs and horses were the smartest they could find. Low sleighs were poorly considered. Sleighs were bought with runners as high as possible, and in the brightest colors. Few British officers had any experience in sleigh-driving. They had to learn the great difference between driving on runners and driving on wheels. When turning corners sharply they might at first make no allowance for the slewing of a sleigh—and a slewing sleigh might easily tip over. Many a Montreal girl, out sleighing with an inexperienced garrison officer, found herself in a snowbank. Such accidents did not deter them. Garrison officers never lacked companionship. The girls who went driving with them were known as "muffins." For those curious about a definition, the correspondent of *The Times*, in Montreal in the winter of 1861-62, wrote: "A muffin is simply a lady who sits beside the male occupant of a sleigh." This dictionary-like definition hardly conveyed the warmth of muffinage. On a long, cold sleigh drive a girl nestled beside an officer was as warm and as cheerful as a muffin served for tea. Though the term "muffin" prevailed, sometimes the girls were called "crumpets," even "scones."

The role of the muffin in a garrison sleigh party was described by a young officer in the 1830s: "Winter picnics were then much the fashion. We used to drive out in our sleighs, each taking a lady—a commonly called a muffin—and a share of the dinner. A band was also sent out, and there were several good rooms in habitants' houses that were used for these parties. After dinner we danced for several hours, then drove home together on the snow roads, all in a long string of sleighs, by moonlight, which was often nearly as light as day. These drives were most charming; and on a still night to hear all the sleigh-bells jingling as the horses trotted merrily along was most fascinating, to say nothing of the young lady who was rolled up in the warm fur robes by your side!"

Only gradually, as the season progressed, would a girl go driving regularly with a particular officer—and only then did she become known as a muffin. The achievement of a state of muffinage required a good deal of time, tact and finesse. Tricks would be played on new officers, unaccustomed to sleigh-driving etiquette.

"Now tell me, what about the muffins?" a young officer, just arrived in the 1860's, asked after dinner in his regimental mess.

"What," they said, "haven't you secured a muffin, yet?"

"No, how could I, when I don't know a soul out here?"

"Ah," they told him, "that's unfair; but you're in luck after all. There's just one left, but she's the nicest girl here. You must secure her at once."

"But who will introduce me?"

"Oh, you don't want any introduction; all you've got to do is to go straight down after lunch tomorrow, ring at the bell, and ask for Miss ——; then introduce yourself, and say you have come to ask her to be your muffin for the season."

The new officer lost no time. He called the next day. As he entered the room he saw a particularly pretty, quiet, lady-like young woman waiting to receive him.

"I arrived a few days ago, Miss ——," he explained, "and have come without delay to ask if you will honour me by driving out with me for the remainder of the season, and I am assured that, fortunately for me, you are still not engaged as a muffin."

Miss —— looked at him in amazement. She reached for the bell to summon the servant. She gave him a bow and he was ushered out of the room. His visit had not lasted a minute; she had said nothing. But suddenly he realized that a girl did not become the steady driving companion of an officer as abruptly as they had made him believe. For the rest of the season, whenever he appeared, a sound like the tinkling of a little bell and a subdued cry of "Muffin!" could be heard. He never quite got over it as long as he remained in Canada.

Many of the garrison officers were young men of private wealth or excellent prospects. A number already had titles or would eventually inherit them. They were regarded as exceptionally desirable husbands by Montreal's girls. Thus, when a true state of muffinage came about, a young officer might be in danger. Many a young officer found himself married to his muffin. When Field Marshal Sir Garnet Wolseley, Commander-in-Chief of the British Army, was a young officer in Montreal in the 1860's, he had realized that one of the problems in muffinage was to stay single. In his reminiscences, written in old age, he recalled the sleighing parties (though in memory the sleighs had become "sledges"):

"Life in Montreal was very pleasant. Of course I bought horses and a sledge, in which I daily drove very charming women ... and many were the sledge expeditions we made into the neighbouring country. Altogether, it was an elysium of bliss for young officers, the only trouble being to keep single. Several impressionable young captains and subalterns had to be sent home hurriedly to save them from imprudent marriages."

The tendency of muffinage to merge into marriage was very real, as young Wolseley had realized. But these marriages, though frequent, may have been seldom happy. "None are so home-sick as the damsels of the free and easy Canadas," a medical officer remarked, "very few of them bear transplanting, as hundreds of English officers know right well." Commanding officers who sent young captains and subalterns "home hurriedly" may have acted in the best interests of all concerned. They left unspoiled the memories of happy sleigh drives.

A few glimpses remain. "On the 'meet' days (generally Wednesdays and Saturdays)," says one account, "it was a beautiful sight to see the grayhaired old commander ... take the lead of the long line of sleighs, each filled with gallant soldiers and beauteous Canadian ladies. Away would dash the General's four-in-hand, followed by the rest of the assembly ... "

And when the correspondent of *The Times* was in Montreal in 1861-62 he wrote for his paper his impression of the garrison tandem club setting out: "On our way we were rejoiced by the sight of the 'Driving Club' going out for an excursion, Sir Fenwick Williams leading. All one could see, however, was a certain looming up of dark forms through the drift gliding along to the music of the bells, which followed one after the other, and were lost in the hazy yet glittering clouds tossed up by the horses' hoofs from the snow."

John Collins

SKETCHBOOK

FIREMEN'S
MONUMENT
—MOUNT ROYAL CEMETERY

EIGHTEEN

Tragedy in the Lane:
The Firemen

THE ALARM WAS sounded at five o'clock in the Sunday morning of April 29, 1877. Fire had broken out in the Oil Cabinet and Novelty Works at the corner of St. Urbain Street and Scott's Lane. It was to be the worst fire, in loss of firemen's lives, in the history of Victorian Montreal.

The building, old and unsteady, was full of varnish and other viciously inflammable materials. Flames streamed up. Heat bursting from the building blistered doors and window sashes across the street. Nearby glass shattered and dropped away.

Firemen tried to force their way in. Heat and smoke rushed at them, driving them out. A special type of firemen's ladder—the Skinner Ladder—was run up in the street. Three firemen climbed up it, pulling a hose up with them. They called for water and poured a heavy stream through an upper window. The flames faded. But the fire was only being driven downward. Suddenly it leaped from one of the lower windows. It seemed to clutch the ladder. The three men were cut off at the top. They could not come down without plunging into a cloud of fire.

A hard April wind blew that early morning on St. Urbain Street. The firemen at the top of the ladder waited for a gust to sweep the flames away, long enough for them to scramble down. One by one they took their chances, none knowing whether the wind would hold off the flames or let them fly at him as he went by. All struggled to the street, alive but horribly burned.

Meanwhile other firemen had been turning a hose on the building from a lane to the north. They had taken up a risky position. The walls were shaky. Some time before, they had been reported by the building inspectors. Now they weakened with the fire and strained under the weight of the machinery. Part of the north wall burst out at the middle. Bricks spilled into the lane. No one on St. Urbain Street knew what had happened until a fireman ran out, shouting: "Get help! The wall has fallen and some of our men are under it!" Firemen ran to the lane. They found several men buried under the wreckage. Part of the remaining wall was tottering.

What happened in the lane in those few minutes was described in Victorian style by Captain William Orme McRobie of the Salvage Corps: "Let us picture to ourselves the position of those men. The first batch covered up to their chins, and some of them covered altogether, with their faces upward, watching the swaying of the high brick wall above them, imploring the rescuers not to leave them. Those noble fellows giving them words of cheer, and telling them that if they could not rescue them they would die with them. What heroism, reader! Can you show a parallel to this? What must have been their feelings, working as they never worked before, with bleeding and bruised hands, in a stooping position, one eye looking up at the tottering wall above them, knowing that it was only a matter of a very short time, when down it would come. The next misplaced beam or the next gust of wind, and then ... At last it came. They saw it. Did they shrink from their self-imposed task? Did they break their word with their comrades? Did they jump to one side, as they might have done, and saved themselves? No! ... When they saw the wall falling they only threw their bodies on those of their comrades, and died there, thereby saving their comrades' lives. Was that not heroism? If not, I do not understand the meaning of the word."

With the second crash of the wall, rescuers crowded into the lane. They tossed away the hot bricks, not caring that they were burning their hands. Several firemen were brought out alive. Six had died, or soon died, of their injuries.

These were among the first deaths in the Fire Department since it was organized in 1863 as a full-time force. The funeral processions to the Protestant and Roman Catholic cemeteries were both so long that citizens were still trying to take their place at the rear when the head of each procession had already arrived at the burial place.

One of the wildest of Victorian fires was in the St. James Hotel, facing Victoria Square, on March 18, 1873. The St. James Hotel, though five stories high, was without fire escapes. As the firemen rounded into Victoria Square at full gallop, they saw the windows "filled with people, some calling for help, others throwing out their trunks, while others could be seen in mid air, suspended by their bed clothes knotted together."

The drama of the evening was provided by Johanna O'Connor. She worked in the kitchen of the hotel. On the night of the fire the watchman and the bookkeeper had come to the kitchen to find out where the smoke was coming from. They looked into the stove. Nothing was wrong there. They went away. Smoke had been in the hotel for several days. Two men had been repairing the flues.

Johanna O'Connor went to bed. She was startled from sleep by the watchman yelling: "Girls, get up, the house is on fire!" She went into the corridor. She saw no light, smoke nearly choked her. She went back, put on some clothes and came into the corridor again. She heard a man shouting: "Where are the stairs?" She caught hold of his coattail and followed him. He found a door and opened it. They went into a room where the gas was still burning. He and another man smashed the glass of the window. One after the other they jumped out. Many guests of the hotel leaped from its windows that night. They came down to the pavement with the same dull thud as the trunks.

The room was on fire. Johanna O'Connor let herself out of the window. She clung to the frame with her right hand, shouting for help. She saw a crowd of men in the square below. "Oh men! Oh men! Help me! Help me!" she screamed. They could do nothing for her except to shout back encouragement: "Don't let go! Don't let go! The ladder is coming!"

Firemen soon put up a ladder. But she was on the fifth floor of the St. James Hotel; the ladder was too short to reach her. Minutes passed. She was still hanging from the window-sill. Fireman John Nolan passed up a second ladder to Fireman John Beckingham, who put one ladder on top of the other. Even the two ladders came short of the windowsill where Johanna dangled.

The crowd by now had filled Victoria Square. It stood gazing in excited silence. Nearly twenty minutes had passed since Johanna had let herself out of the window. Her arms could not support her much longer. It was then that Beckingham stood on the top rung of the main ladder. He put his back against the wall. He braced himself. Then he raised the second ladder in his hands till it touched the girl's feet.

For a moment she hesitated. She seemed to be wondering if she could bring herself to let go of the windowsill and trust her weight to the quivering ladder being held up to her. The firemen were calling to her not to be afraid, but to come down slowly and take care not to miss her footing. She placed her feet on the unsteady ladder and let go her grip on the window. She came down very cautiously, pausing between steps. Nolan was at the top of the main ladder, just below Beckingham. She sank into Nolan's arms. He carried her down to the street. She was exhausted, frost-bitten, cut by glass. "The ice was dreadful," she said, "and my clothes hindered me from going, and I was nearly fainting."

Before the Montreal Fire Department was organized in 1863 fire-fighting in Montreal was done by volunteers. In the early years of the 19th century there were a number of volunteer companies. Names were picturesque, such as Union Company, Neptune Company, Protector Company. To be the captain of a fire company was an honored position in the community. All who joined were honored also as young men ready to risk their lives in the public service.

Methods for years were slow and crude. Warning of a fire usually came from the watchmen, as the guardians of the night. It was their duty to call out the hour at the street corners, suiting their cry to the conditions: stormy night, rainy night, moon night, starry night. And ending with "All is well!" If they happened to see a fire they would shout "Fire! Fire! Fire!" at the top of their lungs. They would hurry to the house of the nearest fire-fighting captain and rap on his door. When the captain came down into the street on a dark night, the watchman would light him to the shed where the engine was kept, for every watchman carried a lantern swinging at the end of his baton—a lantern lit by a tallow candle.

When he had escorted the captain to the engine house, he

would make his way to Place d'Armes to rouse the beadle of Notre Dame Church. The beadle then lived on the north side of the square, where the Bank of Montreal now stands, and the old Notre Dame Church stood across Notre Dame Street, just in front of the Notre Dame Church of today. The sleepy beadle would cross the square, climb the belfry strike a spark with flint and steel to light a lantern, which he suspended out of the belfry on a pole. This was one signal of fire. Next he would hit one of the bells with a mallet, and keep hitting it so long as the fire lasted. The watchmen meanwhile would be helping to spread the warning by whirling loud rattles they carried with them. One watchman is described going about the streets, sounding a gong two feet in diameter.

By these various means members of the volunteer fire companies would be roused and mobilized. When they reached the fire stations they might find the engines were not ready for use. Until the 1840's no station was heated. If it was winter and the engine had been used recently, the hose and the valves on the pumps might be frozen. Warm water had to be fetched from the nearest house to thaw them. Half an hour might pass before the engine could be brought out. The engines were heavy—over a ton. They were drawn by a drag-rope. The speed of arrival could never be great. Yet there was spirit and dash as some thirty or forty young men pulled together to drag their fire engine through the streets. Sometimes a horse was used. A fire company was permitted to commandeer any horse in the street except a doctor's.

Montreal's first fire engines had no supply of water except what could be provided from buckets or puncheons. In serious fires a line of citizens would be formed to the river. The buckets would be handed down the line empty, passed back full. At a great fire near St. Ann's Market (now Place d'Youville) 500 men were mobilized into a bucket brigade to bring water from the river. In many fires water was brought to the engines in puncheons, drawn in little carts by horses or dogs. Fifty cents was paid as a premium for the first puncheon to arrive; subsequent puncheons were twenty cents each. Fire-fighters could not count on a steady supply of water. A member of one of the volunteer companies, George Maclean Rose, re-called: "When the engine exhausted the supply of water, we had to wait patiently until the water carts brought us more."

Volunteer fire-fighters lacked nothing in courage. Most audacious of them all was Alfred Perry, whose interest in fire-fighting was to be lifelong. George Horne had seen him in action: "I have seen him run up the spout of a three-storey building, then crawl from window to window, like a cat, at the risk of his life, to save that of women and children. No extension ladders then, such as we have now. I have seen hundreds of spectators spell-bound, witnessing Perry's acts of daring, expecting to see him drop to his death every moment."

Sometimes the volunteers of Montreal went to fight fires in other communities. On an August afternoon in 1846 a wild glare throbbed in the sky over Laprairie. The captain of the Protector Company in Montreal decided to take his men and their engine to the rescue. No bridge then connected Mont-real with the South Shore; they crossed on the ferry to Longueuil. From Longueuil they dragged their fire engine by its rope along the road to Laprairie. It was a long haul. In the end, exhausted, they commandeered a horse from a field. The fire in Laprairie burned house after house. The Scotch church was gone. The firemen from Montreal arrived in time to save the Roman Catholic church and some houses near it.

Early in the 1860's the City of Montreal took action to estab-lish a regular full-time Fire Department. The volunteers were formed into a sort of reserve force named the City Fire Com-pany. They were to assist the regular Fire Department when-ever needed. The new full-time firemen were named the City

Fire Police. Some police powers were given them. They were sworn in as special constables, "for the purpose of assisting in the maintenance of order in the City, at all times, and more particularly at fires."

Fire alarm boxes were placed about the city. All were locked to prevent false alarms. Policemen carried keys with them. On each box was posted a notice. It gave the address of a "respectable person" living nearby, where a key might be obtained.

To sound the alarm a device was attached to four church bells. The signal was flashed from box to bell by "Electro-Magnetic Telegraph." The number of strokes on a bell indicated where the fire had broken out. The churches had been chosen in the four quarters of the city: Christ Church Cathedral to the north, Notre Dame to the south, St. Jacques to the east, St. George's to the west. In one case at least (Notre Dame in Place d'Armes) the church wardens stipulated that the City of Montreal must assume liability if a bell was fractured in signaling an alarm.

Poor pay and long hours were the lot of Montreal's new firemen. Time off was four hours in every week and a share of Sunday. Even the brief leaves were conditional: firemen had to keep within sound of the alarm and report for duty at once if the alarm was sounded. One man said the hours were so long that he "wouldn't doubt that in many cases children of firemen hardly recognized their fathers, they saw them so seldom."

At first the firemen had to water the streets when not fighting fires. The Corporation wanted to save money and give the men occupation. The arrangement was resisted. As early as 1865 William Patton, in charge of the street-watering service, pleaded with the Fire Committee at City Hall. The horses grew tired in hauling water carts; they could not be expected to dash to a fire with "all speed." Double duty also caused delays. Firemen, hearing an alarm from the nearest church bell, had to get back to the station, unharness the horses from the watering cart and harness them to the engine.

When firemen were relieved of street-watering duties time hung heavily over the stations. The men had no exercise. Their days were spent in "hanging and lounging around." Stations were bleak. Floors were bare boards; furniture was sparse, often broken. At one station chairs were too few for the men. Whenever one man left a chair, it would be occupied at once by another. Always one man was left standing— waiting for his chance.

Dormitories and stables were both on the ground floor and close together. One fireman said it reminded him of what the Irishman said about hanging: "It was all right, when you got used to it." The arrangement was regarded by the authorities as perfectly normal. The Fire Chief, in his report for 1873, was describing the new station on St. Gabriel Street. On the ground floor, he said, seven men "bunk in it, and five horses."

Tedium was relieved by callers. The city was still small; each district had a character of its own. Many people lived, worked and died in the districts where they were born. They knew one another; they knew one another's families—the parents, the grandparents. In such community settings fire stations became community centers. Menfolk dropped in to chat with the firemen and read their newspapers while on their way to work in the morning. They usually dropped in for another visit on their way home at night. The Fire Chief for the department's early years—Chief Alexander Bertram, a former blacksmith—understood the need for such local gatherings. Had he been a stickler for discipline he might have given orders that nobody except firemen should be allowed in a station, unless to report a fire. But he was a generous, human old Scot who felt (wisely, as it proved) that a certain liberality in discipline made for a better response in time of real need.

He would try to visit one station every day. He would sit down with the men, and the outside callers, and talk. Firemen spoke of the "warm genial nature of the lively old man," who presided over the men as the father of "one compact happy family."

At a fire Chief Bertram's easygoing geniality disappeared. Commands were sharp and clear. He was careful of the lives of his men; he frowned on all unnecessary risks. But when the fight had to be pressed, or lives saved, he "expected service to the point of heroism." One fireman remarked that "although Chief Bertram was kind and indulgent to his men, none of those men ever attempted to take advantage of that kindness, or, for a moment, dreamed that they could take liberties on that account. Oh, no! When the old man issued an order or word of command, it had to be obeyed, and it was obeyed with a free, spontaneous willingness . . ."

At a fire Chief Bertram went about with a hickory stick in his hand. If he saw one of his men disobeying an order, he would come up behind him and hit him on the back. "Did you hear me?" he would ask. None of his men resented being hit. All accepted it was one of "the Old Man's" ways. Another officer in the Fire Department tried it, but only once. He was told by the man he hit not to do it again.

Montreal's Victorian firemen had not only to worry about the fires; they had to remember their horses. If the fire lasted long, the horses had to be fed. In winter firemen had to do their best to keep their horses warm. Horses might be frozen to death if left standing where they had been hitched. "The horses had a hard time," said Arthur H. Mann, who joined the Montreal Fire Department in 1892. "They might go out at 11 or 12 at night, get heated up running to a fire, then stand in snow and slush at 25 below zero until 7 a.m., with nothing more than a flimsy blanket over them—if there was time to cover them at all."

Yet the horses were the fire-fighters' greatest pride. When Arthur Mann was appointed captain of Number 1 station in

Place d'Youville, he stabled fourteen majestic grays. Two of them he had insisted on bringing with him from his previous post in another station.

One horse, above all others, won fame in the Fire Department. He was stabled at various stations, though mostly at St. Gabriel Street. He was a dashing fire horse, but one of many tricks. The men at the station had taught him to nod his head by touching him at one spot, to shake his head when touched at another. Visitors to the station went away convinced Charley could hear and answer questions.

In the days when firemen and horses were on the same floor in the St. Gabriel Street station, Charley would wake up the men in the morning when he wanted his feed. He would go to the bunk door and look in and make as much noise as he could. If the men would not stir, he would go over to the reels, take the shank of the bell in his teeth, and swing it backward and forward.

As the Victorian Age advanced, speed in the Fire Department advanced with it. By the 1890's Montreal's fire stations had been fitted with automatic devices. The moment an alarm sounded, the doors of the horses' stalls flew open. Halters unbuckled. Each horse, carefully trained, ran forward and waited in front of its wagon. Harness, suspended over the places where the horses stood, dropped on their backs. A slight pressure snapped the collar round the horse's neck. The belly band was also snapped in place. The reins were made fast to the bit by a flexible steel fastening. The automatic arrangements continued. When the driver mounted the box, he gave the reins a sharp jerk. It not only signaled the horses to go; it opened the street door. The gallop through the streets began.

A writer in *The Dominion Illustrated Monthly* in 1892 described these automatic devices as marvels of Victorian speed. "Eight seconds after the alarm," he wrote, "sees the detachment on the street . . . think of it, eight seconds! Truly this is a fast age."

SKETCHBOOK

John Collins

MOUNT
ROYAL
at the top of
PEEL

NINETEEN

"March Away O'er The Snow"
The Snowshoers

IT WAS THE WEDNESDAY night of March 10, 1869. Twelve members of the Montreal Snow Shoe Club (the "Tuques Bleues") were out on their midweek tramp over Mount Royal. It was the roughest night of the year. Snow alternated with sleet. Drifts were as high as a cottage. A gale pursued and battled anyone out-of-doors.

Snowshoeing was a sinewy sport. Its devotees prided themselves on their hardiness. They tramped out into the worst blizzards, in the most piercing cold. The tramps were tests of endurance—no idlers' stroll, but hard slogging to a swift pace set by the leader.

If any snowshoer on a tramp over Mount Royal felt he just could not stand the pace, he dropped out and went "by the road," which meant Côte-des-Neiges. On this wild night of March 10 two members had fallen out of Indian file and were tramping by way of the road. But on such a night even the road was drifted over and scarcely to be seen. They plunged forward as best they could. It was really a killing night.

The two snowshoers saw a sleigh ahead of them on the hill. It was motionless. They came up to it. The horse was dead, the sleigh deserted. Whoever had been traveling in it had found himself blocked by the drifts and defeated by the pelting sleet. What had happened to him the trampers could not know. No trace remained. The driver of the sleigh had disappeared into the night.

The two snowshoers climbed farther up Côte-des-Neiges. They saw another sleigh ahead. It was not moving either. When they tramped up to it they found, sheltering themselves inside, John Lowe, the managing director of the *Gazette*, and his daughter. For a long time they had been sitting in the stalled sleigh, afraid to leave it to go plunging through the snow of the country road. They had been doing their best to shield themselves from the sleety snow under a buffalo robe, hoping somebody might come to their rescue. But rescue on such a night seemed unlikely. By the time the snowshoers arrived, Lowe and his daughter were exhausted by cold and dread. The "Tuques Bleues" of the Montreal Club helped them to make their way home. It had been a close escape. As a commentator remarked, "but for their timely succor, a sensational article would have been furnished to the papers, and a case for the Coroner."

Snowshoers themselves could be lost in storms on Mount Royal. On the night of December 30, 1857, members of the Montreal Snow Shoe Club—seventeen of them—lost their way in the whirl of a blizzard. Snow conspired with the dark to bewilder them all. Instead of going over the mountain by the accustomed route, they tramped for about an hour in obscurity. Surprised, they came out in Westmount (then part of Notre-Dame-de-Grâces Village). They decided to make their way back to the Côte-des-Neiges Road, for they could follow the road until they were north of the mountain. Later, on the way back to the city, they lost direction again. Half the night they tramped about Mount Royal, not able to see more than a few feet in front of them and missing familiar landmarks. They were not back in town "until cock crow."

This experience disturbed the club. It was bad enough to lose direction, but so long as all kept together they could do something to help one another. The greater danger was that the trampers, moving in long Indian file, might be blinded by blowing snow and lose connection. Precautions were taken. A bugler went on the tramps. His blasts could "call the scattered legions to a common centre for mutual protection and advice."

Such adventures on Mount Royal gave Victorian snowshoers a feeling of risk and challenge that enhanced the sport. Snowshoeing, the club members wished to have understood, was not for weaklings or triflers. It was only for those who could face it, and take it. No storm should make true snowshoers give up or advise prudent postponement. One of the Montreal Club's songs, to the tune of "Dixie Land," vibrated with the words:

"We take our places on the snow shoe trail,
And do not fear the piercing gale.
March away! march away!
March away o'er the snow."

Long-distance tramps put stamina to its severest test. During the season the clubs carried out tramps to Lachine, to St. Johns, to Chambly, to St. Vincent de Paul. In 1876 the Montreal Snow Shoe Club organized a tramp all the way to Cornwall. To set the pace even faster, rival clubs tramped to distant points in steeplechases. On February 7, 1880, the Montreal and St. George's clubs raced from Fletcher's Field, just east of Mount Royal, to Péloquin's Hotel at Sault-au-Récollet. The distance was about five and a half miles. Members of the Montreal

Snow Shoe Club came first and second: George Starke covered the five and a half miles in 43.26½ minutes, A. W. McTaggart in 44.26½. But the victory was still close. T. Davidson of the St. George's Club came in third, with time of 44.41½ minutes.

In long-distance tramps some of the snowshoers sank with exhaustion or were crippled by the terrible cramps (known as "mal de raquet") which seized them in the back of the legs. The "whipper in" was essential. He went at the rear, and his duty was to hurry on whoever was falling behind or to help anyone who had broken down. When the Montreal Snow Shoe Club tramped to the Ottawa Hotel in St. Vincent de Paul in the season of 1876-77 one member collapsed on the ice. The old records of the club note the incident: "The necessity of a 'whipper in' was rendered apparent by the sight of a figure prostrate upon the ice of the Back River, and which turned out to be one of our own men (Aiken) who had unsuccessfully attempted to keep up the 'pace' of the leaders. After a little attention, he revived sufficiently to tramp to the Hotel where a good meal set him upon his legs again."

Mount Royal was the training ground for the clubs. It was good training ground, with a steep climb and hazards along the way that had to be jumped. Each club had its rendezvous at some hotel on the far side of the mountain. Lumkins (on a site not far from today's St. Joseph's Oratory) was the most celebrated. But other hotels beyond the mountain (such as Prendergast's) had each its own following.

Each club had its tramping night. The point of assembly for most of them was at the gates of McGill University (the wooden gates that preceded the Roddick Gates there today). Members strapped on their snowshoes and stood about talking. Though storms did not hinder them, the best nights had the brightest moons. The chimes of Christ Church Cathedral were the signal to start out. "Up! Up!," shouted the leader. Members fell into Indian file. The leader stepped out. The line wound its way after him. They tramped across the campus, past the lighted college buildings. The route was up McTavish hill, across Pine Avenue, then up the mountain path just west of the stone wall of Sir Hugh Allan's property, Ravenscrag.

Snowshoes made a "click-clacking" in regular beat. No lagging was allowed by the leader. Each man had to keep closely behind the man ahead of him. Steam from nostrils puffed out into the icy air. Victorian beards and mustaches grew white in the frost. Grunting and panting came from the very young, the very old. But effort brought its own exhilaration. It is in an account of the 1850's: "The wild blood is careering through the veins with redoubled speed, and we feel all the intoxication of the pure cold air, which we breathe faster as our pace increases. Onward we go; our spirits enlivened, braced up, and mounting higher and higher, as the dark forest seems to invite us on. Excelsior! is the motto; over the snow wreathes, through ravines, round perpendicular rocks —still onwards. Excelsior!"

A grove of trees on the mountain slope, "the Pines," gave somber drama to snowshoe tramps. It was dark, Druid-like. Snowshoers at the end of the Indian file saw those ahead disappearing one by one into the pine gloom, then emerging again into moonlight on the upper side. At the summit of Mount Royal the leader shouted a halt. The roll was called; he had to be sure that nobody had dropped out and needed aid. In this pause the snowshoers looked down over wintry Montreal: "Away below, the moon's rays flash from soaring spires and snow-laden roofs, and lower yet the countless lights of the great city complete an effect that is magical in its strange beauty."

The roll call over, the leader called, "All up!" They set out on the tramp down the far side of the mountain. Thickets, fences, rocks were cleared by jumping. They passed through Côte-des-Neiges Cemetery, among gravestones and vaults drifted with snow and glittering under the moon. In later years members of the Montreal Snow Shoe Club would gather in a circle round the grave of Nicholas Hughes. He had been a grand old figure, almost legendary, in the club's history. "Evergreen" Hughes he had been called, because age had seemed to lag behind him. He had taught and heartened many a young snowshoer who carried on after he was gone. Around his grave the "Tuques Bleues," casting long shadows in the moonlight, paused to sing *Auld Lang Syne*.

When the snowshoers came in sight of their hotel—Lumkin's, Prendergast's, Moore's or whatever it might be—the leader yelled. It was the call to break away from Indian file and to rush, without line or order, to see who could get there first. In their hotel the snowshoers shook off the snow, hung up shoes and coats, lighted pipes and settled down to about two hours of fun. A plain supper was served—biscuits, cheese and ale (never, it seems, any hard liquor). A program of sorts was followed. Songs were sung in solo or in chorus. Someone played the piano. Someone else stood up to tell stories. Jokes passed across the tables. It was two hours of laughing and hearty fellowship.

At ten o'clock the leader called out that it was setting-out time. Members stood to sing "God Save the Queen." Then they started out, up the northern slope of the mountain, down the south side, back again into the streets of the city. The account of the 1850's concludes: "Then, to bed confessing that snow-shoeing is a glorious institution, give a heavy yawn, and sleep, sound as a top, till morning, with no fear of a night-mare before your eyes."

The Mount Royal of the showshoers appeared on the stage. The clubs gave performances in the Queen's Hall or the Academy of Music. On stage were tableaux. Snowshoers could be seen climbing the steep slope of Mount Royal, while white paper snow drifted down upon them. And as a reminder that it was not always enchanting moonlight but often blinding blizzard, W. L. Maltby of the "Tuques Bleues" sang defiance: "Rage, thou angry storm!"

Part Four

Persons
and Places

SKETCHBOOK

John Collins

CHAMP-DE-MARS

TWENTY

Wife Murderer to Stonewall's Sunday:
The Champ de Mars

THE CHAMP DE MARS was the place in Montreal where soldiers were drilled; where citizens promenaded; where criminals were executed; where public meetings took place—even rioters' meetings. All manner of strange lore has gathered about it. Something that happened here even made a Confederate general determined not to fight battles on Sundays.

As its name indicates, the Champ de Mars was intended primarily to be a drill ground—a field dedicated to Mars. Troops were being drilled here back in the French Régime, though at that time it was a far smaller and lower field, just inside a bastion of the town's northern wall. The old wall was demolished early in the nineteenth century to make room for the expanding population. The foundations remained, covered by earth. Before the 1920's, when the field had not yet been paved, the line of the old French wall through the Champ de Mars used to become visible on wet or damp days. W. D. Lighthall, the lawyer and antiquarian, recalled in 1924: "Some years ago, before the asphalt was laid in the Champ de Mars, the old Fortification line was easily visible after a rain, the ground around the wall absorbing the water and leaving an outline of the bastions." It was a mysterious sight, almost as if the old wall of the French Régime returned like a ghost in rainy weather.

The Champ de Mars was enlarged in the 1820's to serve as both a military drill ground and a public park. It was expanded to 240 yards in length, 120 in width. It was also raised with tons of earth and set off handsomely with rows of Lombardy poplars at the borders. "From this spot there is a fine view of the well-cultivated grounds, beautiful orchards, and country-houses towards the mountain," said a writer of 1839.

Montrealers at once took advantage of the amenities that had now been provided for them. The Champ de Mars became Montreal's promenade. It was a place to see and be seen, to stroll about, displaying fashionable costumes. Friends would meet friends for conversation. The exhilaration of the open air and the movement of the crowd was often heightened by the inspiriting airs of a military band. An officer, Lieutenant-Colonel B. W. A. Sleigh, was favorably impressed. "The number of well-dressed people and the assemblage of beauty," he remarked, "would reflect credit on an English city."

But the Champ de Mars did not always present a scene of grace, elegance and social cheerfulness. From time to time it would be overwhelmed by a crowd in an uglier mood. Public executions took place at the rear of the jail. The jail stood facing Notre Dame Street, high on the embankment south of the Champ de Mars. As the back of the jail overlooked the drill ground, an execution carried out from a scaffold erected against the rear wall could be seen clearly by everyone on the ground below, no matter how crowded the ground might be. In the eyes of the law no scaffold could be better placed. At some scaffolds a crowd might have difficulty in seeing. But on the Champ de Mars visibility was perfect. The purpose of public executions was instructive; they were to teach as many people as possible the awful consequences of crime. The size of the Champ de Mars itself and the elevated position of the jail to the south of it made Montreal's public executions singularly impressive. Criminals dropped to their death with maximum effect.

The crowds that turned out to witness Montreal's public executions were composed not only of the morbidly curious. Parents sometimes brought their children in the hope of deterring any criminal inclinations they might have lurking within them. Many upright citizens felt a moral obligation to attend public executions. It was a public way of expressing their abhorrence of crime and their approval of its rigorous suppression. A thin crowd at an execution might be taken as showing public indifference.

The size of the crowd was often in direct proportion to the heinousness of the crime. The biggest crowd on the Champ de Mars (at least the biggest up to that time) packed the ground on Monday, August 19, 1833. It was estimated at 10,000. At ten o'clock that morning Adolphus Dewey was to be hanged.

"It has never yet fallen to our lot," said Chief Justice Reid, in passing sentence upon him, "to address a prisoner, under circumstances so truly afflicting and heart-rending as those which mark your case, nor to see before us the cool and deliberate assassin of an innocent and unoffending wife, a crime so horrible and appalling and of so deep a dye, that it is scarcely possible to find its parallel in the sad story of human depravity, a deed which filled with painful horror and astonishment the entire population of this Province and made the most remote and obscure inhabitant of our forests to shudder . . ."

No one in Montreal had looked upon Adolphus Dewey as

the sort of young man who might turn murderer. He was known as a "man of distinguished traits" with "a frank and open countenance." He "enjoyed a good character."

In the summer of 1832 he became seriously interested in Euphrosyne Martineau, a daughter of Louis Martineau, a cabinet maker. In January, 1833, they were married; her father saw no reason why he should not approve. A friend said that Adolphus "appeared to love her almost to folly."

Dewey rented rooms in Bernard Henrick's boarding house in St. Vincent Street. Other boarders at Henrick's overheard their quarrels. Adolphus would smash crockery. She wept. One day Henrick himself, curious, went to the door of their room. By standing on a chair he could peek through a crack at the top of the door. He saw her crying. He was walking up and down with arms folded. She threw her arms around his neck. "My God! My God!" she cried out. The husband was unmoved; his arms remained folded.

Euphrosyne left Adolphus to live with an uncle. A reconciliation of sorts was arranged. On the Sunday morning of March 24, 1833, Adolphus Dewey and his wife went together to five o'clock mass at Notre Dame Church in Place d'Armes. They kneeled before the same altar where they had been married only about two months before. As soon as they came down the steps of the church he began hurrying her eastward along Notre Dame Street. Passers-by turned to look after them. She, they saw, could scarcely keep up with him. From Notre Dame they turned into St. Paul Street. They came to the shop Dewey had rented and where he carried on a fancy goods business. He pulled out his keys. The shop had two doors: one iron, the other wooden. He opened both and disappeared inside with his wife.

He fetched a pair of candles, lighted them and set them down. He turned to his wife. "We have lived so long in difficulties," he said, "we must finish them here." She thought he must be joking. He reached for an axe.

Adolphus hired a carter to take him over the American border. The driver noticed his passenger was behaving oddly. "I don't want to be seen," he said. "I will get under the robes."

Arrested in Plattsburg and brought to trial in Montreal, Dewey had three of the best lawyers to defend him. But the evidence was overwhelming. The chief justice commented that "an innocent and honest man fears nothing from the laws of his country, which protect him; it is only the dishonest that flee." He was condemned to death, led away to a cell in the Montreal jail and chained to a ring in the wall. He had only one "earthly request." He asked his friends to get him a black coat; he wished to die well dressed.

Adolphus Dewey gave his immense audience in the Champ de Mars a superb performance: "The deportment of the unfortunate young man . . . was firm, resolute and manly, without any approximation to hardihood or heroic effrontery." Standing on the scaffold at the back of the jail, his arms closely bound by a cord, he addressed the crowd. He had his speech by heart; but he asked Constable Malo (the man who had been sent to arrest him in Plattsburg) to hold a written copy of it. Malo would act as his prompter.

Dewey spoke "with extraordinary composure, totally unruffled by the presence of the multitudes . . . and with an emphasis and distinctness, that rendered every syllable audible at an unusual distance."

The hushed crowd could hear the words: "After having asked pardon of God in the bitterness of my heart, I seek pardon from you and from the whole city, for the reproach of which I have been the author . . .

"You perceive my condition and are touched with it; profit by it and learn the nothingness of this world. Oh! my dear fellow countrymen, if you could look upon this matter with the eyes in which I regard it, how soon would you be undeceived as to the vanities and illusions of this world; you would then learn that there is nothing stable but the service of God.

"My hour is come, your's will arrive; do not wait till then to prepare for it. . . . I ask the aid of your prayers; if I obtain pardon, as I hope to do, I shall not forget you before God . . . Pray for me, those of you who have just hearts, pray for an unfortunate being who leaves you for eternity."

The last moments were spent with his confessor. Father Denis said a short prayer; he pronounced a benediction. The biggest crowd ever assembled in Montreal saw Adolphus Dewey drop to his doom. In a minute "all appearance of life became extinct."

Not only public executions brought out big crowds. The Champ de Mars was a natural place for outdoor public meetings, for speeches and protests. Such a meeting, in the spring of 1849, got out of hand, with dramatic and lasting consequences upon the history of Montreal and of Canada. If that meeting had not taken place, Montreal might well be the capital of Canada today.

In 1849 Montreal was, in fact, the capital of Canada, though the name "Canada" then referred only to what are now the provinces of Ontario and Quebec. The Parliament Building stood on the St. Ann's Market (today's Place d'Youville). In that spring the city was torn by controversy. A piece of legislation, the Rebellion Losses Bill, had just passed into law. It was a measure to provide compensation out of the public treasury to those who had suffered property losses during the political rebellion of 1837-38. The Tories had been infuriated. They claimed the bill made no adequate distinction between those who had been rebels and those who had been loyalists. They denounced it as a "revolutionary measure, unprecedented in the history of civilized nations, by which the victorious defenders of the Throne" were "to be taxed to pay the losses of the defeated rebels."

The Tories were determined to protest; they were determined, somehow, to prevent the law from ever taking effect. A mass meeting was planned. Alfred Perry, a young man active in the volunteer fire brigade, jumped on a fire engine and drove pell mell through the streets. On the sides of the engine were placards, printed in huge letters: "To the Champ de Mars! To the Champ de Mars!"

On the Champ de Mars an angry, surly, desperate crowd began to gather. It grew larger and larger until (some said) as many as 5,000 had turned out. Light was provided by torches. The April night was gusty; the flames of the torches swayed and fluttered.

Some of the speakers counseled moderation. A "petition to Her Majesty" was proposed. At this moment young Fred Perry mounted the platform. The crowd called upon him for a speech. He stepped to the front of the platform, took off his cap and used it to extinguish a torch—the torch that was to give light for reading the petition. The time for petitions was passed, said Perry. If those present were in earnest, let them follow him to the Parliament Building. The crowd answered with a cheer. Fred Perry led the meeting off the Champ de Mars. It surged to St. Gabriel Street and along Notre Dame, on its way to St. Ann's Market.

The crowd was screaming and shouting. Torches bobbed in its midst. The Champ de Mars was suddenly dark and vacant, with no sound but the April gusts beating among the bare branches of the Lombardy poplars. The crowd surged into the Parliament Building, where the Assembly was holding a night sitting. In the rioting the building took fire. The crowd swirled about it, in an orgy of political fury. For the riot Montreal was administered a terrible penalty. The Parliament Building never rose from its ashes. Montreal ceased to be the capital.

Meanwhile, down through the years, while the Champ de

Mars was a promenade, a place for executions and angry meetings, it had continued to serve its primary function as a drill ground. Until the beginning of the 1870's Montreal was one of the garrison towns of the British Empire. Here the Imperial regiments (including the most famous of them) served in rotation. These professional British troops at their drill presented the grandest show in town, not only for Montrealers but for visitors. For American visitors, unaccustomed to such precision of drill, the spectacle was amazing.

One of the Americans who saw the troops on the Champ de Mars was Henry David Thoreau. A Yankee so independent that he refused to pay his taxes was scarcely a man to view military discipline with approval. Yet even he, seeing "a large body of soldiers being drilled" in 1850, marveled at the superhuman exactitude. "It was one of the most interesting sights which I saw in Canada," he wrote. "The problem appeared to be how to smooth down all individual protuberances or idiosyncrasies, and make a thousand men move as one man, animated by one central will; and there was some approach to success. They obeyed the signals of a commander who stood at a great distance, wand in hand; and the precision, and promptness, and harmony of their movements could not easily have been matched. The harmony was far more remarkable than that of any choir or band, and obtained, no doubt, at greater cost. They made on me the impression, not of many individuals, but of one vast centipede of a man . . ."

Three years later, on a Sunday afternoon in 1853, another American was watching the British troops at their drill on Montreal's Champ de Mars. His was not the reluctant admiration of Thoreau. He was a professional soldier himself. The opportunity of seeing a British regiment on disciplined display was one he was determined not to miss. He was not aware that seeing that Sunday drill on the Champ de Mars would change his moral outlook for the rest of his life.

This American visitor was Major Thomas Jonathan Jackson. He was then an officer in the army of the United States, teaching artillery at the Virginia Military Institute. Only eight years later, as a Confederate general in the American Civil War, he was to become known as "Stonewall" Jackson, when General Bee of South Carolina, observing his own men wavering, shouted: "Look at Jackson's men; they stand like a stone wall!"

In 1853 Major Jackson was a young man of twenty-nine, visiting Montreal on his honeymoon. Traveling with him and his wife Eleanor was his sister-in-law Margaret. This rather unusual arrangement is explained by the fact that Eleanor and Margaret had always been devoted to each other. Much alike in temperament, they even went so far as to wear identical clothes, as though they were twins. They also had identical views on the strict observance of the Sabbath day.

Major Jackson had gone that Sunday in Montreal to see a Highland regiment on the Champ de Mars. Eleanor and Margaret at once closed ranks against him. They took him to task for desecrating the Sabbath. His conduct in going to watch the drill, said Margaret, "was a matter of surprise to the rest of us." Major Jackson stood his ground. He did not agree with them about the iniquity of watching troops drill on Sunday. Margaret (in her account) said that "he defended himself stoutly for having done so, giving as a reason . . . that if anything was right and good in itself, and . . . he could not avail himself of it at any time but Sunday, it would not be wrong for him to do so."

Despite the honeymoon mood, Eleanor "quietly but firmly" branded her husband's reasoning as nothing more than sophistry; he was evading the true issue. Jackson began to give ground. "It is possible that my premises are wrong," he conceded; "when I get home I will go carefully over all this ground, and decide the matter for myself."

237

In making this concession Jackson had still preserved his independence. He would come to a considered opinion about Sabbath observance; but it would be his own decision, not his wife's or his sister-in-law's. His own opinion, when he had arrived at it, went far beyond anything Eleanor or Margaret had urged. He became a fanatic over Sabbath observance.

He did his best never to travel anywhere on a Sunday. He would never post a letter, if he believed it would travel, for any part of its delivery, on a Sunday. His letters would not be mailed late in the week; he would keep them for mailing on Monday morning. Among all his preoccupations during the Civil War, he found time to follow, with interest and approval, the proceedings of a committee of the Confederate Congress—a committee that submitted a report condemning Sunday mails. He wrote to his friend, Colonel J. T. Preston, one of the delegates to the General Assembly of the Presbyterian Church. He begged Colonel Preston to influence the Assembly to petition the Confederate Government to repeal the law permitting the Sunday movement of the mail.

At the same time he wrote to his pastor: "I trust that you will write to every member of Congress with whom you have influence, and do all you can to procure the adoption of the report, and please request those with whom you correspond (when expedient) to do the same." The letter ended with his belief that the blessing of God on the Confederate cause would be affected by what was done about transporting mails on the Sabbath: "I believe that God will bless us with success if Christians will but do their duty." Jackson himself had sold stock he held in a railway because the company insisted on transporting mail on Sundays.

Stonewall Jackson made a practice of refraining from all worldly conversation on the Sabbath. If "secular topics were introduced," he would say, "we will talk about that tomorrow." In camp he insisted that religious services be conducted regularly, and would spend the rest of the day reading his Bible and pondering religious themes. As a commander in the field he tried not to open a dispatch that reached him on the Sabbath but would rise with the dawn to read it. He did everything he could to avoid fighting a battle on a Sunday. When he felt compelled to fight for fear of losing a military advantage, he tried to keep several later days in a row, as if they were Sundays, to make up for having violated the Sabbath calm and having neglected his religious duties.

He repeatedly said he wished to die on a Sunday. And on Sunday, May 10, 1863, he died. He was asked on his deathbed if he would be willing to die that day, if it was God's will. "I prefer it," he replied. Then, as if fearing that his reply might not be fully understood, he said again, more emphatically "I prefer it!"

In these words was the last echo of the summer afternoon in 1853, after he had gone to watch the Highland regiment being drilled on the Montreal Champ de Mars and was charged with desecrating the Sabbath.

The Champ de Mars continued to be used as a drill ground long after the British garrison was withdrawn. It became the drill ground for Montreal's militia regiments. An immense drill hall, or armory, for the militia was built on Craig Street. Here the various volunteer regiments assembled on different nights or at different hours. For outdoor drill they had only to march out of the armory, cross Craig Street, and come onto the Champ de Mars.

Changes came with the twentieth century. The old Craig Street armory was used less and less; the militia regiments were being provided with armories of their own in different parts of the city. The Champ de Mars came to have a neglected appearance. The Government of Canada had given it over to the City of Montreal in 1889, at a rent of a dollar a year, though with the right to reclaim it for military purposes if the need ever arose. Sir Wilfrid Laurier, the prime minister, on a visit to Montreal, complained to the City that the Champ de Mars was ragged and untidy. The City responded by cutting down the rotting Lombardy poplars, then about ninety years old. The ground looked neater but bleaker.

Some new function had to be found for the Champ de Mars. No longer was it useful as a fashionable promenade, or as a gathering place for public executions or political meetings; it was even ceasing to be a drill ground. For a number of years it was put to use as a market, accommodating the overflow of farmers' wagons from the Bonsecours Market nearby. But a new need was arising. With the increase of automobiles, demands began to be made for parking space in Old Montreal. In 1926 the Champ de Mars became an immense parking lot.

It was a prosaic end. Only old guide books recapture the earlier glamor, as in *The Canadian Handbook and Tourist's Guide* for 1867: "The Champ de Mars, in front of the Court House, is a splendid parade ground, and kept in excellent order; and the visitor should not fail to view the exercise and parade of the different regiments in the garrison, which daily takes place here in summer. At night, too, there is generally a military band playing here ... making ... a fashionable lounge, with its enlivening strains."

John Collins SKETCHBOOK

240

The OLD PEW of DARCY McGEE

TWENTY-ONE

"He Had His Faults, Every One Knows": Thomas D'Arcy McGee

ON SUNDAY, SEPTEMBER 8, 1867 Thomas D'Arcy McGee said to his wife: "Tell the grocer tomorrow, to come and take every drop of wine and liquor out of the cellar. I have made up my mind to have nothing more to do with it."

The cellar where that wine and liquor were stored was in the Montmorenci Terrace—a row of gray limestone town houses at the southeast corner of St. Catherine Street and Drummond. That house had been a gift to McGee from the constituents of the Montreal riding he represented in Parliament and from friends and well-wishers in many other parts of the country. They had made the house a distinctive gift by having shamrocks carved in rows in the stone windowsills. Those shamrocks could still be seen, above the lower, added shop fronts, until the house was ruined by fire in the 1960s.

D'Arcy McGee's teetotal resolution was variously regarded among his friends and enemies. Many, in both camps, were amused and cynical. They thought they knew D'Arcy McGee. His good intentions would never last; self-indulgence had seemed part of his nature, the recurring pattern of his life. It was late in the day to reform.

Others, however, praised and honored him, and wished him well. They even prayed for him. Within a few weeks, McGee's resolution was discussed at a temperance meeting in Montreal. It was reported in a newspaper item headed: "MR. MCGEE'S CONVERSION TO TEETOTALISM." The item read:

"At the religious Temperance meeting last Sabbath, one of the speakers said, that, having business with Mr. McGee, he took occasion to congratulate him upon the noble stand he had taken, and to assure him of the joy he had given to all good men, and of their earnest desire that he would prove faithful. Mr. McGee said he had made up his mind before the election to become a teetotaler, but he had delayed till after that had taken place, fearing that his motives might be construed into a desire to make political capital. . . .

"The chairman suggested that Mr. McGee should be remembered in the closing prayer—a suggestion which was heartily and earnestly complied with, and the prayer was joined in by the audience with peculiar interest."

McGee had had phases of alcoholism even as a young man, before he settled in Montreal in 1857. After he had entered Canadian political life his weakness gained immensely in publicity. The very prominence he achieved as a statesman made his want of self-control all the more conspicuous. Since he could not hide his light under a bushel, he could not hide his weakness either.

To make matters worse, he was the close political colleague of John A. Macdonald. They gained a mingled reputation as tipsters. Often, in fact, they were drinking companions. During election campaigns they sometimes went on tours together. On the hustings they made a powerful combination. But when the day's electioneering was over, they withdrew to share a bottle—even more than one. An old squaw had once remarked to Macdonald that "too much was just enough." Macdonald and McGee tended to agree that it was.

If their drinking had been reserved for the evenings and behind closed doors, the public notoriety might have been less serious. The trouble was that they both had a reputation for drinking bouts; they might remain tipsy for days on end. Such prolonged indulgence could not be concealed, and the lightheadedness of their sprees made them less aware of the danger to their careers.

Their sprees were not always concealed even from the House of Commons. John A. Macdonald sometimes came to the House with a thick voice; he might be scarcely intelligible. When he rose to speak, he might feel compelled to lean on the desk in front of him for support.

D'Arcy McGee showed greater sense. He generally absented himself from the House when unfit to appear. But his absences were often conspicuous; the explanation of them was soon rumored. McGee himself often confirmed the rumors at such times by going about town, visiting his friends in newspaper offices, joking with the boys and ending up in a drunkard's sleep on a pile of old papers in a corner.

At times McGee's wife, Mary Teresa, was called from Montreal to the capital to sober her husband. She could do little. One day in 1863 she was writing to a friend: "As my visit . . . has not been productive of any good result, and as my staying here is not the least check to Mr. McGee's unfortunate propensity, I have come to the conclusion to return today . . .

"He has just come in, and from his appearance, it is just a repetition of yesterday, so that I have given up all hope."

Inevitably the convivial habits of Macdonald and McGee played into the hands of their opponents. The Toronto *Globe* denounced their conduct as scandalous. The *Globe* was taken to task for indulging in "personalities," and invading private lives. It retorted that the degrading habits of public men could not be considered as private. The public welfare was endangered when men in posts of responsibility might be carrying on public business with impaired judgment.

John A. Macdonald viewed his own failings with an indulgent eye. His attitude toward himself was almost invariably charitable. He tolerated his own weaknesses. D'Arcy McGee felt differently. Though he easily gave in to his weaknesses, he felt the shame of them when he had recovered himself. While Macdonald's conscience was seldom disturbed, McGee's was seldom at ease. Macdonald in his cups never felt himself to be other than Macdonald. McGee, however lively his geniality, knew he was leaving himself behind, that he was failing himself, and sinking.

When Macdonald and McGee appeared before their voters, they had to admit their weakness, as it was so well known, and would be used against them. Macdonald's admission was jaunty and without apology. In a campaign against his chief political enemy, George Brown, he said he was sure the voters would rather have John A. drunk than George Brown sober. McGee's admission to his Montreal constituents had no such flippancy. "If you wish to have me as I am," he said, "personal faults and all—and God knows I have my share of them—I am ready to serve you."

Macdonald could joke about McGee and himself as a pair of tipsters. The problem came up in the Cabinet. Someone said, "This sort of think is a disgrace." Macdonald turned to McGee. "Look here, McGee," he said, "this Cabinet can't afford two drunkards and I'm not quitting."

McGee saw the humor of it, but he saw the tragedy also. In his days in Ireland he had witnessed the curse of drink among the people. As a temperance speaker he had begun his career as an orator. He was then very young—only about four-teen or fifteen. Father Theobald Mathew had set out on his great life's work as "the Apostle of Temperance" in Ireland. Young Thomas D'Arcy McGee was one of his followers. The temperance harangues by "little Tommy McGee" became one of the chief attractions of the Wexford Temperance Society. After listening to one of Tommy's eloquent appeals, Father Mathew had patted him on the head and been full of praise and encouragement. He was delighted to find a supporter so gifted, so promising.

An Irishwoman, Mary Banim, wrote of young McGee in her reminiscences many years later: "Tommy McGee's first speeches made him quite famous as a lad. They were on temperance, and were delivered at tea-parties held in con-nection with the society, and when the boy, then only sixteen, decided on seeking his fortunes in America, a special tea-party was given in his honour, gentlemen of the best social position in town and country attending to show their regard for the talented and high-principled youth."

McGee soon fell away from his early commitment. Tem-perance tea parties knew him no more. Lapses as sot and clown interspersed his new achievements in oratory, statesmanship and literature. But in the last months of his life his veneration of Father Mathew revived, though Father Mathew had been dead more than ten years. McGee was returning to his boy-hood vow when he cleared the wine and liquor from the cellar of his Montreal home.

He even went so far as to appear again in public as an advocate of temperance. He wrote a long account in two in-stallments on "Father Mathew and His Work." It appeared in a Montreal magazine, *The Dominion Monthly*, in the last issue for 1867 and the first for 1868. The founder and chief editor of the magazine was the Presbyterian John Dougall, the leading Apostle of Temperance in Montreal. Dougall kept a vow of total abstinence for the last fifty years of his life. His daily newspaper, the Montreal *Witness*, aggressively attacked "the liquor interests." He had been one of the founders of an earlier periodical, *The Canada Temperance Advocate*.

McGee needed courage to come out publicly as a writer on temperance in one of John Dougall's publications. To the skeptical, well acquainted with his bouts of drunkenness only a few months earlier, his sudden transformation into a campaigner for abstinence seemed delightfully risible. But McGee's new resolution was so firm that not even his physician could prevail against it. McGee had been seriously ill. His physician recommended some alcohol as a medicinal stimulant. McGee refused to take it. "I have made my resolve," he said, "and not to save my life will I break through it."

This abstinence from alcohol was part of a revival of his religious feelings. He was taking his duties as a Roman Catholic more seriously. He was seen more regularly in his pew in St. Patrick's Church in Montreal—the same pew that still stands, number 240, in the "Pulpit Aisle." He was in that pew for an Easter service on the day before he left Montreal to attend the session of the House of Commons in Ottawa.

In the early morning of April 7, 1868, he made his last speech in Parliament. He walked in the moonlight to his boardinghouse on Sparks Street. His landlady, Mrs. M. A. Trotter, heard someone putting a key into the lock. She opened the door slightly. A flash burst across her face, a smell of gunpowder. She thought it might be a firecracker.

She shut the door, then cautiously opened it again. In the dark she saw the figure of a man leaning against the right-hand side of the doorway. She went back to the dining room for a lamp. When she next looked out into the street, the lamplight shone on the same man leaning against the door-jam. He was a little more stooped than before. Then he collapsed and fell back across the wooden sidewalk, straight from the door.

Mrs. Trotter had just witnessed the death of her boarder, Thomas D'Arcy McGee. Someone had silently stolen up behind him as he bent at the lock. A bullet from a pistol tore through the back of his neck, fired so near that it singed the hair. Only a few days before McGee had said to his friend, Brown Chamberlin, editor of the Montreal *Gazette*: "If ever I were murdered it would be by some wretch who would shoot me from behind."

McGee's body was brought back to Montreal—to his stone house in the Montmorenci Terrace on St. Catherine Street. For three days it lay in state in the dining room. "By the especial request of the community and the considerate permission of his widow," says a contemporary account, "his house was open to all who desired to see him in that fatal sleep . . ." A funeral service was held in St. Patrick's Church on Easter Monday, April 13, the forty-third anniversary of his birth. The sermon was preached by Father Michael O'Farrell, the young priest who had been McGee's confessor. Father O'Farrell spoke of the great achievements of McGee as statesman, as orator, as author, all within that brief life of fewer than forty-three years.

At the close of the sermon Father O'Farrell spoke of another achievement, perhaps the greatest of them all. "He had his faults, every one knows," said Father O'Farrell. But toward the end had come a change: "This change might . . . be seen in the resolution which he kept so inviolably until the day of his death, to abstain from those social excesses which would mar so considerably the effect of his talents. Let those who are tempted as he was, appreciate the amount of self-sacrifice which such a resolution involved."

Whatever influence young Father Michael O'Farrell, as confessor, may have had on D'Arcy McGee's last months, the real influence had come from a more distant past—from Father Theobald Mathew, the Apostle of Temperance far back in

McGee's Irish youth. At the close of his last article in the Montreal magazine (which had appeared in print only three months before the assassination in Ottawa) D'Arcy McGee had quoted words from John Francis Maguire's biography of Father Mathew—significant words to express exactly what McGee himself wished most to say:

"Father Mathew taught his generation a great lesson . . . that . . . there is no possible safety for those liable to excesses, and unable to resist temptation, save in total abstinence . . . there is no fear that the lesson will not be applied, or that Providence will not inspire, or even raise up, those who will put it into practice as Father Mathew did, for the sake of religion, humanity, and country."

John Collins SKETCHBOOK

LACHINE WATERFRONT

TWENTY-TWO

The Little Emperor of The Fur Trade: Sir George Simpson

ANYONE ENTERING HUDSON'S Bay House, the headquarters of the Hudson's Bay Company on the waterfront at Lachine, would see portraits of the Emperor Napoleon hanging conspicuously on the walls. It might seem odd that Napoleon would be so prominent a presence in Hudson's Bay House. But the overseas Governor of the company, Sir George Simpson, had a Napoleonic complex. He collected pictures of Napoleon and read anything about him he could find.

Presiding over the Hudson's Bay Company's territories in Canada, his was a greater empire than Napoleon ever ruled. He clung to his dignity and authority with Napoleonic tenacity. They called him the "Little Emperor of the Fur Trade," or the "Emperor of the Plains." Like Napoleon, Sir George Simpson was a little man. He was once compared to the squat, thick stone pillars of an old English country church—not elegant, perhaps, but wonderfully sturdy and capable of bearing an immense weight. No doubt, being a little man, he insisted all the more on his dignity. And this little, vain, arrogant figure, through the long period from 1826 to 1860, directed and intimidated the operations of the vast company, in its lands from the Atlantic to the Pacific and from the American border to the Arctic seas.

Hudson's Bay House, where the "Little Emperor" sat behind his desk, studying piles of papers and giving his curt interviews, stood overlooking Lake St. Louis, exactly where the chapel of the convent now stands. Old photographs reveal the house as imposing and mansion-like in its proportions, with a stately porch and pillars. Very likely it was extended and embellished under Sir George; but it must have been large even when the company bought it from William Gordon, for it had been used as an inn.

Sir George Simpson used to attend services at St. Stephen's. It was conveniently situated for him—just around the corner from Hudson's Bay House. But even in church Sir George remained the "Little Emperor." A diary kept by Albert Parr records the Governor's refusal at St. Stephen's to listen passively if the preacher made him angry: "Being Governor of such an august body apparently gave him the idea that he could take instant dislike to anything said in a sermon with which he did not approve. One Sunday morning the then Rector did that very thing and Sir George whipped up his cushion off the seat, tucked his books under his arm, and strode angrily from the church—and no Warden dared to hinder him!"

His abruptness in religion was also seen in his manner of saying grace. It was not his habit to say grace at the table. But one day his wife insisted it must be done. They were having guests to dinner who were accustomed to grace at meals, and would be distressed if none were said. She had done her best to include a clergyman among the guests, but had failed. This time Sir George promised to say a grace if he could remember one. As this was scarcely reassuring, she arranged that his brother-in-law should sit next to him and remind him. Sir George was about to commence a graceless dinner when the brother-in-law played his part and put in his reminder. The Governor exclaimed: "Lord have mercy on what is now before us." He looked quite satisfied, but his wife could not regain her self-possession for the rest of the evening.

This strain of oddity appeared in his only known accomplishment in music. Lord Mark Kerr, the aide-de-camp to the Governor General, Lord Elgin, wrote in his journal on April 24, 1847: "I make acquaintance at this time with Sir G. Simpson, of the Hudson's Bay Company . . . he is an extraordinary man and besides his greater qualities plays many tunes on the fire-irons, poker, tongs, &c."

In his office in Hudson's Bay House at Lachine, as elsewhere, Governor Simpson could be smooth and suave and courtly with persons of position, or with those he aimed to influence in his own or the company's favor. But with his subordinates he "took delight in the outward show of tyranny."

The innate force of his personality is seen in the very fact that he was so young a man when he was given the company's top post in North America. He was not only young, but had little experience, having come only recently into the company's employment. And he became Governor at a uniquely difficult time, just when the Hudson's Bay Company had won its long, harsh struggle against the North West Company, and had absorbed the Nor'Westers in what was called a merger. Over men far older, more experienced, long seasoned by a hard and dangerous life, and divided by old and bitter rivalry, this young and inexperienced little man was placed as their ruler. It was the sort of appointment that seemed inexcusable, even incredible, and bound for disaster. Yet only a short time after his appointment, everyone in the company felt the change.

One of them remarked that "the North-west is now beginning to be ruled with an iron rod."

How Sir George Simpson ruled from Hudson's Bay House in Lachine was learned by young Donald A. Smith (the Lord Strathcona of years to come). Donald Smith, having letters of introduction, was brought into the Governor's awful presence at Hudson's Bay House. Within a few minutes he was appointed an apprentice-clerk in the company's service at Lachine at a salary of £20 per annum. "You will begin at once, sir," said Governor Simpson, "to familiarize yourself with your future duties. Call Mr. Mactavish." A clerk named Mactavish appeared, full of the required humility. He was told: "Mr. Mactavish, have the goodness to take Mr. Donald Smith to the fur-room and instruct him in the art of counting rat-skins."

Donald Smith had the misfortune to annoy the Governor. The Governor's wife took a friendly interest in the "indentured young gentlemen," as the clerks were called. She invited Donald Smith to tea in the parlor of Hudson's Bay House. When she went on boating excursions on Lake St. Louis she "commanded him" as her escort. The Governor returned from an absence at the Red River. He was angry. He was overheard, in his high-pitched treble, declaring he was not going to endure any "quill-driving upstart apprentices dangling about a parlor reserved to the nobility and gentry." Donald Smith, however, seems to have recovered from this setback. He gained some measure of the Governor's approval, perhaps by following his uncle's advice and showing the Governor "not only strict obedience but deference to the point of humility." One day in the spring of 1841 he was called away from invoicing bales of furs in the storeroom at Lachine to appear in the office at Hudson's Bay House. "You are appointed to Tadoussac," said the Governor. He paused, then added: "It is now Monday; you will leave by the Quebec stage Wednesday morning."

To maintain his imperial sway in the Hudson's Bay Company's territories, Sir George Simpson made regular tours of inspection. When he arrived from his headquarters at Lachine at the company's posts in the far wilderness he did not wish to appear as just another traveling trader. No doubt should remain that an imperial personage was drawing near and was about to land. In 1828, when approaching the post at Norway House near the head of Lake Winnipeg, he called for a halt. His men were ordered to put on a clean change of clothes; the voyageurs were to deck themselves out with new feathers. In his canoe he had brought a Highland piper. As they paddled toward the post about seven o'clock in the evening the piper gave a blast; from another canoe a bugle sounded. Then the voyageurs (about eighteen of them) broke out into one of their most lively songs. As one in the Governor's party remarked, their arrival "was certainly more imposing than anything hitherto seen in this part of the Indian country."

Sir George's journeys were not only to visit and inspect the company's trading posts; he was ready, at times, to turn explorer and risk his life on rivers never traveled before and even said to be impassable. In 1828 the company had to find out if there was another route by water from its posts in the interior to the Pacific. It had been using the Columbia River; but the Columbia might be assigned to the United States in the boundary negotiations. If this happened, the company might be shut off from the coast. The Fraser River, and its great tributary, the Thompson, had never been fully explored. Simpson was warned he could never hope to descend them alive. But he was determined to find out for himself, in a small boat. These rivers might provide the alternative route the company had to have.

Simpson's experiences on the Thompson River were horrendous. He admitted that its series of relentless alarms made "whitened countenances of the boldest among us." He could find "no comfort in the whole passage of this turbulent River, as the continual plunging from one Rapid into another kept us as wet, as if dragged through them . . ."

The Fraser River was even more appalling. The rocks of the shorelines reached into the clouds. Often they were nearly perpendicular. They offered no ledge for landing to appraise the rapids ahead. The rapids had to be entered without knowing how they were to be taken. He said his boat "shot like the flight of an Arrow, into deep whirlpools which seemed to sport in twirling us about, and passing us from one to another . . . and leaving our water logged craft in a sinking state." At times the rocks hung over them, darkening the river and sending it leaping through a narrowed channel like water in a millrace.

Simpson had proved the Thompson River to be "exceedingly dangerous." As for the Fraser, it could "no longer be thought of as a practicable communication with the interior; it was never wholly passed by water before, and in all probability never will again . . . I should consider the passage down, to be certain Death, in nine attempts out of Ten."

Simpson's experiment on the rivers had been, in a way, a negative achievement. But if he had proved them practically impassable, he had also proved his own imperious will, and his readiness to risk his life in the company's service.

In the spring of 1841 Governor Simpson set out from Lachine on a very different sort of journey. He was going around the world, eager to be the first man to circle the globe by what was called "the overland route." He was to complete his tremendous journey and (with a ghost writer) to bring out a book about it.

A journey so unusual called for even more pomp than ever. Sir George also was anxious to depart with a flourish because he was taking with him, as far as the Red River, two members of the British nobility, Lord Caledon and Lord Mulgrave—army officers who hoped to hunt buffalo on the prairie. His orders went out to maintain a mood of state and dignity. The voyageurs were to be "kept as sober as voyageurs could be kept on such an occasion." Each man was to have a feather in his cap. Flags were to be kept ready to be unfurled in a moment and flown from the prow of every canoe. Unfortunately this grandest of all Sir George's departures from Lachine did not come off with the intended pageantry. The day was savagely cold. Lake St. Louis was tormented by a gale. No flags could be unfurled in the wild gusts. At about ten minutes before eleven in the morning the brigade left the Lachine shore. The Governor's friends, crowded near the Hudson's Bay Company's post, did their best to raise a cheer. The voyageurs started a song as their paddles struck the water. But it was still a dismal setting out, with the wind rolling waves on the pebbled beach "like the waves of the sea" and driving the spring snow into their faces.

Even as Sir George Simpson grew old he was determined to remain "Emperor of the Fur Trade" to the end. And he was also determined to maintain the company's headquarters at Lachine. The time had long passed since Lachine was the point of departure for trade and travel to the west. Roads, railways, canals, improved steamboats—all had changed the pattern. But Sir George would not change. Without logic or convenience Hudson's Bay House was still at Lachine.

Fate gave him one last chance for ceremonious display. This man who had cherished associations with the nobility and gentry now had his opportunity to be host even to royalty. The young Prince of Wales, Queen Victoria's son and heir, came to Montreal in 1860 for the official opening of Victoria Bridge. Sir George was host at a luncheon given to the Prince at his country house on Dorval Island. Then he took him back to Lachine in a brigade of canoes manned by Indians. It was an imperial spectacle. The canoe carrying the Prince of Wales, with the Royal Standard fluttering from its bow, was followed by all the others in line abreast. From a canoe about the center of the line old Sir George directed the movements.

The excitements of the royal visit were too much for the aged and ailing Governor. Only a few days later, driving in his carriage from Montreal to Lachine, he was stricken by apoplexy. He was taken to Hudson's Bay House. There, on September 7, he died. The Indians sang "a weird and doleful but solemn dirge" as his body was put aboard the train for Montreal. But the ending was not altogether doleful. Dugald Mactavish, who had risen under Sir George to become Chief Trader in the Hudson's Bay Company, sounded the right note for the end: "The little Emperor's light has gone out, just after he basked in a final blaze of glory."

Now that Sir George Simpson was dead, no need lingered to maintain the company's headquarters inconveniently at Lachine. Hudson's Bay House was up for sale. The contents were disposed of at auction. Details give glimpses of his style of living. The auctioneer was offering sleighs and carriages, two neat bark canoes, a cellar of fine wines, a tame macaw parrot, eight peacocks and pea-hens. Hudson's Bay House itself was sold in 1861 for 8,000 dollars to the religious community, the Ladies of St. Ann. The sale had the condition that the land would never be occupied by any other proprietor. The Hudson's Bay official, Edward Martin Hopkins, made a little ceremony of handing over the keys to the Mother Superior. He had always been close to Sir George; he had entered the service of the company in 1841 as the Governor's personal secretary and assistant. He told the Mother Superior that "his old master would be happy with the succession." Before the year was out the Ladies of St. Ann had established in the old Hudson's Bay House a "pensionnat," or boarding school for girls. Other convent buildings were added. Hudson's Bay House was demolished to make room for the convent's chapel in 1888.

With Governor Simpson's death Lachine underwent a rapid transition. Its fur-trading days were over. "Lachine, in summer," said *The Montreal Weekly Witness* in 1868, "is a favorite residence for Montreal families, on account of the facilities it presents for boating and fishing, and its easy access by rail from the city; but it possesses scarcely a vestige of the importance and prosperity it enjoyed in the early part of the present century ... And here the Hudson's Bay Company had its headquarters in the New World; an arrangement which, with the conservatism characteristic of that company, or rather of its late Governor, Sir George Simpson, continued long after it was either necessary or convenient."

On the other side of the road to the convent, on a narrow strip of land between the little canal and the lake, a stone warehouse of the company still stands. It is a lingering reminder of Lachine's fur-trading traditions, when "the little Emperor" used to set out with his brigade of canoes to tour, as ceremoniously as possible, his kingdom in the productive wilderness.

JOHN COLLINS SKETCHBOOK

MOUNT ROYAL PARK

TWENTY-THREE

The Mountain That Was Too Far Away: Mount Royal

NEAR THE HEAD of the valley to the east of Beaver Lake in Mount Royal Park stands a large stone house. It was built by H. B. Smith in 1858. According to a dubious tradition, the extraordinary thickness of its walls is explained by a belief, held at the time, that this massive construction would fortify its inhabitants against infection from epidemics. The house, however, would seem to have been sufficiently isolated, without additional precautions. It stood in its broad and lovely valley of 156 arpents (French acres)—a country property, high above the city.

The Smith house is a reminder that Mount Royal was not always a public park. It was once divided among private owners. In 1872, when expropriation for the park began, these private owners numbered about sixteen.

In those earlier days, before the city began to expand northward from the waterfront, the mountain was seen as a whole and to far better advantage. No near tall buildings fragmented the view. Visitors used to describe it as "overlooking the city" or "standing like a bulwark against storms." Nothing obscured the drama of its rugged summit. As a visitor of the 1830's wrote: "At the top of the mountain is a thick wood, whose richness imparts life to the whole landscape."

Not only was the view of the mountain uninterrupted; it was finely set off by fields, orchards, gardens, country houses. Green with its own foliage, it was surrounded by a wide sweep of greenery. The slopes of the mountain were renowned throughout the country and even abroad for their superb fertility. Something about the climate on the southern slopes was peculiarly favorable to growing apples. Town and mountain were separated by a mile or more of open land. The view was always described as "out from the city toward the mountain."

As the 19th century moved into its middle years the city still tended to grow eastward and westward (especially eastward) along the waterfront, rather than to the north. The open country near the mountain underwent a change: it became more sophisticated. The farms were turning into villas— villas still separated from one another, and "embowered" in lawns and gardens. Here and there the villas were even developing into mansions. Sir Hugh Allan, the shipping magnate, went high up on the mountain when he built his mansion "Ravenscrag" beyond the top of McTavish Street about 1861. When Mount Royal was expropriated as a park by the City of Montreal, a portion of his grounds was claimed. But "Ravenscrag" itself was far too huge and costly a building for expropriation. The Allan mansion (now the Allan Memorial Institute of Psychiatry) is almost embedded in Mount Royal Park.

So long as Mount Royal remained remote from the city, interest in acquiring it as a public park remained slight. A vast sum of money would have to be spent to buy out the private owners; and if it were made into a park, it would only be adding an amenity for the people who lived near it—a privileged few who were already living in villas or mansions, surrounded by wide grounds and gardens. As late as 1870 even so enlightened a citizen as Honorable John Young, a leader in civic improvements, gave the expropriation of Mount Royal a low priority. He argued that "from the narrowness of the strip of land between the Mountain and the River, it is evident that whatever increase of the city does take place, it must be east and west of the present limits . . .

"While, therefore, the more wealthy citizens will occupy the mountain slope and the higher levels of the city, the great bulk of the people will live on the lower levels, as they do now; and it is in this space also, where the business and trade of the city must be carried on . . .

"But this Park on the Mountain-top would be comparatively inaccessible to the poorer classes of society and others who live in the valley below, who must require change of air for themselves and families. By inaccessible, I mean that without a carriage, men, women and children could not get to the Park; for on a hot day many could not walk there, while their means might, to a large extent, prevent the hiring of carriages."

Though everyone knew that Montreal was growing, and growing fast (Honorable John Young prophesied a growth from 150,000 in 1870 to 750,000 in 1910), nobody seemed to foresee that the mountain would one day be encircled by streets and buildings until it became the hub of a Greater Montreal. Meanwhile, as the "Mountain Park Project" was debated without action, life in Montreal went on as usual. It was hard to see where the urgency lay. The mountain, though divided among private owners, remained unspoiled and beautiful. Public use, to a certain extent, was tolerated. Before the end of the 18th century a carriage road—"a good road of very easy ascent"—had been made on the mountain. Montrealers and visitors were free to drive on it and enjoy the view. But private owners did not welcome strangers who left the carriage road to invade their property. In the summer of 1815 they combined to give public warnings that trespassers would be rigorously prosecuted. In 1850, when the New England philosopher, Henry David Thoreau, went one evening for a solitary ramble on Mount Royal he scrambled "across lots in spite of numerous signs threatening the severest penalties to trespassers."

Such warnings, however, were directed against mischief-makers and hoodlums from the city, rather than those who might wish to come to the mountain for respectable recreation. The tradition of tolerating the respectable went back to the close of the 18th century. It is seen in Isaac Weld's description of the summertime picnics of a club of citizens on the mountain's southern slope: "Two stewards are appointed for the day, who always chuse some spot where there is a spring or rill of water, and an agreeable shade: each family brings cold provisions, wine, &c.; the whole is put together, and the company, often amounting to one hundred persons, sits down to dinner."

Long before Mount Royal was expropriated as a park, consideration was given to expropriating it for military defense. To the military mind, its height and its commanding view over vast distances would make it suitable as a citadel for Montreal. It could become a bastion, a stronghold, its slopes and access roads easily defended against all enemies. If batteries were set up there, the guns would have full sweep. They could bombard enemies coming up the river or approaching over any of the surrounding fields. In 1826 fortifications on Mount Royal were actually commenced. Foundations were dug, apparently not far from today's Lookout.

The works were never completed. By the 1860's the defenses of Montreal were being reconsidered. The arts of war had changed. Increased use of explosive shells, after the earlier era of cannon balls, discouraged the use of heights for forts. The new military wisdom was to be as inconspicuous as possible, to offer the least possible target for artillery. The old idea (almost medieval) of a tall citadel, or keep, had to give way to the new idea of digging earthworks, with a low profile, close to the level ground, and far in front of a city. Montreal, it was now thought, would best be defended, not from the mountain, but somewhere on the South Shore of the river. Had Mount Royal been acquired for military defense, its use by civilians might have been prohibited. But military planners were looking in other directions.

Mount Royal became a park for the dead many years before it became a park for the living. In the 1850's two of the mountain farms were bought for cemeteries. The remoteness of Mount Royal—used as an argument against acquiring it as a public park—was the reason why large portions were acquired for burials. Remoteness seemed to offer protection for the dead—protection from the encroachments that were overwhelming the old burial grounds in town.

The new concept of the "rural cemetery" had just come to North America. Mount Auburn Cemetery near Boston had been laid out with ample space, with freedom from expropriation, in a setting of parklike loveliness and peace. Montreal's rural cemeteries soon followed. In 1851 the new Mount Royal Cemetery Company bought "Spring Grove," the mountain farm of Dr. Michael McCulloch, one of the professors in the Medical Faculty of McGill University. The Roman Catholics of Montreal, no longer able to use their crowded burial place in what today is Dominion Square and Place du Canada, also acquired part of Mount Royal. In 1853 they bought Dr. Pierre Beaubien's farm in Côte-des-Neiges, where eighty-five arpents were under cultivation, about twenty-five in woodlands. A

267

guidebook of 1856 recommended tourists to visit these cemeteries to see how near they were to natural beauty. Much work remained to be done at the Côte-des-Neiges Cemetery, but at Mount Royal Cemetery 120 acres had been enclosed and "laid out into one of the most romantic and secluded burying grounds in the world."

Who first suggested that the mountain be made into a park for the living is now obscure. One of the earliest proposals was made by a visitor, Dr. Benjamin Silliman, professor of chemistry in Yale College. After touring the mountain in 1819 he wrote: "Nothing is wanted to render the mountain of Montreal a charming place for pedestrian excursions, and for rural parties, but a little effort, and expense in cutting and clearing winding walks, and in removing a few trees from the principal points of view, (as they now form a very great obstruction;) a lodge or resting place on the mountain, constructed so as to be ornamental, would also be a desirable addition."

Visitors were seeing the park possibilities better than Montrealers. Another proposal was made about 1850 by Sir James Edward Alexander, an officer on the staff of the commander-in-chief of the forces. He examined the mountain "at no little cost of time and personal fatigue." As an officer in the Royal Engineers, he viewed it practically. He urged the City to make it a park.

Montreal's Mayor, Dr. Wolfred Nelson, supported Sir James' proposal: "I beg leave to recommend this project to the serious consideration of the council, which will not lose sight of it, big as it is of promise to the city of the future, because some comparatively trivial expenses may be entailed by it at the moment."

The City Council may not have lost sight of the proposal, but it scarcely occupied the center of its attention. Nor was the Council altogether convinced that the expenses would be comparatively trivial. In any case, the public seemed indifferent. Demand was growing for a park, but the demand was not centered on Mount Royal. The argument about the inaccessibility of most of it seemed strong. The City would be spending its money on buying a cliff that few could ever scale. Buying a park on level ground would be preferable.

One of the principal sponsors of Mount Royal in the City Council was Major A. A. Stevenson—"Sandy" Stevenson. He ran a printing business and spent most of his spare time with one of the city's militia units, the Montreal Field Battery (which, as Lieutenant-Colonel, he later commanded). He laid a secret plan to prove how accessible the mountain would be, if a proper road to its summit were built. He made arrangements to take his battery, without benefit of a road, up to the height the City Councillors were declaring to be beyond reach. There, on the official birthday of the Prince of Wales, he would fire a royal salute.

Despite all his carefully laid plans, Major Stevenson found himself facing a problem he had not foreseen. On that morning of November 10, 1862, the ground was covered by a foot of snow. He had planned to take the wheeled gun carriages up the mountain; now he remounted the guns on sleighs. He would have to take the guns through private properties, but he had already obtained permission. They went up by way of John Redpath's avenue. This was not difficult. Then came the hard climb to the plateau on the summit of the mountain above Ravenscrag. Horses were struggling with the heavy sleighs. To ease the climb they were led from side to side, gradually zigzagging upward. Stumps were in the way. Some sleighs ran upon them, toppled over and had to be righted—not easy, from the weight of the guns. On other stumps sleighs stuck; the stumps had to be cut away to free them. In ravines Major Stevenson ordered his men to tramp ahead to beat a path for the horses. Openings through thick bushes were cut with axes.

At noon precisely, on the plateau above Ravenscrag, the first round was fired. Round followed round. Then, as Stevenson would say, in telling the story, "we partook of the sweetest meal of our lives." It was fairly substantial: "Cold roast beef, ham, etc., with bread and hot coffee." Having reached the summit, Major Stevenson wished to drive his point home. He ordered his men back to the guns. One hundred rounds were fired in about twenty minutes. He gave his men a short rest. Then, as a parting gesture, he ordered three salvoes.

Montrealers had always lived with a quiet, remote mountain. They were shaken into alarm by the thunder from the heights. Rumors ran about that the Fenians (the Irish activists of the day) had invaded Canada and were bombarding the city. But as no part of the city was destroyed—not even by the three salvoes—the happier news spread that Major Stevenson was proving the accessibility of Mount Royal. The major was a persistent man. He was aware that some people would say that his expedition up the mountain proved nothing. It was the sort of thing that might be done once but would be too difficult to repeat. To answer them, he took his battery up the mountain again on March 10, 1863.

His sensational demonstration had immediate results. The City Surveyor, Patrick Macquisten, referred to it in his annual report for 1863. A new road, he said, would make access to the upper mountain easy: "Major Stevenson showed this, by taking his artillery on the 10th of November, 1862, and on the following 10th of March, 1863, by way of Messrs. Smith and Redpath's portion. Every person who has been on the summit of the Mountain admits that the view from this point is magnificent, and that a park there would be equal if not superior to any other in North America."

About this time the project received sudden impetus in an unexpected way. One of the proprietors had been disturbed by rumors that his part of the mountain might be expropriated.

He realized the asset he had in the timber and decided to cut it down and sell it before his land could be claimed by the City. Trees went down by the score just west of Ravenscrag. A shocking gash was ripped up the mountain's face. Over the years the appearance of the mountain had not been injured by the private owners. Now public ownership took on a new urgency. The mountain had to be saved while there was still time. The newspapers took up the cry. A public meeting was called. An injunction was taken out to prevent the further cutting of trees.

City Council was at last pressed into action. In 1869 the Quebec Legislature amended the Montreal Charter to permit the City to borrow up to 350,000 dollars "to be designated the Mount Royal Park loan, for the purpose of acquiring and establishing a public park on and in the vicinity of the Mountain of Montreal." But the procedures of expropriation did not go ahead rapidly. Some of the owners agreed to yield up their portions for the sums offered; everything was settled, as far as they were concerned, by "amicable agreement." Other owners had no wish to surrender their mountain holdings. So fiercely did they fight expropriation that the Mayor of Montreal, Aldis Bernard, wondered in 1874 whether the City should go on with the struggle. It had already acquired a substantial area of the mountain; perhaps it should let the rest go. "In view of the apparent reluctance of the owners to part with their property for park purposes," he said, "of their utter refusal to accept the awards of competent and honourable Commissioners, and of the determined manner in which they persist in throwing every possible obstruction in the way of fair and legitimate expropriation proceedings, it has been a question in my mind whether it would not be wise and proper to allow them to retain their respective properties. They are by no means indispensable to a magnificent Mountain Park ..."

By this time, however, the City had spent less than a quarter of the one million dollars Mount Royal eventually cost. The legal battles went on until all the desired properties had been acquired.

The properties differed greatly in size. The biggest, by far, was acquired from the estate of H. B. Smith. In addition to the valley of 156 arpents (with the old stone house), the Smith property extended over adjoining parts of the mountain, reaching a total of 186 arpents. Another large property was acquired from the estate of Benjamin Hall, in the Fletcher's Field area: it comprised 96.28 arpents. Other expropriations were small: 33.94 arpents from Sir Hugh Allan's old "Ravenscrag" property; and 20.54 arpents from the Ladies of the Hôtel Dieu.

Before the end of 1875 the City of Montreal had completed the purchases and expropriations. It was ready to begin the work of developing the mountain into a park. The fact that the country was sinking into a financial depression did not delay the work; it even aided it. Building the new roads would provide relief for the jobless; especially, it could be a winter works program. Labor was cheap; the mountain could be developed at depression rates. The unemployed, no matter what their previous trades or occupations had been, were glad to take up a pick or shovel. They were paid sixty-three cents a day for nine hours' work, or seven cents an hour. Carters were paid $1.25 a day for man, cart and horse.

To mark the beginning of the work some ceremony seemed called for. It was performed by the three aldermen who composed the Park Commission. All had to be done as simply as possible; it would have been unseemly to waste money in a time of depression. The three aldermen met with William McGibbon, the first park ranger, near the high-level reservoir. It was November 12, 1875—"a bleak, cold, miserable day." No band played; no speeches were delivered. Each of the aldermen turned a sod, not an easy thing to do in the frozen ground. McGibbon used to recall that "they were all jolly as the circumstances permitted, but a joke would have frozen stiff if anyone had uttered it."

The ceremony was over. Alderman Nelson turned to the park ranger. "McGibbon, have you the courage to start this job?" he asked.

McGibbon replied: "I've got to do it—it's got to be done."

They all went slowly away through the November chill.

The park ranger did what he could to make the work a little less grim for the depressed laborers. He saw the men coming to work in the bitter weather with bread-and-butter dinners wrapped in newspapers. At the meal hours they would sit down to eat them frozen. The park ranger heard that one of the laborers had been a cook in the French army. He put him in charge of a cookhouse. McGibbon got a 75-gallon boiler. He gave the cook split peas by the bag, barley by the barrel. He ordered meat at a cent and a half to two cents a pound, together with two dozen dippers, cheap plates and spoons. The men now had a hot meal every day. The park ranger, with satisfaction, saw the change: "Each gang got a pail of the hot soup and the largest gangs two pails, and it would have done your heart good to see these fellows take their meal. They would soak their frozen bread in the hot soup, and many a blessing they gave me, poor men."

When the City Council looked for a planner to design the new Mount Royal Park it went to the top. It sought the services of Frederick Law Olmsted, the greatest landscape architect in North America, and one of the greatest of all time. Many of the principal parks on the continent had been, or were to be, designed by him: Central Park, and the Riverside and Mount Morris parks in New York; the park at Niagara; the grounds of the Capitol in Washington; the Back Bay Fens of Boston. He was the first commissioner of the National Park at Yosemite. And for the world's fair—the World's Columbian Exposition in Chicago—he anticipated the design of Montreal's

Expo '67 with a "serviceable, and at the same time charming commingling of land, buildings, verdure and waterways."

The City Council had difficulty in persuading Olmsted to design Mount Royal. He was preoccupied with other projects; Montreal seemed too far away for him to give the work adequate supervision. When correspondence failed, a delegation from Montreal went to New York. They persuaded him in the end partly by giving him assurances which, he believed, were never carried out.

Olmsted had fixed convictions about what should be done with Mount Royal. "Small as your mountain is," he said, "it presents in different parts no little variety of mountain scenery." Its value as a park would lie in preserving for all generations to come a place of peace and natural beauty, where citizens could find relief from the pace and fatigue of city life. He set himself emphatically against all "developers," who would crowd it with "prospect-towers, club-houses, and fanciful houses of entertainment." If this was all Montrealers wanted, they had no need for his services as a landscape architect. All they needed would be an engineer and a jobbing gardener or florist. And they would find the whole park deteriorate, until they would have nothing more than another vulgar amusement park.

Frederick Law Olmsted tried to impress on all his clients that the value of Nature was for her own sake. Nature did not need to be improved. Instead of placing jaded and nerve-wracked citizens under the necessity of traveling far away to find Nature unspoiled, the greatest value of a park was to make it available to them close at hand. This, he argued, was not being unpractical; it was being supremely practical, unless one assumed that Nature is really worthless and tired people want to go to a park only to hear the jangle of noisy entertainment and to see a burlesque show.

In his plans he urged Montrealers to have nothing to do with mere ornaments or with artificial flowerbeds. The art of designing Mount Royal should be that of altering Nature as little as possible. He gave an example in the building of roads on the mountain. It was not enough to adopt the ordinary city methods of following the shortest route from one point to another. The mountain roads should offer the best views of natural scenery, even if they must be turned this way and that, to make the most of fine prospects, or to avoid the destruction of Mount Royal's good features.

The City Councillors did not find Olmsted an easy man to deal with. He was opinionated, impatient, contemptuous. On the other hand, the motives of City Hall politics had sorely tried him. He found no stability. He dealt with one group of Park Commissioners, only to find them changed and new ones taking their place. They all had ideas of their own about what ought to be done to develop the park; or they were, as politicians, pressing ideas from someone else. When he proposed his plans for preserving the natural loveliness of the mountain, they would oppose him, not directly, but by saying to him, in a kindly, advisory, confiding way: "We, who are paying the bills, have an interest in economy, you know." This was particularly irritating. His recommendations, aimed at preserving the mountain as far as possible as it was, would cost far less than the artificial and elaborate improvements these same representatives of City Hall were trying to press upon him.

Olmsted in the end was embittered by his experience in Montreal—by the "prolonged labor, and the poor results of it." Yet his aims, seemingly frustrated at the time, were still largely achieved. Though parts of his plans were marred then, and have been marred further over the years, as much of natural and unspoiled bauty as Mount Royal retains is due to his philosophy of what such a park should be.

He had left Montreal with the words (half-plea, half-command): ". . . follow an intelligent purpose to bring out the latent loveliness of mountain beauty, which you have bought with the property, in such a manner as to make it of the highest distinctive value." His parting warning was: bring the park to the city, but do not bring the city into the park.

John Collins SKETCHBOOK

GATES OF
COTE DES NEIGES

TWENTY-FOUR

It Took Six Years to Bury Him:
Joseph Guibord

BETWEEN TWO AND three o'clock in the afternoon of September 2, 1875, a funeral procession (a hearse and a number of carriages) drove up to the gates of the Roman Catholic Cemetery at Côte-des-Neiges. It arrived with peculiar speed—at a trot. At the gates of the cemetery surged a crowd, angry and alert. Ringleaders harangued their friends, "gesturing violently." As the hearse came up the roadway, the gates were swung shut, "very hurriedly and very bunglingly." The crowd, though determined, was nervous.

The funeral procession halted outside the gates. Those in charge of it hesitated. With this delay the crowd grew bolder. It thrust props against the gates, fortifying its position. Murmurs expanded into shouts. "Like madmen" the leaders were now screaming: *"Ils n'entrent pas! Ils n'entrent pas!"*

The driver of the hearse was in the most dangerous position—seated high up, exposed like a target. He was having trouble with his horses, startled by the roar and stir. The crowd moved from defiance to attack. It rushed for the horses. The driver, William Seale (a young man in his early twenties), tried to turn the hearse round, to escape. The crowd forced him off the road. He had to make the turn between a tree and the gates. Stones dropped about him. Some rattled against the side of the hearse. He had all he could do to lean back on the reins to keep the horses from breaking out of control.

The mourners stood about on the road outside the gates, discussing what could be done. The volley of stones grew heavier. Several of the mourners were hit; some were reported "severely injured." A few of them, in indignation, reached for their revolvers. George Martin, the photographer and poet, was in the funeral party that day. "The rumor had spread," he wrote, "that we would meet with violent opposition, that we were risking life and limb. For the first time in my life I carried a revolver in the breast pocket of my coat. I think that most of my companions did likewise ... A friend of mine from Côte St. Paul lost command of himself; his indignation burst with flame; his voice was 'for open war.' I rushed upon and seized him by the arms; remonstrated, blew a loud whisper in his ear, signifying the fearful reckoning that his indiscretion would precipitate. I knew that a single shot would be the signal for a general conflict, and would add more than one corpse to that in the hearse. Cooler heads averted the storm ..."

The sight of the rearing, quivering horses inflamed the crowd. William Seale drove the hearse still farther from the gates. An hour passed. The funeral party gave up. Hearse and carriages drove off. The crowd lingered at the gates, ready to confront the procession if it returned. Meanwhile some of the demonstrators went to the open grave. With two shovels they pitched the earth back into it.

The body in the hearse, the cause of all the disturbance, was that of the printer, Joseph Guibord. He was described as "a man of irreproachable morals, of the steadiest habits, of rigid honesty, and altogether a model workman." As a printer he was progressive and scientific. He was said to have turned out the first book stereotyped in Canada. For many years he had been an exemplary Roman Catholic. He had done printing for the Church.

Joseph Guibord got into trouble when he joined the Institut Canadien, and he joined it soon after it was organized in 1844. The Institut had created centers for reading, lectures, discussion, companionship. These purposes would not in themselves have been considered objectionable by the Church, had the members been willing to accept a general supervision and direction by the clergy. The difficulty arose from the Institut's assertion of independence. It encouraged freedom of opinion, a library not subject to censorship, the admission of non-Catholic members, the invitation of lecturers with viewpoints far beyond Catholic orthodoxy. In general, the Institut Canadien in Montreal represented the liberalism that had been sweeping over Europe.

The membership was varied. Some were anti-clerical, even agnostic or atheistic. But most of them were Roman Catholics hoping the day had come for a broader interpretation of Catholic principles, a closer association with the non-Catholic world and a more tolerant acceptance by the Church of modern scientific, social and intellectual attitudes. They were convinced the isolation of the Catholic Church from contemporary thought and movements would render it incapable of dealing with the modern world, alienate it from men of more active intellects and tend to make it an obstruction to progress. These members were both Catholic and liberal. They hoped that a reconciliation would make possible a Liberal Catholicism.

The Institut Canadien was proving successful. It was something new in the life of the province; it was meeting a need.

By the 1850's it had about a hundred branches. More important than the rising total of its membership was the high intellectual quality of the men it was attracting. Among them was the young, ambitious lawyer, Wilfrid Laurier.

The headquarters of the Institut on Notre Dame Street in Montreal had a large library. The choice of books had been broad. Members had access to the works of Voltaire, or they could peruse Florente's *History of the Inquisition*. On the tables of the reading room they could browse freely among the latest magazines and newspapers, even the aggressively anti-Catholic Montreal *Witness*. The headquarters also had a commodious lecture hall—a forum for free expression, free debate.

Confrontation was inevitable. The Roman Catholic hierarchy was mounting a massive counterattack on liberalism. Pope Pius IX was denouncing it as a compendium of all evils. He saw liberalism not as evolution but as heresy. Its whole tendency was to make men more and more the judges of their own thinking, their own conduct. The role of the Church as the divinely appointed guide of minds and morals (an institution always aware of mankind's natural sinfulness and frailty) would be eroded and eventually destroyed.

The liberals of the world were insisting on a clear separation of Church and State. They would exclude the Church from all external and social matters and would limit her authority to matters of faith and conscience. But the Pope could not agree that the Church should silence her voice on issues of public concern or political policy, where her guidance might be needed and in which her own future might be seriously involved. Moreover, it seemed, even with regard to conscience, that liberals were ready to set up revised standards of their own. If the Church were to "come to terms" with liberalism, to become tolerant and accommodating toward it, she would be exposing all Catholics to the modern skeptical, cynical, irreverent influences that would endanger the great simplicities of spiritual welfare.

An attempt by the Institut Canadien to promote a Catholic Liberalism at the very time the Pope was condemning it was hardly a promising enterprise. The difficulties were greater still because Msgr. Bourget happened to be Montreal's bishop. He was working, with impressive zeal and strength of will, for a very different kind of religious revival. His emphasis was on family piety, an absolute, unquestioning submission to the Church's divinely inspired instructions, a vigorous rejection of anything that might try to rival, dispute or undermine faith in the Church's sure guidance.

Bishop Bourget was also the outstanding leader in Canada of the religious movement known as Ultramontanism—the belief that ties with the Papacy needed to be everywhere strengthened. The spirit of Ultramontanism was particularly needed among French Catholics in Canada because they were a distinctive and isolated group, likely at any time to be overwhelmed and assimilated in the vastness of North American life. In his enthusiasm for Rome he planned his new cathedral as a replica (though on a reduced scale) of St. Peter's itself. He discouraged the building of any further Gothic churches in his diocese, and favored the Italianate style as far more representative of Roman tradition and allegiance. Under his energetic leadership the Diocese of Montreal prospered. Catholic churches, Catholic orders and institutions proliferated.

To Bishop Bourget the appearance in his diocese of the Institut Canadien, as an institution cherishing its independence and committed to the propagation of liberalism, was a calculated defiance of his authority and aims. He was to become convinced that "Catholic Liberalism is a thing to be regarded with the abhorrence with which one contemplates a pestilence." This pestilence had already appeared in his diocese; it was spreading; it was likely to spread still further. His duty as a bishop, as the servant of the Pope, was first to quarantine it, then eradicate it. He could not do less. He could not seek a compromise with a pestilence.

The confrontation was made all the more massive by political animosities. The Institut Canadien was made up largely of members of the "Rouge" party—those French Canadians aiming to form a French Liberal wing of the Canadian Liberal Party. Bishop Bourget supported the Conservatives. His interest lay in encouraging a French Catholic and Ultramontane wing of the Canadian Conservative Party. The Rouge members were so conspicuous in the Institut Canadien that in 1854 more than a dozen members of the Institut were elected as Rouge members of Parliament. The Institut was also indirectly involved in the paper *Le Pays*—one of the "bad papers" the Bishop warned his people not to read.

One of the Bishop's first actions against the Institut was to condemn it for having irreligious books in its library— books that were, in fact, on the Index of Prohibited Books in Rome. The Institut took a firm stand. "The Institut," it declared, "has always been, and is alone competent to judge of the morality of its library, the administration of which it is capable of conducting without the interference of foreign influences." Later an attempt was made to reach an understanding. The Institut sent a delegation to interview the Bishop. But the Bishop was not interested in negotiating a settlement; he was insisting on total submission.

Meanwhile the Institut was making itself vulnerable in another way; it was providing Bishop Bourget with the weapon he needed. In its *Annuaire*, or yearbook, printed by Joseph Guibord, it was publishing texts of addresses delivered by speakers invited to its lecture hall. In one of these addresses Horace Greeley, the eminent editor of the New York *Tribune*, had lauded freethinking and the supremacy of individual opinion in the search for truth. Greeley was warmly thanked by the lawyer, Christophe-Alphonse Geoffrion, who turned to him and said: "Your presence here is a solemn approval of the path the Institut has followed ever since its foundation, without deviating from it one iota, despite the countless obstacles piled up on that path."

Horace Greeley's address, and similar materials, were published in the Institut's *Annuaire* for 1868. Bishop Bourget sent copies to Rome. On July 14, 1869 that *Annuaire* was placed on the Index. The Bishop, now armed with the papal authority he needed, ordered a pastoral letter to be read in all the churches of the Diocese of Montreal. All Roman Catholics were required to leave the Institut Canadien immediately or they would be refused the sacraments, even if at the point of death. Nor was the condemnation aimed at members of the Institut only. Any Catholic who so much as read, or even possessed, a copy of the *Annuaire* would be liable to the same penalties.

Membership in the Institut in Montreal rapidly melted. Some members had kept hoping for a reconciliation between Catholicism and liberalism. One of them, Gonzalve Doutre, even went to Rome in October, 1869, still seeking for broader interpretations of Catholic doctrine than Bishop Bourget could be expected to allow. Such efforts were futile when the Pope himself was dedicated to the extirpation of liberalism. Wilfrid Laurier, though he had been an office-holder in the Institut in Montreal, escaped the crisis because he had moved to Arthabaskaville in 1866 to practice law and edit a newspaper.

A hard core of members refused to renounce the Institut or its principles. Among them was Joseph Guibord. If Catholics could be condemned for even reading or possessing the *Annuaire*, far more serious was his position as the *Annuaire's* printer as well as a member of the Institut of long standing. Guibord had ceased to be a practicing Catholic, but his sense of alienation from the Church at times weighed heavily on him. In the autumn of 1869 he fell ill and feared he might be dying. He called a priest to his bedside. The priest told him that he must withdraw from the Institut. If he would not, he could not receive the last rites of the Church. Even under the shadow of death Guibord's loyalty to the Institut could not be shaken. The last rites were not administered. Guibord grew better. For several weeks he seemed likely to recover. Suddenly he died of apoplexy. The stroke was so swift that no priest could reach his bedside.

The question then arose: where was he to be buried? Bishop Bourget was away in Rome, attending the Vatican Council. The parish priest of Notre Dame Church, M. Benjamin-Victor Rousselot, consulted the Vicar-General, Canon Alex-Frédéric Truteau, who was administering the diocese in the Bishop's absence. "You tell me that M. Guibord was a member of the Institut," Canon Truteau replied, "and that he died without having left it; therefore it is impossible for me to grant him ecclesiastical burial." The friends of Guibord, applying to Curé Rousselot, were twice told that Christian burial would be forbidden.

The Institut had decided, however, to make Guibord's burial the supreme issue—a test case between civil rights and ecclesiastical authority. As a first step, it would take the body to the Roman Catholic Cemetery, just as if his burial there was normal and unquestioned.

On the Sunday afternoon of November 21, 1869, more than 200 men met at Guibord's "humble dwelling" on Panet Street. They accompanied the hearse to Notre-Dame-des-Neiges Cemetery (commonly known as Côte-des-Neiges Cemetery). The procession passed through the gates. It paused in front of the chapel. The superintendent of the cemetery was asked to bury the coffin "in the ordinary way, common to Catholics."

286

The superintendent spoke civilly. But he said he had instructions "from gentlemen connected with the Bishop's Palace to refuse burial in ground intended for the burial of Catholics." This did not mean that he was refusing any burial at all. He had been informed that he could bury Guibord's coffin in the little adjacent cemetery, an area reserved for unbaptized children and persons who had died beyond the pale of the Church.

Guibord's friends asked if they could see this area. The superintendent led the way; a large number of the funeral party followed him. The superintendent was asked if this unconsecrated area did not contain the bodies of executed criminals. That depended, he replied, on whether they submitted before death to the requirements of the Church. He pointed with his finger to the nearby consecrated ground. "There," he said, "lies Beauregaud; here is Barreau." They had been executed for murder, but had made a confession and been reconciled with the Church.

The friends of Guibord discussed among themselves what they had seen and heard. They reached a decision. The funeral procession was formed again. It proceeded out of the gates of Côte-des-Neiges and went on the Protestant cemetery, Mount Royal. At Mount Royal Cemetery the coffin was placed in the stone vault. This vault still stands, on the road that branches to the right from the cemetery gates. It had been built to accommodate bodies during the wintertime, for in those years no winter burials took place. The vault, now used as a shed for gardening equipment, has two iron doors. Guibord's coffin was carried through the west door.

Standing in front of the grim vault Guibord's friends made speeches. "We honor him," said one member of the Institut Canadien, "because in the supreme hour he did not desert the cause and for having left an example of moral courage . . ." Another speaker alluded to the struggle between the Institut and the Bishop. He said there were two movements within the Church. One aspired "to attract all who belong to other creeds." The other appeared "to repel all the most distinguished adherents from the bosom of the Church."

The last speaker summoned up the real significance of what had happened on that November Sunday in 1869. The Institut Canadien was going to the courts to defend Guibord's right to burial. His body would rest in the vault at Mount Royal Cemetery only "during the period required to obtain from the Courts an order" directing the authorities in the Diocese of Montreal "to give the deceased that burial insisted on by his friends and family."

Joseph Guibord, lying in his coffin, became the symbol of the struggle between the Institut Canadien and all it stood for and Bishop Bourget and all he stood for. The Institut, especially through one of its lawyer-members, Joseph Doutre, persuaded his widow, Henrietta Brown, to become the plaintiff. Three days after the first attempt to bury Guibord in Côte-des-Neiges Cemetery a suit was brought against the Church. The Bishop had tried to make the Institut Canadien bow to his will. Now the Institut, in the Guibord case, would try to bend the will of the Bishop. Legally speaking, the Bishop could not be brought into the case, though it was really against him that the suit was directed. As the matter concerned Côte-des-Neiges Cemetery, action had to be taken against its owners and managers, the Curé and Churchwardens of Notre Dame. The principal defendant was the French-born Sulpician and Curé of Notre Dame, the Reverend Benjamin-Victor Rousselot.

In the course of the legal proceedings that followed, lawyers for the Curé of Notre Dame submitted a startling affidavit. In this statement the curé declared: ". . . Madame Guibord came to the parlor of the Seminary, and there, I asked her if it was true that she did not want the lawsuit that they had launched against me. Here is what she said to me in reply: 'No, Monsieur, I do not want them to involve you in a lawsuit—neither you nor the Bishop. I told this to these men who have led me, in spite of myself, into the court. I have told them, and repeated it a number of times, that I did not wish a case made, either against the Seminary, or the Bishop.' I asked her then if she hadn't signed a proxy that authorized some of these gentlemen of the Institut to proceed against us. 'No, Monsieur,' she replied, 'I never signed anything. All that happened was that they led me before a judge, and I didn't understand why I went there, or what I said there."

It appeared from this affidavit that the case was really between the Institut Canadien and the Church, and that Guibord's widow, an illiterate, had been pressed into the role of plaintiff, against both her will and her understanding. But this affidavit sworn by the curé was not accepted in court as sufficient grounds to prevent the case from proceeding.

Action had been taken for a writ of mandamus to compel the burial of Guibord in the land acquired for his grave. The application was heard by Judge Charles Mondelet. The Institut was fortunate in having Judge Mondelet at this first stage of the proceedings. He sympathized with independence of spirit. He had defended captured rebels of 1837-38 at their trial in 1839, though the Church had condemned their revolt; and he had also shown his independence by marrying outside the Church. After hearing legal arguments for seventeen days, Judge Mondelet gave his ruling. He sustained the action in favor of the plaintiff. He ordered a peremptory writ of mandamus, requiring the curé and churchwardens of Notre Dame to bury Joseph Guibord in the consecrated ground within six days.

The struggle in the courts over Guibord's burial was, however, only beginning. The delay in his burial was not to be merely the six days prescribed by Judge Mondelet. It was to stretch out to six years. The case was taken to the Court of Appeals. Here, by a unanimous judgment, Mondelet's decision was reversed. The Court of Appeals, on September 30, 1870, ruled that the clergy of the Roman Catholic Church, in performing their duties, were entirely independent of civil tribunals. The Institut was declared to be legally mistaken in trying to bring a purely ecclesiastical matter before a civil court that had no possible jurisdiction over the internal administration of the Church.

Now it was the Institut's turn to appeal. The case was taken before the Court of Queen's Bench. Joseph Doutre, as the lawyer for the Institut, moved that the Roman Catholic judges should be barred from hearing the case. He argued that they could not reach an impartial decision in a conflict between civil and ecclesiastical interests. Doutre's motion was indignantly rejected, as it reflected seriously on the integrity of Roman Catholics as judges. The Court of Queen's Bench, on September 7, 1871, sustained the judgment of the Court of Appeals: civil courts had no jurisdiction in such ecclesiastical matters.

For the Institut Canadien only one hope remained: the Guibord case could be taken to the Privy Council in London. The costs would be heavy. The Institut had already paid the costs of three court hearings. By now, however, the case had become of such wide interest that supplementary funds were raised by subscriptions from Montreal citizens outside the Institut, both Catholic and Protestant.

On November 28, 1874, the Privy Council rendered the final, irrevocable judgment in the Guibord case. It based its conclusion largely on the Quebec Act of 1774—the historic measure by which the British Government assured the Roman Catholic Church in Quebec that it would have essentially the same rights as it possessed under the French Régime. The Privy Council, however, pointed out that these rights had not been unlimited. The kings of France had followed the policy known as Gallicanism—they had tended to exclude the clergy from temporal or civil affairs, and to recognize the right of appeal to the civil courts from ecclesiastical rulings. The Quebec Act of 1774 had perpetuated both the authority and the limitations of the Roman Catholic Church in Quebec as they had existed under the French Régime. Moreover, the Index of Prohibited Books, and the penalties imposed on Catholics who disregarded it, had never been recognized in France or in Canada. Guibord, then, could not be affected by them. No ecclesiastical sentence based on the Index could remove from him his right to Christian burial.

The case had gone on so long that Madame Guibord had died in the meantime. Despite what she was alleged to have said, according to the curé's affidavit, her sympathies had evidently remained with the Institut Canadien. In her will she not only gave her property to the Institut; she appointed it her universal legatee. With her death some question had arisen whether an appeal to the Privy Council would be possible, now that the plaintiff in the case was dead. The Institut had been permitted, however, to carry the case to the Privy Council in its own name. In this way, in the final proceedings in court, the Guibord case became in law what it had always been in fact: a direct confrontation between the Institut and the Church. Legally speaking, the Institut had won—and had won completely. The Privy Council had ordered the curé and churchwardens ("la Fabrique") of Notre Dame to inter the body of Joseph Guibord in that part of Côte-des-Neiges Cemetery where Roman Catholics normally received ecclesiastical burial. Further still, they were obliged to pay the court costs— not only the costs of the appeal to the Privy Council, but the costs in all the lower courts as well.

Winning a decision in Privy Council was one thing; carrying that decision into effect was quite another. The Guibord case had always been more than an attempt to assert private rights. It was a symbolic case—something far bigger than Joseph Guibord, far bigger even than the Institut Canadien. The whole question of Roman Catholic Liberalism was at stake. The audacity of the Institut in taking the Bishop to law (which was what the case amounted to) was provocative enough. The stubbornness of the Institut in carrying the case through four courts, and over six years, had tightened tensions to the breaking point. The real climax had now arrived. Would the Institut, armed with nothing more than a court order, and a few revolvers for self-defense, be able to force its way into the cemetery?

The Institut put its rights to the test in the afternoon of September 2, 1875. The attempt was a disaster. The funeral party had not been able even to get through the gates but had been forced to retreat under a shower of stones. The Institut then appealed to the state to exert its full power. If an army would be needed to bury Guibord, then an army would have to be mustered. But the law had to be enforced. Such appeals to force, even though it was force in the name of law, brought warnings. The newspaper *Nouveau Monde* prophesied that any attempt to storm the gates of the cemetery would simply drive the people to revolt.

The majesty of the law, backed by irresistible civil power, was set in motion. November 16, 1875, was the day set to enforce the burial of Joseph Guibord. The morning was dark and gloomy. A massive military force was assembling to sweep aside any opposition. As early that morning as seven-thirty, militiamen in their winter uniforms could be seen hurrying to the Drill Hall on Craig Street, across the road from the old drill ground, the Champ de Mars. They seemed "really apprehensive of such serious trouble as to warrant very serious faces."

About nine o'clock the force was reviewed on the Champ de Mars. It was a formidable muster. Artillery was provided by the Montreal Field Battery and the Montreal Garrison Artillery; engineers by the Company of English Engineers; cavalry by the Montreal Troop of Cavalry (the Hussars); infantry by the Victoria Rifles, the Prince of Wales' Rifles, and the Hochelaga Light Infantry. Estimates of the number of men called out differed; about 1,200 had been mobilized. Each of the infantrymen was served twenty rounds of cartridge. At nine-fifteen the military moved off the Champ de Mars. The men marched north by way of St. Lawrence Main. Meanwhile the Montreal Police were being mobilized. About a hundred constables assembled at the Central Station. About sixty were armed with Snider rifles. They marched north also.

Nobody knew what might happen. Rumors flew about town. Men were said to be coming in from the surrounding villages; they might be rallying to block the burial. Other rumors were that small parties of youths were moving from the Tanneries (now St. Henri). They were said to be armed with muskets and revolvers.

The public official who had to see the Privy Council's judgment enforced was the mayor of Montreal, Dr. William Hales Hingston (later Sir William). Ironically, he happened to be one of the most devout, eminent and obedient Roman Catholic laymen in the diocese. As Mayor of Montreal, however, he considered himself as a civil officer, obliged by the law to see the law enforced. He was a man of tact and discretion. He wished to see the Privy Council's judgment carried out with as much finesse as possible, and with as little provocation as circumstances might allow. He sought wider powers, for the day's proceedings would lie largely outside his geographical authority. He obtained from the mayors of Outremont and Côte-des-Neiges a delegation of authority, to act as he saw fit within their jurisdictions. And he kept himself mobile by riding horseback that day. He was a good rider, a member of the Montreal Hunt Club.

Mayor Hingston had quietly planned to keep the military in reserve. He would use it if necessary, but he would not parade it in such a way as to inflame existing anger. While the military was still marching north to Mile End, he went with the hearse and the armed police to Mount Royal Cemetery. There the coffin of Joseph Guibord was taken from the vault where, by courtesy of the Protestants, it had been kept since he died in 1869.

While the hearse was on its way to Côte-des-Neiges, Dr. Hingston rode on ahead. He wished to see what was happening at the Roman Catholic Cemetery. He found that no resistance to the burial seemed intended. In the cemetery about a thousand people had gathered. They appeared to have come out of curiosity only. They just stood about, smoking and chatting. He could see no signs of any organized defiance of the law. Some small boys were pretending to shut the iron gates. Detectives, aided by a few cemetery employees, lifted the gates off their hinges and laid them to one side.

Mayor Hingston at once rode back to meet the military. He informed the commanding officers that there seemed to be no likelihood whatever of having recourse to their services. They should halt where they were unless they received from him a call to help. He then joined the funeral procession and entered the Côte-des-Neiges Cemetery, accompanied by the friends of Guibord and the police armed with rifles. The procession encountered no opposition, no demonstration. At the open grave the armed police formed a square. Quickly, quietly Guibord's coffin, enclosed in a large box painted "Rouge," was lowered into the grave while "one of the most cheerless of miserable drizzles steadily fell."

The crowd stirred. A carriage was driving up. Inside was a priest and the detective Cinquemars. The carriage door was opened. The Reverend Benjamin-Victor Rousellot stepped out. This sudden appearance of the curé of Notre Dame was a surprise. Some supposed he must have come to prohibit the interment. Others wondered whether the Church had relented at the last moment; perhaps some religious ceremony was to be performed over Guibord's coffin after all. The curé explained that he had come only as a civil officer. He asked a member of the Institut whether the coffin had been identified as that of Guibord, and whether the grave had been dug to the required depth of four feet. When he had been assured on both points, he turned away, entered his carriage and drove off.

Before the funeral procession arrived, workmen had come into the cemetery by a back way. They carried with them bags of Portland cement. While waiting for the procession they had been busily mixing it. Already they had poured cement into the bottom of the grave. Guibord's coffin was lowered into it. More cement was shoveled on top of it at once. When the cement reached about halfway up the sides of the coffin, pieces of iron and tin were tossed in. Cement and metal would harden together, into an impenetrable mass.

No speeches were made at the graveside. But as Guibord's grave was being filled a French Canadian printer stepped forward, and spoke: "If there is nobody to say a word for him, I would like to do so; he taught me my trade, and I would like to make the Sign of the Cross for him." He made the sign and retired into the crowd.

When the grave was nearly filled, a layer of earth was laid over the steel and concrete mixture. The earth was packed down. The police formed ranks and marched away. The funeral party left after them. The crowd dispersed. Only about a dozen curious spectators lingered. Word reached the military forces that the burial was over. They passed, in their ranks, by the gates of Côte-des-Neiges Cemetery, as they marched back to the city.

Mayor Hingston received one last request from the Institut Canadien. It asked him to order "a squad of police to remain on the spot all night if possible," or it would be "most certain" that the body would be snatched. The mayor had received a similar request from the cemetery authorities. He sent Sergeant Burke, with five constables, to maintain an all-night vigil at the graveside. Nothing happened. To increase the security of Guibord's grave the Institut later covered it with an immense boulder.

The absence of any physical resistance to Guibord's burial on that gloomy November day in 1875 had been due neither to the intimidating mobilization of the military, nor to the mayor's resourceful tact. It had come about because Bishop Bourget had devised a way of safeguarding the freedom of the Church, while avoiding open conflict with civil authority. He had issued a pastoral letter to the Catholics of his diocese. He instructed his people not to oppose the burial. The sacred cemetery must not be profaned by the shedding of blood. This did not mean, however, that he was bowing down before "this criminal unsurpation" of his episcopal authority by the Institut or the courts. As Bishop of the Diocese of Montreal he possessed "full power . . . to bless and to curse." He would deconsecrate that part of the cemetery where the body of Joseph Guibord would be laid. It would become only "a profane place." In taking this action he was only exercising his unquestioned powers "to hand over to Satan those who hear not the Church." The faithful of the diocese, therefore, need no longer be outraged that the cemetery, which they justly venerated as a holy place, "might be profaned by the burial of a man dead in the disgrace and under the anathema of the Church." That man would lie in cursed ground.

On the Sunday after the funeral Bishop Bourget issued another pastoral letter. He commended the people for having allowed the wretched Guibord affair to end without bloodshed. And he said that anyone visiting the Côte-des-Neiges Cemetery in the years to come would view the grave of Joseph Guibord with a shudder: " 'Here lies,' he will exclaim in the recesses of his soul, 'the body of the notorious Joseph Guibord, who died in rebellion against the common Father of the Church, under the anathema of the Church; who could not pass the gates of this sacred place save escorted by armed men, as if for battle against the enemies of the country . . . for whom the priest obliged to be present could perform no religious ceremony; could utter no prayer for the repose of his soul; could not say a single word of *requiescat in pace*; could not, in short, sprinkle a single drop of holy water, whose virtue it is to moderate and quench the flames of that terrible fire that purifies souls in the other world.' "

So it was that the consecrated ground became unconsecrated after all. And there the body of Joseph Guibord, the printer, still lies, in its weird sarcophagus of cement and iron and tin.

John Collins SKETCHBOOK

PHYSICS
BUILDING -
—McGILL

TWENTY-FIVE

The Man Who Changed
The World:
Ernest Rutherford

THE MACDONALD PHYSICS Building on the campus of McGill University is one of the most historic buildings in the world. Here Ernest Rutherford carried out his research into radio-activity; here he evolved his theory of the disintegration of radio-elements. This theory revolutionized scientific under-standing of the atom. In the space of a few years' work in this building Rutherford ushered the world into its Atomic Age. His discoveries at McGill had given the world its greatest risk of doom and destruction or its greatest hope of peace and plenty. He had presented the world with a relentless, in-escapable challenge. In that building the whole world was changed forever.

Ernest Rutherford was a very young man when he came to McGill in 1898; he was only twenty-seven. He had been surprised that McGill had chosen him to be its Macdonald Professor of Physics. He was a New Zealander doing research

in physics at Cambridge. Principal William Peterson of Mc-
Gill and Professor John Cox of McGill's Physics Department
had come to Cambridge looking for a suitable physicist for
the Macdonald professorship (recently left vacant when Professor H. L. Callandar had resigned to return to England).
McGill had chosen Rutherford because he was highly recommended by his chief at Cambridge, Professor J. J. Thomson.

Rutherford had been aware one day that he was being
pointed out to the McGill delegation; but he could not believe
he would ever be selected. When the appointment came, he
was astonished. "I am only a kid for such a position," he said.
Such appointments were simply not "thrown about for men
of my age."

When Rutherford arrived on the McGill campus he seemed
to be a somewhat puzzling person. He had no academic manner; he made no attempt to impress; he was rather clumsy,
"like a farmer just in town." "I remember him," wrote one
McGill professor, "as a tall, slim man, slightly bent, with very
long arms, causing a kind of ungainly gait." His manner was
amiable good-natured, accommodating. He was likely to burst
into loud laughter. He had no careful dignity, no cultivated
voice, no inclination to develop a presence.

His general appearance was unmistakably English; but unmistakably English in the middle-class tradition. "Prof. Rutherford," wrote a Montreal newspaper reporter, "is to the outward
eye simply a typical blue-eyed Englishman, with rather high
cheek bones, and an angular head. He is a New Zealander as
a matter of fact, but they are very English in New Zealand.
His tongue is the tongue of middle-class England—middle-
class London even—not that of the universities; it has no drawl
and is sharp rather than broad . . . not in the least thrilling."

Only one feature of Ernest Rutherford was impressive; but
it was enough to suggest that here might be a young man of
genius. No one could forget his eyes. "The one thing that

fascinates you when he is talking," said one observer, "is his eyes, which have always an extraordinary attentive and penetrating look, such as seems natural enough in a man who deals in atoms of which millions are needed to make a visible speck." Much the same was the impression those eyes made on Dr. A. S. Eve (later to be Macdonald Professor of Physics at McGill): "My own first meeting with Rutherford was at McGill in January 1903. . . . At this first interview I realised that Rutherford's eyes had a curious fascination. As you looked at them, you began to understand the saying: 'If thine eye be single, thy whole body shall be full of light.'"

The rapid series of fudamental discoveries in atomic research by Ernest Rutherford at McGill came not from his genius alone. He had at his disposal a building with laboratories and equipment unrivaled in the world. All these facilities had been provided by Sir William Christopher Macdonald, the founder, owner and head of the Macdonald Tobacco Company. Sir William, who lived around the corner from McGill, at Number 3 in the Prince of Wales Terrace, was a middle-aged bachelor. He lived a withdrawn, ascetic life, spent exceedingly little on himself and hardly ever took a holiday, yet gave prodigious sums for the development of the university. Among other large gifts were the three limestone science buildings down the east side of the campus: the Macdonald Engineering Building, the Macdonald Chemistry and Mining Building, and the Macdonald Physics Building. He not only erected the buildings; he established the professorships, endowed the maintenance, furnished the equipment.

At the Macdonald Physics Building young Ernest Rutherford realized everything had been provided "regardless of cost." The building, in fact, had been so uniquely planned for its purpose that not a piece of metal had been introduced into its construction, so that no metallic disturbance would interfere with the experiments to be carried out within its walls. The laboratories were well equipped. If Rutherford needed anything more—such as a supply of radium or a machine for producing liquid air—Sir William Macdonald did not hesitate; they were immediately forthcoming.

Though a severely practical businessman, Macdonald had an intellectual love of science—not only science in its practical applications, but science as a field for the imagination of man. He was fascinated by the idea of these researchers "voyaging through strange seas of thought alone." He bought a series of fine engravings of the great men of science since classical times. These he had hung as inspiration in the corridors and lecture halls of the Physics Building. When someone sent him photographs of stars, taken through a giant telescope, he had them framed and would study them, feeling an expansion of mind from trying to imagine the vastness of the heavens. In such a businessman as this Rutherford was sure of a helper, both sympathetic and generous.

Sir William, however, had his eccentricities. These had to be scrupulously respected. For one thing, he was disposed to be far more generous with buildings and equipment than he was with the professors who used them. "The salaries are small compared with the endowment of the laboratories and the enormous money spent on them," said Rutherford, "but that is chiefly due to the fact that the money has been advanced by Macdonald ... he lives on £250, so he reckons a professor should live on £500. However £500 is not so bad and as the physical laboratory is the best of its kind in the world, I cannot complain." Rutherford and Macdonald had much in common in their plain unpretentiousness. Rutherford's comment on Macdonald was: "He is a grey-headed Scotsman, simple and unassuming, and I like him very well."

Rutherford soon learned, however, that he had to be alert to Sir William's eccentric abhorrence of tobacco. His millions had been made as a tobacco manufacturer, but he was revolted when he saw anybody using it. Warnings flew about the Physics Building whenever Sir William arrived on a visit. Cigars and cigarettes had to be extinguished in a hurry; windows were flung up to let the aroma escape. It would never do to let this manufacturer of tobacco smell it in the building tobacco had built. "Disgusting habit!" would be Sir William's comment. Anyone who heard him saying it knew he had received the ultimate rebuke.

Ernest Rutherford gave himself to his research in the Macdonald Physics Building with magnificent abandon. The work did more than interest him; it exhilarated him. It was as though he had slipped out of himself, to become part of his own discoveries. A McGill teacher in a very different line of study—John Macnaughton, the Professor of Classics—happened one day to attend a meeting when Rutherford was lecturing: "We found that we had stumbled in upon one of Rutherford's brilliant demonstrations of radium. It was indeed an eye-opener ... Radioactive is the one sufficient term to characterize the total impression made upon us by his personality. Emanations of light and energy, swift and penetrating ... appeared to sparkle and coruscate from him all over in sheaves. Here was the rarest and most refreshing spectacle— the pure ardour of the chase, a man quite possessed by a noble work and altogether happy in it."

As Professor Macnaughton said, Rutherford's happiness in his work was ebullient. Dr. H. M. Tory chanced to come into the laboratory one day; he saw Rutherford skipping and prancing about the floor, carried away by his excitement at some new insight into radioactivity. Rutherford's total abandonment to his work was also observed by the Reverend J. L. Morin, McGill's Professor of French, at whose house Rutherford boarded for one winter: "He was nervous and very active, devoting all his time working in the physics laboratory. Sometimes, I should say often, he got up during the night and went to his laboratory.

"Once I asked him why. 'Are your students wide awake at that time?' He smiled, and told me something to this effect. 'I am seeking to know Nature, now I am part of Nature, therefore, I should be able to infer her laws, and to make sure I don't make any mistake. I lay snares for her, so I go at any time, day or night, to see if I have caught her.' "

Rutherford's revelations of the atom came not from one great discovery. They came from a series of discoveries, theories and experiments in the laboratories of the Macdonald Physics Building. He was aided in much of his work by his chief assistant, Frederick Soddy (later Professor of Inorganic Chemistry at Oxford). Again and again, within a few years, the scientific world was bombarded with books and papers. The old ideas were destroyed; the new concepts were startling.

Ideas so revolutionary were not easily accepted. Some of the leading scientists in Great Britain and elsewhere opposed him. Even at McGill considerable uneasiness might be sensed. At one meeting at McGill the value of his work was openly questioned. If he should be proved wrong in his wild break from hitherto accepted theories, it was said, McGill would become laughingstock of the learned world. Rutherford, disturbed by these critics, replied poorly. His colleague, Professor Cox, came to his support; he stated the case effectively in his defense.

Before long, however, the highest honors began to come. In 1904 Rutherford was awarded the Rumford Medal—one of the supreme scientific awards of the Royal Society of London. "What the devil is the Rumford Medal?" asked Rutherford with customary lack of pretension. But McGill felt a glow of pride and achievement. Next morning the students gave him an ovation when he arrived at the Physics Building.

Sir William Macdonald made arrangements to honor

Rutherford at a tremendous banquet in the Windsor Hotel. It was a complimentary dinner; Macdonald paid for all the guests. Some 130 of the principal personages of town and gown were invited. "Loads of flowers" decorated the tables; an orchestra played triumphal music as Rutherford entered. The banquet went on till two in the morning. Rutherford was gratified, though it was an ordeal to hear himself "talked at" for hours on end. At the dinner Sir William Macdonald was absent. He knew that he, too, would be praised. He shunned public tributes.

In due course the inevitable happened. Ernest Rutherford left McGill to return to England. He left with regret. "I have been granted exceptional opportunities to carry out my research work . . ." he explained. "In arriving at a decision as to the course I was to take I may say that the determining factor was that it was necessary for me to be closer in contact with European science than is possible on this side of the Atlantic."

Yet Rutherford's main work was already done. He never excelled his achievements at McGill. As his old chief at Cambridge, Sir J. J. Thomson, said, Rutherford was "never greater than when he was in Montreal."

Rutherford himself certified that the Atomic Age was born in the Macdonald Physics Building at McGill. In 1932, five years before his death, he wrote: "I would like to take this opportunity to emphasise that the credit of the first definite proof of atomic transformation belongs to McGill University. It was in the Macdonald Physics Building in the years 1902-1904 that Soddy and I accumulated the experimental evidence that the radioactive elements were undergoing spontaneous transformations. The disintegration theory, advanced in explanation of the observations, has stood the test of time and has formed the basis of all subsequent developments.

"The next stage in advance was a proof that certain elements could be artificially transmuted by bombardment with the *a*-

rays from radium, and it should be noted that it was at McGill, in 1903, that the true nature of this radiation, which played such a big part in the development of physics, was first disclosed. There is a saying that 'it is the first step that counts,' and it is clear that to McGill belongs whatever credit is due for the early ideas and experiments which opened up the way into the unknown that all subsequent investigators have followed."

Rutherford had been aware, in his researches at McGill, that he was engaged in something more than abstract physics. The practical application of his discoveries was already looming before his eyes. He realized this application would one day give mankind access to a power never known before. In a lecture at McGill he said that "if the process whereby the radioactive group develop energy, could be quickened by some artificial method, the world would be endowed with a new and enormous source of power, derived from a comparatively small quantity of matter."

On the evening of the August day in 1945 when news reached Montreal that the first atomic bomb had been exploded over Hiroshima, a reporter from the Montreal *Gazette* went to the Macdonald Physics Building, hoping to interview Dr. John Stuart Foster, who was then the latest successor to Ernest Rutherford as Macdonald Professor of Physics. The building was deserted and dark, except for a light here and there in the shadowy corridors. Dr. Foster was found sitting alone, his arm resting on a table in one of the lecture amphitheaters. A light shone over the table; the rest of the amphitheater faded into darkness. "It all began right here, in this building," he said, rapping his knuckles on the table. He pondered aloud, as though half speaking to himself. Perhaps this terrible demonstration of atomic power might bring peace to the world at last, just because war had become too devastating in its reach ever to be endured. It might not mean merely the end

306

of World War II, but freedom from all world wars, forever. But he felt the awesomeness of the hour. The world, living on a trembling hope, would never be the same again.

The reporter, leaving, glanced back. Dr. Foster was still sitting, hunched, in the big silent building, where Ernest Rutherford had foreseen, forty years earlier, "a new and enormous source of power, derived from a comparatively small quantity of matter."

INDEX

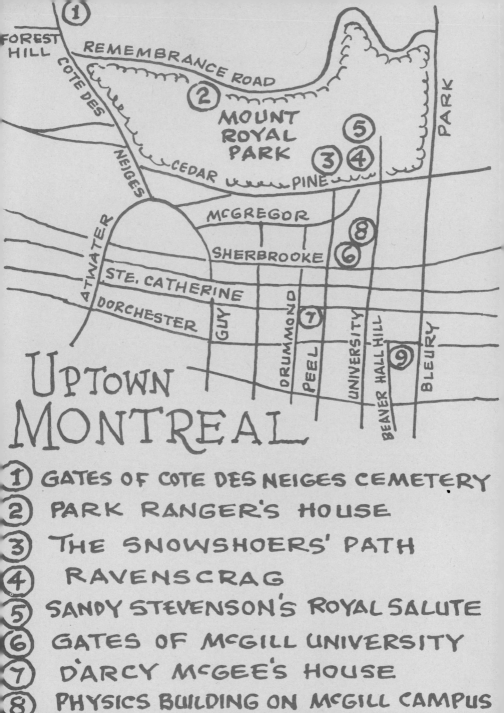

UPTOWN
MONTREAL

1. GATES OF COTE DES NEIGES CEMETERY
2. PARK RANGER'S HOUSE
3. THE SNOWSHOERS' PATH
4. RAVENSCRAG
5. SANDY STEVENSON'S ROYAL SALUTE
6. GATES OF McGILL UNIVERSITY
7. D'ARCY McGEE'S HOUSE
8. PHYSICS BUILDING ON McGILL CAMPUS
9. ST. PATRICK'S CHURCH